TURN IT UP!
AMERICAN RADIO TALES
1946 ~ 1996

BOB SHANNON

austrianmonk publishing
Bainbridge Island, Washington

Copyrights

austrianmonk publishing
P.O. Box 10187
Bainbridge Island, WA 98110

ISBN 978-1-61584-545-3

Library of Congress Cataloging-in-Publication Data is available.

Visit my website at www.americanradiotales.com

For information about special discounts for bulk purchases, please contact austrianmonk publishing at 1-206-755-5162 or business@americanradiotales.com.

Printed and manufactured in the United States of America
First Printing: October 2009

Book and cover design by Jeanette Alexander Graphic Design of Bainbridge Island, WA. *City Radio,* a digital Illustration by Ultra-Generic, was purchased through Istockphoto.com, and is incorporated into the cover design.

DEDICATION

To Patti, the love of my life;
to Jessica, the light of my life; and to
Eli, Jacob, Thomas, Sarah and Joel,
the stars of my life.

FOREWORD

By Bob Henabery

Media critics and historians applaud radio's Golden Years that began in 1933, with FDR's first fireside chat to an economically depressed nation, and ended in 1949 when "Stop the Music," the last big radio network show, switched to TV. All told, 16 years. That was the radio Granddad listened to.

The Golden Years I knew and worked in were from 1956, when Elvis Presley spectacularly emerged, to 1987, when the Government deregulated radio — 31 years altogether. Bob Shannon's book tells of that second era of Golden Years through his wonderful stories of its programmers and air talent, many of whom I knew. Bob absolutely *nails it*.

And, when he had asked me which of those he writes about had the most impact, the names Rick Sklar and Bill Drake immediately came to mind. There would have been no second Golden Years era without them. Rick Sklar was the program director at WABC New York in the '60s. In the summertime WABC's chime-time ID echoed along Jones Beach and Coney Island and re-echoed all along the East Coast shore — from a million transistors simultaneously. Amazing stuff! Amazing and literally true! Chime-time was the audible cue that *proved* that everybody on the beach who wasn't totally deaf *was in fact listening*. For a decade WABC reached over five million in the metropolitan area, alone a third of the New York population, and more than twice the circulation of its biggest newspaper.

Bill Drake was responsible for the greatly improved quality of Top 40 stations beginning in 1965. His flagship station, KHJ/Los Angeles, set the tone. He applied the architectural aesthetic, "Less is more" — *less talk — more music*. The jingle "more music, 93-KHJ" promised and delivered more songs and the KHJ jocks surfed on the perfect wave of hit music. Production was fabulous and promotions like "The Big Kahuna" involved listeners all the way from The Valley to East LA.

When reading Bob Shannon's wonderful book, the common quality that runs like a thread through each is how much his radio guys loved what they did. It was never the money. It couldn't be. There wasn't that much.

FOREWORD

It was 1950, a year before "I Love Lucy" went on TV, and I was a 20-something, just named program director of WBEC — a 250 watt AM station in the factory town of Pittsfield, Massachusetts. We gave that community of 50,000 an original mix of music, news, sports and fun. I was so happy that I used to run to work every day.

No, that's not right. As a matter of fact, I never really worked a day in my life.

B. H.
November 21, 2008
Gainesville, Virginia

CONTENTS

CHAPTERS

INTRODUCTION

Radio was dead. Everyone who was anyone said so.

At the end of World War Two mid-century media executives chose pictures over sound and in the years that followed diverted their funds and energies to television. In New York, actors with faces made for radio filled unemployment lines while the Golden Age radio stars that could — big names like Jack Benny, George Burns, and Fibber McGee and Molly — jumped to television, and radio, once a giant, faced a bleak, if non-existent, future.

Then, from the ashes, it rose again.

"What happened next was *called* radio, but it wasn't anything like the radio that had come before," says Chuck Blore. "It just had the same name."

Local radio station owners, faced with a pressing need to replace the programming the networks were taking away, discovered that disc jockeys playing records — men like Alan Freed, Dick Biondi and Murray the K — made good financial sense. That rock 'n' roll was inventing itself at the same time seemed simply a coincidence. In hindsight, however, it was both serendipitous and transformational.

By the mid 1950s AM Top 40, the invention of Todd Storz, Gordon McLendon and their disciples, was cutting through the ether with the power of a hundred teen idols and, by 1960, when Sony introduced the first transistor radio and Blore's KFWB/Color Radio-Channel 98 was the darling of Southern California, AM radio was the undisputed source of "music and news" for America's baby boomers, and even some of their elders.

But, change was in the air.

FM radio had been invented by Edwin H. Armstrong in 1934, but for more than a generation radio station owners and network executives had ignored it because it didn't fit into their business plans or, more precisely, because David Sarnoff and RCA didn't want it to gain any traction. But, on July 1, 1965, when the #1 record in the country was a Bob Dylan song (*Mr. Tambourine Man* by The Byrds), the Federal Communications Commission (FCC) issued a ruling prohibiting FM stations from simulcasting more than fifty percent of their co-owned AM's programming.

The implications were immense. Broadcasters were told they had to create new programming for their FM stations with no guarantee new revenue streams would follow. Within a week Pacifica owned WBAI-FM/New York began to experiment with what they called "free-form progressive" programming and over the next 24 months other FMs, each with its own take on this "free-form" idea, began to appear in cities across the country; most notoriously KMPX-FM/San Francisco on April 7, 1967 and WBCN/Boston on March 15, 1968.

In 1971 Top 40 first surfaced on the FM dial on Bartell Broadcasting's WMYQ/Miami, but it wasn't until 1975 that an FM station, WXLO (nicknamed 99X) delivered winning ratings in New York City and grabbed the advertising community's attention. WXLO-FM was Top 40, but the music it played was "hipper" and less teen oriented than its main format competitor, AM station WABC. Adding insult to injury, 99X promised it was playing "more album cuts" and, whether it was or not, New York's audience believed it. Their ratings success was a game changer and, from that day forward, anyone programming or listening to music on the radio knew FM was the place to be.

(Sadly, inventor Edwin Armstrong wasn't around to celebrate the vindication. After years of legal battles with Sarnoff, who'd insisted the patent for FM belonged to RCA because Armstrong invented it while he was employed by the company, Armstrong killed himself. On January 31, 1954 he dressed warmly in an overcoat, hat, scarf and gloves, kissed his wife goodbye, and walked out the window of his thirteenth floor Manhattan apartment.)

By the 1980s, music radio had migrated to FM and AM was struggling. Some savvy broadcasters re-discovered the big bands of the '30s and '40s, but just as with (the barely surviving) '60s music formats still on the air in the '90s, it was widely understood that nostalgic programming had a limited shelf life and would eventually fade away, along with its aging audiences.

In 1985, deregulation of the radio industry began, starting with a relaxation of ownership rules which allowed an individual company to increase the number of stations it owned in any given market. The idea was that it would stimulate competition. It didn't. Two years later the FCC took another step to loosen things up and unwittingly, perhaps, rescued AM from extinction by eliminating an obscure FCC regulation called the Fairness Doctrine.

The doctrine, articulated in 1949, had been an attempt to ensure that all coverage of controversial issues by a broadcast station be balanced and fair. Long before Fox News inverted the phrase ("fair and balanced") the FCC took the view "that station licensees were public trustees and had an obligation to afford reasonable discussion of contrasting points of view of controversial issues." Granted, that's a mouthful, but it was effectively spit out in 1985, when an opinion appeared in "The Fairness Report" stating that "the doctrine was no longer having its intended effect and could, in fact, be in violation of the First Amendment." In reaction, FCC Chairman Mark Fowler quickly and publicly vowed to kill the doctrine and, by 1987, the courts (in Meredith v. FCC) declared the doctrine wasn't mandated by Congress and that the FCC didn't have to continue to enforce it. Congress, however, disagreed and both houses voted the doctrine back into law, a move which caught Ronald Reagan's attention. The president quickly responded with a veto and, with the stroke of a pen, the Fairness Doctrine was dead. Reagan's signature, along with the invention of the seven-second delay and the introduction of satellite distribution, set the stage for the emergence of new American voices, including Rush Limbaugh, who launched his nationally syndicated program in August of 1988 and single-handedly brought AM back from its coma.

The 1990s began with deregulation fever. By 1994, when Republican majorities were elected to both houses of Congress, media consolidation was a foregone conclusion and a little more than a year later, on January 3, 1996, the 104th Congress passed the Telecommunications Act of 1996 and sent it on to President Bill Clinton for signature.

Merger mania began with a bang. Medium size companies swallowed up smaller ones and big companies, with venture capital money, ate up the mediums. Eventually, only the big boys were left standing and since those at the top of these conglomerates were, more likely, accountants instead of broadcasters, radio rapidly became a real estate business. As a result, educating, informing and entertaining the public became a thing of the past.

·

This book was written because radio people, more often than not, tell their history in bars, not on paper. The stories they tell aren't about industry wide initiatives, results and consequences, they're more personal: about places they worked, people they knew and things that happened along the way. Between the lines a picture appears of a time gone by, one that will never be repeated, when radio was an important part of American life, disc jockeys were stars, and their listeners cared about them.

Today, as the first decade of the 21st century is coming to a close, the definition of media is changing at a pace that's almost unrecognizable. It's an exciting time, with unlimited possibilities and opportunities for re-invention. But, it would be sad to forget, or worse yet, to never know what came before and how and why it set the stage for the future.

Believe it or not, once upon a time a young boy named Paul Harvey dreamed of running away to "join the radio." As it turns out, he wasn't the only one.

That's what this book is all about.

"To those of us who stand on the threshold of radio's tomorrow, these years have been but the closing of a brilliant chapter. The pages of radio's next years will prove once again that there are still sounds worth a thousand pictures."

Gordon McLendon
Dallas, Texas

TURN IT UP!

AMERICAN RADIO TALES

1946 ~ 1996

Karen —
How very kind of you
to buy this. Radio is a
very strange world — as
you're about to find out.
    Warmest regards,

Bob Shannon

BOB SHANNON

austrianmonk publishing
Bainbridge Island, Washington

CHAPTER 1
LEE ABRAMS ~ SUPERSTAR

Al Casey laughs. Not a chuckle, but a real laugh; one that ripples from the corners of his eyes all the way down to his shaking, skinny belly. He's remembering the first time he set eyes on Lee Abrams.

"We thought he was a narc," Casey says.

Casey and his partner in crime, Rob Walker, had rolled into South Florida from Memphis. They'd been working for RKO Radio at WHBQ, but Bartell Broadcasting had an FM station in Miami, WMYQ, and they'd been called in to save the day or re-invent it, whatever came first.

The company put them up in a hotel. "I wouldn't call it seedy," says Casey, softly, "but..." He goes no further. Casey's a nice man.

Sequestered behind closed doors, dressed in Levis and record company tee-shirts, the two men, with their hair down to there, were filling the air with plans for the FM rock 'n' roll invasion of Miami. Suddenly someone knocked on the door. "We weren't expecting anyone," explains Casey.

Quick, hide the "plans."

Once that was done he opened the door. "Yes?"

Abrams looked like a boy. He was five-six, maybe five-seven, dressed in a pin-striped suit and had short hair. Before Casey could open his mouth, the kid began. "Hi, I'm Lee Abrams and Buzz Bennett sent me."

Casey stared; Abrams kept talking. "He said he was the music director of WQAM, but that he really wanted to work for us," Casey explained.

Abrams recalls the conversation, too. "I had to convince them that I didn't usually wear a suit and that my hair was normally a lot longer."

Eventually he was invited in. Casey remembers Abrams saying that he conducted research by hitchhiking around South Florida. "He told me he'd ask anybody, anywhere, 'What are you listening to? Why are you listening?' "

Walker and Casey were taken aback, but after an afternoon of talking, driving around Miami, and "planning," Casey says he agreed to give Abrams the job he wanted, the job as WMYQ's Music Director. "I gave him two weeks to get the music library together, but he had everything we needed in a week-and-a-half. It was amazing."

Then, they — by "they" I mean most of the disc jockeys who were hired to work at WMYQ *and* their new Music Director — rented a mini-mansion in Coconut Grove, named it The Q-House, and began to live the communal life. It was good, they thought.

It was 1971, the year that marked the beginning of FM Top 40 penetration.

•

Lee Abrams was born and raised in Chicago, and by the time he was twelve, he knew FM was going to be the next big thing. "I knew rock 'n' roll would sound incredible in stereo," he says. But, despite his enthusiasm for the potential of FM, in 1963 AM was still king and Abrams was still hooked. "I thought the entire staff at WLS was fabulous."

It wasn't just Chicago radio that rocked his boat. At night, he dialed for faraway AM signals — KFI/Los Angeles, WABC/New York, and any signal in between he was able to pick up. His interest was primarily radio, but he was also deeply into the music, and by high school he'd already begun compiling playlists for the great rock 'n' roll FM station he heard in his head — the station that didn't exist yet. "But, by then," he says, "I knew it wasn't a pipe dream."

Biding his time, Abrams began managing and booking local bands all over Chicago, and even started a small record label (GEM

Records; look for *Three For Love* by The Moving Violations). He had no radio connections, but that didn't stop him from calling radio people and writing them letters. He did whatever it took to get himself noticed. And it worked. In Chicago, Gene Taylor let him run errands at WLS, and in Miami, where his family summered, he snagged a job at WQAM. "I just loved that station," says Abrams today. "But, it was a tight ship and I was paid with money allocated for the News Tip of the Week." (He only got paid during a slow news week.)

In 1966, before radio trade magazines began sharing programming ideas, Abrams started a newsletter he named "Radio Promotion Concepts." He wrote about how music was changing. "We got our first taste of underground in 1968, and I got totally into it," he says. And, to keep his head above water, he sold classified ads and solicited subscriptions. "I had seventy-five to a hundred," he recalls.

•

Abrams thought underground FM disc jockeys "breathed" and Top 40 AM jocks "screamed." (KHJ Programmer Ron Jacobs expressed the sentiment a different way: "Rock 'n' roll radio was either too hip or too hype," he wrote.)

By 1970 Abrams had identified a group of people he called *vulnerable Top 40 listeners.* "They'd hate Gary Puckett and Herb Alpert, but would stick around for The Moody Blues," he explains. His guess was that until FM programmers figured it all out, most listeners would stick with the AM stations they'd grown up with. "One song out of three that you loved (on AM) was better than one out of ten that you recognized (on FM)," he explained.

The point was that he was thinking about FM as a mass appeal delivery system at a time when no one else seemed interested. Granted, he was beginning to think beyond Top 40, but his ideas still impressed Buzz Bennett, the man in charge of Bartell Broadcasting's programming, and that led to Al Casey, who gave him the job at WMYQ.

His ambition didn't stop in Miami. "He wrote letter after letter to ABC," remembers Casey, "and, finally, I think they just gave up and offered him the job programming WRIF-FM/Detroit."

Abrams was ready to try his ideas out, but when he arrived in the Motor City he encountered mayhem. WRIF was totally free-form, which meant the DJs played pretty much what they wanted when they wanted; Abrams figured he could fix that. There was, however, a larger issue: the station had, seemingly, fallen under a political/sociological spell. Today, Abrams explains that WRIF's internal agenda had been taken over by The Rainbow Peoples Party, whose vision was anarchy. "I was eighteen and it was scary," he says.

So, he concentrated on getting the music right and kept his head out of the politics. It wasn't easy. Eight months into it, a friend named Dan Henderson mentioned he had another friend who owned an FM station in Raleigh, North Carolina. "I've told him about what you're doing up here and he wants to talk."

This was a tipping point.

•

Lee Abrams signed his first consulting deal with the Carolina station, WPTF-FM. Quickly he changed the call letters to WQDR and, with no political agenda to hem him in, launched the mass appeal FM format he'd been hearing in his head for years. Unlike many of the "progressive" FMs of the day that played a wide and largely unfamiliar library, Abram's format featured groups and artists you'd recognize: The Beatles; The Stones; Led Zeppelin; Chicago; Crosby, Stills, Nash and Young. (In truth, his ideas reflected much of what Bob Henabery had been preaching to the ABC FM programmers.) "When the ratings came out," says Abrams, "the station was #1 in the market, and got huge press." He also says his bosses at ABC weren't happy about his moonlighting. "They told me, 'It's either us or them.' "

Abrams opted for them, and left ABC.

You think you know what happened next, don't you?

He hung out a shingle: *Lee Abrams Consulting.* He continued to write letters to anyone who would listen to his story. He signed his second station, WRNO/New Orleans, and was packing for a trip to the Crescent City when he got a call from WEFM/Chicago. They said they weren't looking for a consultant. They wanted to talk with him about becoming the station's new Program Director.

Abrams figured he couldn't turn the job down. "It was my home town," he explains. So, he talked himself into putting his consulting business on hold, went in to pitch the job, and was hired. What happened next is a classic radio story.

WEFM was a classical music station with loyal listeners and supporters vehemently opposed to the format change. Abrams says he always understood he might be stopped, but says he put on blinders, ignored the outcries, and stayed focused on preparing for the new rock format. Until the very last minute he was convinced he'd be allowed to do it. Then WEFM was served with an injunction.

Three weeks later a disappointed Abrams returned to consulting. He was disillusioned and not just a little introspective. He wasn't quite sure what to do next. Then the phone rang again. On the other end of the line was Kent Burkhart. "Look," Burkhart told him, "I'm on the way to Minneapolis to see my client, KSTP. Can you get on a plane and meet me there? Let's see what kind of relationship we can come up with."

They met in the MSP airport lounge, talked, connected, shook hands and, based on this one meeting, decided to join forces.

They called the company Burkhart/Abrams, with Burkhart working with AM clients and Abrams concentrating on the FMs. In the years that followed, Abrams' FM album format, marketed as "Superstars," became the prototype for Album Rock in the '70s and '80s. "Superstars" wasn't the only format of its kind — Mike Harrison, John Sebastian and Jeff Pollack all had their own successful initiatives — but it was, in sheer station numbers, the most successful syndicated album format of its day. What Burkhart/Abrams promised their clients was that the format would deliver a specific and highly desirable target audience, 18-to-24 year-old men. It did.

•

In 1988, after fifteen years with Burkhart, Abrams decided it was time to look for a new challenge. In short order, he took on some non-radio projects: "Rolling Stone" magazine, Swatch Watches, and even British rockers, The Moody Blues and Yes. "I was an American culture interpreter," he jokes. From there he joined ABC's Satellite Music Network, based in Dallas. He cast himself as an in-house consultant and developed a format for the network called "Z Rock."

In the spring of 1999, Abrams joined American Mobile Radio Corporation, a company based in Washington D.C. One of only two companies licensed by the federal government to create multi-channel satellite radio, AMRC, which would become XM Satellite Radio, named Abrams its Chief Programming Officer. He was, according to sources, the architect of XM's attitude, which went a long way towards differentiating the company from its sole satellite competitor, Sirius Radio. (This, of course, was before the two companies merged in July, 2008.)

Just before the millennium, as Abrams was getting ready to join the satellite company, he was quick to point out two things:

1) It'll be a content war and the best content wins.

2. Nothing is sacred. It's time to re-think everything.

Nine years later, I think he still means it.

(From The Chicago Tribune)

CHICAGO March 11, 2008 — The sweeping change underway at Tribune Company today took another giant leap forward as the media giant announced the appointment of music and radio industry icon Lee Abrams as Chief Innovation Officer. Abrams will be responsible for innovation across Tribune's publishing, broadcasting and interactive divisions, and will assume his duties April 1. He is the first person to hold the position in the company's 160-year history.

"There is a remarkable opportunity for Tribune to design the future of American media with passion, intellect, and imagination that meets the spirit of the 21st century," said Abrams. "We have the resources to pioneer a new age of information and entertainment that re-invents and enlightens — and that is exactly what we are going to do!"

(On March 26, 2008) Abrams posted this blog.

Effective April 1, I will be heading to Chicago. (I) heard a lot of rumors about why I am leaving XM for the Tribune. There is only ONE reason: A remarkable opportunity. I guess I have this thing for danger. Going with FM at a time when FM was literally housed in closets playing Doctor's Office music...Going with XM at a time when no one said people would pay for radio (almost 20 million are, FYI)...and now going to a business that *some* say is on life support. I think Randy Michaels, myself, and the people I'll be working with are pretty good media surgeons...with high confidence that we'll do our part to help create a renaissance and a new level of health, happiness, well-being and prosperity with the people and brands of Tribune. Lofty words, but that's the plan. THAT's why I am leaving XM. It has NOTHING to do with: Mergers, Firings, or any other high drama. The Tribune mission is an opportunity that you just can't pass up.

Leaving XM is hard. There are way, way too many memories (bad, good, strange, whacked and funny) to reminisce in this forum, but I can't think of a place I've been that has been more memorable and magical.

There WILL be a book.

CHAPTER 2
JACK ARMSTRONG ~ THE WORLD'S FASTEST TALKING DJ

"You're listening to The Jack Armstrong Experience. It's where all the good music is!!!"

For Jack Armstrong, the music might have been fine, but the money wasn't. It was 1973 and Armstrong, a man whose on-air energy was enough to keep a small city going for days, was working seven to midnight for 50,000-watt WKBW/Buffalo, a station with a night-time signal that covered the entire eastern seaboard.

"So, I went in and told the boss I needed a raise," said Armstrong.

Hem-haw, hem-haw, management shuffle. The long and short of it — "No, Jack, but you can still work here. We like what you do."

"I had a lot of fun at 'KB," Armstrong told me. "It's just that I was poverty-stricken." He pauses. He knows back then there was no such thing as Howard Stern money. But, he's peeved. Still. "People (he means radio executives) don't understand that a lot of personalities would probably do better air work if they weren't looking at their checkbooks between the records." This comment is made thirty years after the fact, but he still means it and still thinks it applies.

The plain fact is Armstrong never got rich doing radio.

•

One evening the request line at WKBW rang. Armstrong answered. "KB."

"Jack Armstrong, please."

"You got him."

"It's Buzz Bennett, Jack."

"Yeah," replied Armstrong, sarcastically. "And I'm Rick Sklar."

"No, man, it really *is* Buzz Bennett. I'm calling from Pittsburgh."

"What the hell you doing down there, man?" Armstrong asked, warming up a bit.

"I'm starting a station," answered Bennett. "And I'm interested in hiring you."

Armstrong, having just gone through the money dance and having his feet stepped upon, cut to the chase. "So, what I said was, 'Look, Buzz, let me tell you upfront. It's all about the money.' "

"What are we talking about?" Bennett asked.

Armstrong didn't answer quickly. He had a wife and a couple of kids. He had to do this right. "$28,000," he said, firmly.

"Well," said Bennett. "That's a lot of money for a night-man. But, I reckon we could do it."

Armstrong's heart started pounding. It was more money than he'd ever made. His record was running out and he had to go back on the air. He didn't want to give Bennett time to take the offer back.

"Good God Almighty. I can't talk to you anymore, man. I'm busy packing."

•

Jack Armstrong's parents were highly educated and had set certain expectations for him. "My father was the world's authority on parasitology, the study of tropical diseases," Armstrong told me. "And my mother had a master's degree in botany by the time she was eighteen." In other words, John Charles Larsh, his real name, had a family full of, "Go to college, or you're nothing."

So he tried. He enrolled at Guilford College, in Greensboro, signed up for pre-med classes, and almost made it through a semester. But, it never felt right to him. "I still remember what happened when I told my Dad I was going to quit," said Armstrong.

"I was in the backseat of the car and he turned around, that big cigar sticking out of his mouth, stuck his finger right in my face and said, 'Kid, in this world you gotta have one of two things: education or talent. You sure as hell ain't going to have any education, so you better hope you have some talent.' "

•

In 1966 Armstrong went to Cleveland. It was his third radio job in as many years. He'd been hired to work for WIXY, a Top 40 station owned by Norman Wayne.

"When I got there I sat in my hotel room and listened to the station and it sounded pretty much 'coat and tie' to me. I remember thinking, 'What they're doing doesn't fit the music.' " (Big hits in 1966 included *Paint It Black* by The Rolling Stones, *96 Tears* by ? and the Mysterians and *Good Vibrations* by The Beach Boys.) So, quickly, in a spur-of-the-moment move, Armstrong decided his on-air approach on WIXY would be "wide open and crazy." He knew it was risky, but he figured, 'Why not? I'll try it. It'll either work or it won't. My career will end suddenly or I'll have found the answer.' "

He was a maniac. He talked as fast as he possibly could. The goal was to get noticed and stand out; to be electrifying. WIXY's audience, mostly teenagers, responded like teens of another generation in the same city had responded to Alan Freed and in a very short time Armstrong became Cleveland's undisputed night-time radio leader. "We went from a 4.0 share to a 22.0," Armstrong told me. By the time his WIXY numbers hit the mid 30s, Armstrong was contemplating his future. "I wanted to stay in the business forever," he said, "and I began to think that if I could work on one of those 50,000 watt flame-throwers, like WKYC, the station across town, then tens of thousands of people would hear me."

His confidence was growing. "I'd sit back and listen to what I was doing and think, 'Nobody else is close.' "

In 1967, when Jack Armstrong was twenty-one, he broke his contract at WIXY and crossed the street to do nights at WKYC.

Now, the challenge was to beat his own ratings, which wasn't going to be easy. "When you've honked someone else's call letters up into the thirties, and then you try to get those ratings back… it's, well, very difficult to do."

Before the ride was over Armstrong got within striking distance of his WIXY ratings, but he never actually beat himself. Still, his reputation was spreading. "I was driving to Mobile," Scott Shannon told author Ben Fong-Torres (in "The Hits Just Keep on Coming"). "On the way, I picked up a 50,000-watt radio station out of Cleveland, and I heard a fellow by the name of Jack Armstrong, who was a screaming maniac. And I said, 'You know what? I like his style…that sounds a little bit more like where radio is going.' "

•

Influenced by Jack Gale, the PD and morning man of WAYS/Charlotte, Armstrong created two on-air characters that eventually became a large part of his act. One, named "Gorilla," had a raspy voice and was known to proclaim that he liked, "women, banana juice, and whiskey." The other, "The Old Timer," wheezed, told corny jokes, and always got shot after delivering a lame punch line.

Armstrong's on-air execution – the play between the characters — was seamless, and most listeners assumed there was another person doing the voices. There wasn't.

By 1971, Armstrong's act was so refined and so fast that "The Guinness Book of World Records" named him the world's fastest talking human. Really.

•

In 1997 Jack Armstrong returned home to North Carolina and for the next six years did the morning show at WMQX/Winston-Salem. Gary Weiss, the station's General Manager, remembers the day Armstrong signed his contract. "It stipulated six to ten a.m. But, when he signed it, he handed it back to me and said, 'Hey, do you mind if I go on at five-thirty instead?' "

In 2003, Jack Armstrong was invited to return to WKBW, the station many still think of as his home. He wasn't actually in the Buffalo studio — he voice-tracked the show — but, according to those who heard him, Armstrong projected the same level of energy he'd exhibited three decades before. Then, in 2006, WKBW changed format, dropping oldies for syndicated talk. In an instant, Big Jack Armstrong was silenced.

Two years later, on March 22, 2008, after a fall at his home, Armstrong died at High Point Regional Hospital in North Carolina. He was only sixty-two.

In 2001 Jack Armstrong and I spent an afternoon talking. After telling me his stories, he confessed a strong belief. "I don't think anybody cares about what we did and what it was like to be on the radio back then."

I remember saying I disagreed and asking if he'd given any thought to how many lives he'd impacted. "I'll bet there's someone out there right now, in Buffalo, in Cleveland, Pittsburgh or San Francisco. Someone sitting in a chair, drinking a beer and listening to the Rolling Stones on the radio. And, just as *Satisfaction* is fading out that someone is subconsciously waiting for the grand finale, you know, YOUR sign-off — the words you used to say every night at the end of your show — the words that helped them understand who they were and helped them face the world."

"I believe it's true, Jack. I really do."

(Here's a transcript of Jacks Armstrong's sign-off. Read it fast.)

> "Don't get none on ya, do it twice, be nice. It's very nice to be important, but more important to be very nice. Let it all hang out, drag it in the sand, and make a deep rut. People who live in glass houses shouldn't...A bird in the hand makes it hard to blow your nose. One good turn takes most of the blankets. You can lead a horse to water, but don't push him in. Nothing smells any worse than a wet horse, or you can lead a horse to water, push him in and teach him the backstroke, then you've really got something. Wash your face in the morning, neck at night. Love

is life, life is love. Light your own candle and the world will be a much brighter place. When you get to the end of your rope, tie a little knot, hang on and swing. Stay calm, try to adjust. You can't live with 'em or without 'em. HOO HEE, HEE HOO! Don't let your six-gun get rusty. It's been a business doing pleasure with you, it's been real... and your LEEEEEEADAAAAAAAAH loves you-ah!"

Thanks, Jack. You were always a hard act to follow.

CHAPTER 3

DICK BIONDI: THE WILD EYE-TRALIAN

I was in the lobby of Seattle's Paramount Theater talking with a very tall man. He, his wife, and my wife and I had just shared a taxi from the Bainbridge Island ferry. No, we didn't know each other, and the shared ride was simply a matter of convenience. But, as we sipped wine in anticipation of the Randy Newman concert we were there to attend, we started to chat.

"So, what do you do?" he asked, looking down at me.

"Well, a little of this and a little of that," I said. "One of the things I do is write a column about the history of radio."

"Really? What does that mean?"

"Well, I do biographical sketches; I try to capture who these people are, what they did, and, you know, why they're important."

"For example?" he asked.

I looked up at him. "Um, where are you from?"

"The Midwest," he answered.

"Oh. Ever hear of a radio station called WLS?" I asked.

A smile appeared on his face. "Sure!" And then, right there, in the middle of the lobby, he sang the jingle. "Eighty-nine.....Double U LLLL SSSSS."

People stared. Too much wine, they must have thought. "So, who did you interview from WLS?" he asked.

"Ever heard of Dick Biondi?" I responded.

His face lit up. "You mean you actually talked with Dick Biondi?"

I nodded, yes.

"Wow, that's incredible!" he responded. "You know, I remember when I was a kid ..."

The next night, under completely different circumstances, Biondi's name came up again. It was as if I couldn't go anywhere without running into someone who knew who he was and had a remembrance or two. And, in case you're missing the point, these weren't radio people, they were radio listeners, people who'd been touched by Biondi.

I wonder if this happens anymore.

•

Dick Biondi is from Endicott, New York and came of age five or six years before the dawn of rock 'n' roll. Rhythm and blues — the phrase was coined by Billboard's Jerry Wexler to describe what had been called "race" records — was still a secret to most whites and only known to listeners who dared migrate to the top end of the AM radio dial where they found the music on far away radio stations like WLAC/Nashville, KAAY/Little Rock, WKBW/Buffalo and WLS/Chicago. Biondi says those distant AM signals still live in his memory and hold a special place in his heart. "Young guys, today, don't have a chance," he says.

What he's talking about is the chance he had, the chance to be a young kid playing rock 'n' roll records on a 50,000 watt AM radio station with a signal so large that it covered the entire east coast, two countries and twenty-two states. "That kind of thing will never happen again," Biondi says, sadly.

Biondi was sixteen when he started in radio at WCBA/Corning, New York. He did what was called a split shift — a few early morning hours; then a few more in the afternoon. His salary was one hundred dollars a month and he spent seven dollars a week for lodging and another seven bucks for a meal ticket at a local Italian restaurant. It was 1950. After three months, his bosses fired him. "I guess they didn't think I was strong enough," he explains.

He placed an ad in "Broadcasting" magazine and, after a few weeks, accepted a job offer at KVOB/Alexandria, Louisiana (VOB stood for Voice of the Baptists). Moving to the south from New York was a culture shock, he says. "Everybody thought I'd get eaten by alligators, but it was a full-time job that paid forty-five dollars a week. Back then, all I wanted to do was go on the air and run my mouth."

He did a late night show that he called "Nightwatch." "At seventeen, I thought I was real sexy. You know, talking with a deep voice, playing the pop hits of the day." He also did a rhythm and blues show called "Jammin' Jive." "I called myself Daddio Substitute, and part of my Saturday show included a segment of religious gospel music sponsored by the Progressive Funeral Home." Another sponsor was Old California Brand Wine, and Biondi, excited by the energy of the music, would, as often as not, flip open his mic and lay out a line like, "A little OCB is good for the soul."

He was finding his voice. But, in 1954, after four Louisiana years, an eternity for a young man barely twenty-one, Biondi was forced to move on. "I was coaching a little league football team and one of the guys, a big-shot local politician, decided he was going to run up the score on my guys. Well, I, uh, sorta, blew up."

This blow up, he admits, didn't earn him any new friends or get him any help from those who might have stood by him. So, after five years in Alexandria, he packed his bags and headed back toward the east coast, landing in York, Pennsylvania, where he was hired by Susquehanna Broadcasting. But, that job didn't last long, Biondi says. "I was fired for being too goofy."

His next stop was Youngstown, Ohio, where he signed on with a young self-starter named Myron Jones. Jones was an engineer based in Erie, Pennsylvania, who'd founded WJET, a station well known, at the time, for its commitment to rock 'n' roll and local news. Biondi says he was totally blown away.

"It was the first time I'd seen real Top 40."

In 1958, WKBW, Buffalo, an AM giant with a signal that covered twenty-two states along the eastern seaboard and, up into Canada, too, changed its format to Top 40. It was a move that didn't please everyone, especially George "Hound Dog" Lorenz, one of WKBW's star disc jockeys. Lorenz thought Top 40 was restrictive. "It hurts the recording industry, lowers radio listening and decreases a new artist's chance to make it," he told "Billboard" magazine. The indignant Lorenz quit. His replacement was Dick Biondi

WKBW changed format for business reasons that included: (1) The announced loss of its NBC network affiliation, (2) The crosstown success of WBNY-AM, Buffalo's first true Top 40 (programmed by a man named Dick Lawrence who would become PD of WKBW) and (3) The recognition of changing demographics that made young adults an attractive audience. Three weeks before the new format hit the air the station began teasing Buffalo with promos promising the pending arrival of "Audio Activity" and "FutureSonic Radio."

Then, on July 3, twenty-four hours before the format actually debuted, twelve beautiful girls hit the streets, each proclaiming she was "Miss KB" and each handing out the station's new Top 30 survey, accompanied by a flier that stated, in big bright bold letters:

It's Hot!
Friday, July 4th, is Independence Day,
And WKBW goes K-Boom!!!

At high noon, on July 4, 1958, the station exploded with a two-hour sneak preview high lighting the music AND the new personalities. "The first day was awesome," remembered one of the jocks, Art Roberts. "KB was a hit from day one!"

•

Neither of them knew the honeymoon was over.

Biondi had been at WKBW for two years and, in that time, had virtually reinvented Top 40 night-time radio. His boss — no, I won't give you his name — was a newlywed and, on the night he and his bride came home from their honeymoon, the bride decided to throw a pajama party for her girlfriends. "It was kinda weird," says Biondi. "I mean, can you imagine a woman coming home from her honeymoon, calling her girlfriends and kicking her husband out of the house?"

So, anyway, this all-girl soiree didn't exactly float the young manager's boat. He left his home and began to drive around town, looking for something to do and somewhere to go. "Aha," he must have thought, "I'll go to where I'm the boss of everybody."

He arrived at the station, ran into Biondi first thing, and started yelling at him, giving him hell.

"The guy was a bug," Biondi remembers. "So, I went on the air and casually said, 'If you see my boss driving down Main Street in a grey Chevy Impala convertible, throw stones at him.' "

As he was about to find out, 50,000 watts is no place to do a throwaway line. Why? Because his devoted listeners heard him and did exactly what they'd been asked to do.

Rocks through a windshield, one baby DJ out the door.

•

For the 500 watt radio station owned and operated by Sears-Roebuck & Company of Chicago, April 9, 1924 was a red-letter day. The station began its test runs with the call letters, WES, but these were only placeholder calls and, three days later, when the station formally debuted, it had a new name — WLS — initials that stood for World's Largest Store.

Actress Ethel Barrymore, on hand to witness the occasion, was so frightened by the microphone placed in front of her that she lost her composure and demanded that the "damn thing" be turned off. A week later, WLS introduced "The National Barn Dance," a live country and western show (that preceded WSM's "Grand Ole

Opry" by eighteen months). Two weeks after that *The New York Times* ran this headline:

NEW RADIO TELEPHONE STATION
OPERATING IN CHICAGO

It's difficult to overstate WLS's influence in the decades that followed. From The Barn Dance, featuring one of country music's first stars, Patsy Montana, to its farm programming, patriotic features and its ensemble of variety shows (featuring a very young Andy Williams, Patti Page, Rex Allen, and Homer and Jethro), the 50,000 watt signal at 890 was a constant companion for much of the Midwest.

But, by the end of the '50s, rural America wasn't the important or desirable audience to advertisers it had once been. The country was on the move and television, super highways, baby boomers and rock 'n' roll all signified a new and shiny consumer-focused future. In New York City executives at ABC Radio were paying attention. They, after all, were the same folks who'd given Dick Clark the green light for TV's "American Bandstand" and, when it came time to make a change at WLS, it had been these execs who decided the station should take its programming focus from the back 40 — to Top 40.

•

Biondi, who'd just been fired at WKBW for inciting rock throwing, got a phone call. On the line was Sam Holman, the new Program Director at WLS. Holman knew all about Biondi and his act (including the rocks) and, even though his plan called for WLS to project a midwest friendly attitude during the day, he wanted a wildman at the air at night. Biondi fit the bill.

On May 2, 1960 WLS became a Top 40 station. The air staff included Bob Hale, Gene Taylor, Mort Crowley, Jim Dunbar, Ed Grennan, plus Biondi and three newsmen — Jerry Golden, Harvey Wittenberg and Jerry Mitchell. Holman commissioned the Anita Kerr Singers to do new jingles and, with the new staff in place and very little promotion money, he put the new format in play.

Biondi says Holman gave him free reign. "Well, within reason," he chuckles. "Sam only called me on the air one time. Bobby Darin was in town and came by the station, and I put him on the air. After he left, the hotline rang.

"This is Sam. What the hell did you just do?"

"Well, I just interviewed Bobby Darin."

"Whadda you mean? You interviewed him without asking me!? Don't you ever do that again!" Holman slammed down the phone.

Biondi had two hours before his shift ended and started sweating bullets. "That's it," he thought. "I'm going to get fired."

At midnight he walked out of the studio full of trepidation. To his surprise, he found his boss standing by the elevator. "C'mon," said Holman. "Let's go have a beer."

"So, we went downstairs to The London House and sat for two and a half hours," Biondi recalls, fondly. "Never once did he mention what happened. He just talked about how well the station was doing. He was a gentleman, a guy who gave the seven of us the biggest break of our lives."

Despite his paranoia, Biondi was a superstar at WLS and Holman knew it. If you were a listener who lived under the umbrella of the station's monster signal and were under thirty, Biondi was all that mattered. He ranted, he raved, he sang between the records and he even had a hit of his own, *On Top Of A Pizza* (sung to the tune of *On Top Of Old Smokey*), which sold over 11,000 copies.

"He was a madman," says Tribune Broadcasting's Lee Abrams. "I'd never heard anything like him before. He did knock-knock jokes and dedications." Biondi, claims Abrams, is why he was sucked into the radio life. "When Dick hit the air, it was electric. And, you also kinda knew that half of America was listening at the same time, so you felt you were part of a community."

Biondi's audience didn't stop at the Canadian border, either. In an interview on PBS, where he discussed his roots, Neil Young said that one of his bigger influences was listening to Biondi.

During his three years at WLS, Biondi was named The Best Disc Jockey in America twice. His on air act bordered on the inane and insane but there was more to it than just zaniness. "There was a fire at a church in Anderson, Indiana," he told me. "I went on the air and said, 'You know, everybody's talking about how bad teenagers are. Well, wouldn't it be nice if everybody listening tonight would just take a dime and send it to the church?' Well, the church collected so much money that, when it was resurrected, they named a new wing The Teenager Building."

During the summer of 1961, when it appeared that the United States and Russia might be on the verge of nuclear war, Biondi took to the air again. Like many Americans, he was troubled by what he was hearing and conflicted by what he felt, although he knew he couldn't address his feelings on the air. But, he says, he tried. "Did you see that beautiful sunset we're having?" he asked his audience. "It's still out there a little bit. Go take a look."

He paused, then continued. "If you don't believe the sunset means God is going to make everything alright, then there's something wrong."

Remembering the moment over forty-five years later, Biondi says that's just the way he said it and that there's more to the story. "A week later I got a letter from a lady in Michigan, who wrote that her husband had been arrested for arson and was facing forty years in prison. She wrote that she'd had a gun and was so distraught she was going to shoot herself and her three children. But, when I said that everything was going to be alright, she looked out her window, saw my sunset, put down the gun and called her pastor."

The letter went on to say that two weeks later the real arsonist confessed, and her husband was exonerated. "You never realize that what you're saying is actually touching people," Biondi says.

"I still get chills when I think about it."

In 1963, Biondi's WLS show ran from nine to midnight.

"In my ten o'clock hour, I had five minutes of news at the top of the hour, five minutes of Dick Clark at 10:25, and twenty-two minutes of commercials," he says. "So, one night I complained on the air. I mean, yeah, I had fun with it. But, c'mon — twenty-two minutes of commercials!"

The next day Biondi arrived at the station. He remembers it was Friday, May 3. Entering the building, he was greeted by WLS's Sales Manager, clearly a mad man with a mission. The manager began to yell about what Biondi had said on the air the night before. "Every filthy word you could think of," says Biondi, "He accused me of taking food out of his children's mouths."

Biondi was taken aback and didn't know how to respond. So, he kept on walking with the manager in pursuit. "I ran into the production studio," says Biondi, "and he went into the control room, pushed the talk-back button and went at it again."

By now Biondi was agitated and, when the manager entered the production studio and threatened him physically, he lost his composure, picked up something on the table, and threw it. Only afterwards did he realize it was a letter opener.

PD Sam Holman, attempting to calm things down, ran into the studio, separated the men and told Biondi to go home. Biondi did. What happened next is the strangest part of the story.

Dick Biondi left WLS that day and never returned. He says he thought that he'd been fired. Only later, after he had another job in Los Angeles, did he discover that all Holman intended was that he go home and cool off.

•

Biondi was a hot property.

Within weeks of the letter opener incident he joined KRLA/Los Angeles. It was still May of 1963. Boss Radio, KHJ, was two years away from launching (so, not a factor yet), and KRLA's only Top

40 competition was KFWB, Color Radio, Channel 98.

Biondi arrived in LA just before summer hit. It was nine months before the British Invasion — which, for some unknown reason, KFWB would chose to ignore, to their demise. (By the way, Biondi had been way ahead in the Beatle game. As early as February of 1963 he'd played *Please Please Me* on WLS, when Music Director Art Roberts found it, and he'd brought the record with him to Los Angeles. "I played it on KRLA and the phones started to ring," he remembers. "They told me to get that crap off the air and play The Beach Boys!")

Biondi's stay at KRLA only lasted three months because, shortly after arriving, he was offered and accepted a job hosting the first-ever-national rock 'n' roll show on The Mutual Broadcasting System. Based in New York City, the program was scheduled to debut in late fall, but when President Kennedy was assassinated in Dallas, the network pushed the launch back to early 1964. Biondi parked himself in Binghamton, New York, and waited for the call. When it finally came, he reported for duty.

The new national show was music and artist intensive and Biondi says, "I did a lot of artist interviews." One of the first featured a virtually unknown English band called The Rolling Stones. "It was their first day in the United States," says Biondi. Before meeting with Biondi, the Stones had been at WMCA, where they'd been asked to record some drop-ins ("Hi, this is Mick Jagger and you're listening to WMCA.") Apparently things hadn't gone very well. "I found out that every time Jagger recorded a line, someone at the station would tell him to do it again," says Biondi.

Jagger wasn't used to this kind of treatment and got angry and frustrated. The last straw came when the station thanked him for his efforts by giving him a WMCA T-shirt. "He was furious," Biondi told me. "When the band hit the street, Mick walked over to a car, put his foot up on the bumper, and shined his shoes with the shirt. Then he threw it into a gutter."

The Rolling Stones' interview with Biondi went smoother despite a gathering of network bigwigs who stared at the group, aghast at the length of their hair. Afterwards, Biondi was invited to join the band back at their hotel. "So we're sitting in the suite and the record company promo guy comes over and says, 'Dick, you ought to hear what Jagger just said about you.'"

"What?" asked Biondi

"Well, he wanted to know if you were really a disc jockey. He says you weren't loud and boisterous like the other guys he met today."

In the years since, Biondi says that whenever he runs into the Stones, Jagger remembers exactly what happened. He also says his love for their music became so well known that he was the only disc jockey in America to ever be booed at a Beatles concert.

•

In 1967, Dick Biondi returned to Chicago to work for WCFL. Six years later, in 1973, he joined WNMB/Myrtle Beach, South Carolina, and stayed in the sunshine for ten years. Still, Chicago was always in his heart.

In 1983, WBBM-FM/Chicago, a CBS station, brought him back to the Windy City but, after only a year, someone suggested WBBM wasn't the best fit for Biondi's talents and CBS transferred him to sister station WJMK-FM, where Biondi became the signature voice of the station's oldies format. This move made sense, and Biondi stayed at WJMK-FM for the next twenty-two years.

•

Dick Biondi is still on the air in Chicago, at WLS-FM. He says it's exactly what he's supposed to be doing at this stage in his life. "I still can't wait to turn on the microphone every night," he explained.

I asked him how the world has changed since he first went on the radio. "The times are more explicit," he responds. "But, what they're saying about gangsta rap today is exactly what they said about rock 'n' roll in the '50s."

"So, when you think back over the years," I asked, "what makes you most proud?"

"The connection I have with my listeners," he replies. "To be able to touch someone like the way I did, when I told people to look at the sunset that night long ago."

He pauses. (As I wait for him to gather his thoughts I started thinking about the man I met at the Randy Newman concert, and how excited he was when I mentioned Biondi's name.) Finally, Mr. Biondi decides how he wants to end our conversation. He takes a deep breath. "Radio," he says, "is the greatest medium in the world."

In 1998, Dick Biondi was inducted into the NAB's Radio Hall of Fame. From my perspective this gesture of respect was long overdue and despite its righteousness, it doesn't even come close to capturing the affection — no, that's not the right word; the word is love — the *love* that his listeners have for him. Still, and forever.

I don't think relationships like that happen anymore.

P.S. The Ron Jacobs *Cruisin'* Series (1960) includes a re-creation of Dick Biondi's program on WKBW/Buffalo.

CHAPTER 4

CHUCK BLORE "GET STAN FREBERG..."

Chuck Blore. Who is he, and why should you care?

"His innovative pioneering of emotions as the living center of great radio changed radio advertising forever," says Dick Orkin, the creator of *Chickenman*. Orkin then amended his statement. "Hell, make that all advertising."

(If you're skeptical, google Chuck Blore, hit on The Chuck Blore Company site, skip the intro, go directly to the speaking link, and watch Blore do a show-and-tell to the Hollywood Chamber of Commerce on how an innocuous subject, like testing for cancer, can be turned into cinematic audio magic.)

What I'm trying to say is Chuck Blore looks at things like nobody else. Always has, still does.

•

LA disc jockey Al Jarvis created "The Make Believe Ballroom" on the west coast (WNEW/New York's Martin Block copied the idea and went national with it) and, because Blore grew up in Los Angeles, it was Jarvis he looked up to and who inspired him to get into radio.

Blore began his career at a little radio station in Kingman, Arizona, a town famous for Route 66, its proximity to Hoover Dam, and for temperatures that climbed over one-hundred degrees. But, it was the early '50s and he was young, still in his early twenties, and hot to trot.

After only three months, he slid south to KTKT/Tucson and it was there that a radio exec named Gordon McLendon, driving to Dallas from Los Angeles, heard him on the air and engineered a job offer that led Blore to KTSA/San Antonio. Blore accepted, but before reporting to the Alamo City was told he had to attend "bible" school in Dallas.

Gordon McLendon had a vision about how to run a radio station that was specific, disciplined and neatly chronicled in a policy book, and everyone who worked for him was required to learn it. Blore remembers the sessions well. "Gordon would arrive in the morning, tell us to study the book and then say, 'There is nothing more you have to know and nothing less you have to know.' "

Cram time over, young Blore headed south to KTSA and immediately went on the air. He says he was troubled by how he sounded. "I've never had the kind of voice that would put you on the radio," he confided.

To differentiate himself from the "golden-voiced performers," he created little theater pieces — short audio plays lasting twenty, thirty or forty seconds. Within a short time his audience grabbed onto them and, as it turned out, so did McLendon. Much to his surprise, Blore discovered HIS theater pieces were being copied and bicycled around to the other McLendon stations. Blore wasn't happy about this turn of events and the more he brooded, the angrier he got. He decided to confront McLendon directly, in person. "I didn't know you were putting my things on your other stations," he told the Man. "I think I should be paid."

"No," replied McLendon. "You should be a Program Director."

"I don't want to be a Program Director. I want to be the greatest disc jockey known to man."

"No," said McLendon. "You're going to be a Program Director and I think you've made a wise decision."

The next thing Blore knew he was headed west to El Paso. He'd been named Program Director of McLendon's KELP. He says he still remembers the drive and how scared he was. He says his mind was racing. "At one point I glanced over at my wife and said, 'I only hope when I hear this station I'll know whether it's good or bad.' "

{ 28 }

Turn It Up!

In 1957, El Paso, Texas was a sleepy, little border town with eight radio stations. Four of the stations broadcast in Spanish, but KELP, the English speaking Top 40 station, was the undisputed leader, despite one of Gordon McLendon's golden rules — always play two Glenn Miller records per hour.

McLendon had purchased the station from a pair of brothers who were traveling evangelists. "When they were on the road preaching they'd just switch the station off," says Bob Gourley. Gourley, General Manager of KELP during the early '70s, also says McLendon bought the station for less than $15,000 (plus line haul fees owed him for Liberty Network baseball feeds) and used it as a laboratory. "Gordon figured El Paso was large enough to get a decent sample size. With Tucson three-hundred miles to the west, Albuquerque three-hundred miles to the north, and Midland/Odessa three-hundred miles east and south, he figured he wouldn't have to worry about competitors stealing his ideas."

Blore followed McLendon's programming bible as instructed and, over a period of months, created what many feel may have been the purest example of McLendon's ideals. But, then the station was sold. At first, Blore was upset. McLendon's group, after all, was one of the most admired in the industry and he didn't want to leave. But, when it turned out his contract transferred with the station sale, he took advantage of the cards he'd been dealt. "As soon as I was no longer under the McLendon yoke, I stole Todd Storz's music format," says Blore. (The Glenn Miller records disappeared.)

Virtually overnight the playlist at KELP got very short. (While McLendon and Storz are both recognized as "The Fathers of Top 40," most radio scholars give Storz credit for recognizing the benefits of a short playlist – listeners hear their favorite songs more often — and McLendon kudos for understanding the value of promotion.) Blore's short playlist yielded big numbers; in fact, KELP's ratings were so huge – seventy percent of the available audience listened to the station — that they're hard to even fathom today.

Blore was in the office on the day after Thanksgiving in 1957 when the phone rang.

"Are you the Program Director?" a voice asked.

"Yes," Blore answered.

"You have amazing ratings."

"Yes, I do. You're right."

The voice belonged to Bob Purcell, an executive at Crowell-Collier Broadcasting, the owners of KFWB/Los Angeles. "Would you like to come to Los Angeles and talk to us about a job here?" Purcell asked.

"Hell, yes," responded Blore. "LA's my home. I'll go visit my parents."

•

Blore arrived in Los Angeles twenty-four hours before his meeting so he could listen to the station. He knew Purcell was interested in talking about "modern radio," the term the radio industry was calling the new Top 40 format breaking audience records in Dallas, Houston, New Orleans and, yes, El Paso. He also knew that if KFWB was going to be successful he'd have to make a lot of changes, but that convincing Purcell to let him do it was going to be an uphill battle. "I had this yellow pad full of stuff and during our first meeting I started telling him what was wrong with the station."

On Blore's list was a fifteen minute afternoon sports program in the afternoons and a thirty minute block in the morning devoted to the Teamster's Union. Both made KFWB a lot of money. Still, Blore told Purcell they had to go.

"Oh my God! No! No! No! That's a quarter of our billing!" Purcell exclaimed.

Blore insisted and, when Purcell gave in, says he knew they were really going to go with his idea, and that he had the job.

The launch date was set for January 1, 1958.

Blore decided to call the station "Color Radio," an idea he admits he appropriated from McLendon. "McLendon changed things on KLIF every three or four days and didn't stick with any one name for long. He had "Hi Fi Radio" and "Stereo Radio," and one that lasted about a week was "Color Radio." I thought it was the best thing he'd ever done."

In 1958, Los Angeles didn't have a full tilt boogie Top 40 station. KDAY was playing the music and had some disc jockeys, but it was only a daytimer, and XEAK, "The Mighty 690," had a giant signal blowing in from Tijuana, but it was just playing music — so it was basically a jukebox with no personality. "There were lots of stations *almost* doing the format," says Blore. "But, no one was really putting it all together."

Putting it all together meant the right music, the best personalities and the biggest promotions — whatever it took to make Los Angeles aware of the station in a hurry. Blore says KFWB's owners came through with the money he needed to make a big splash. "We were #1 within three months. It was really a phenomenon." KFWB's original on-air staff featured Bruce Hayes, Al Jarvis (Blore always pays his debts), Joe Yocam, Elliot Field, B. Mitchell Reed, Bill Balance and Ted Quillan. These were the guys on the stage. But, behind the scenes, KFWB was about executing Blore's vision. He insisted the station should have a heart, be fun, and always sound like, and be, a winner.

In the five years that Chuck Blore programmed KFWB — a time that found Beach Boy, Brian Wilson, cruising around Hawthorne, California, in his car listening — KFWB was the #1 radio station in Los Angeles.

•

"No, no, no."

These three words expressed Newton Minnow's sentiments about one broadcasting company owning a large number of stations. Forty years before the broadcasting industry deregulated, Minnow, an FCC Commissioner, took a dim view of one company having the power to reach so many ears. "We can't have one corporation talking to that many people," he commented.

Around the same time Minnow was making these comments, Crowell-Collier Broadcasting, Blore's employer, was making moves to buy a New York City radio station, WMGM, and another in Washington D.C. The company planned to add these two to the three they already owned — KFWB/Los Angeles, KEWB/San Francisco and KDWB/Minneapolis — and turn the company into a five station group. For Blore, this growth meant he inherited a mountain of paperwork. "I was left hiring PDs for all the other stations," he says. "After a while, I wasn't doing anything except writing memos and telling other people what to do. The fun was gone."

He says he started looking around for something new to do. "At the time Crowell-Collier wanted to start an audio/visual division and asked me if I'd like to be creative head," he says. It seemed like a good move but, as time passed, Blore discovered designing film strips wasn't anywhere as much fun as building radio stations. One day, acting on impulse, he just upped and quit.

The company was not amused and were quick to point out that he was still under contract. So, for the next eighteen months, Blore collected a check in exchange for agreeing to not work in broadcasting. Not just in LA, but anywhere.

He spent his time playing golf and played at drawing a comic strip.

He twiddled his thumbs and waited for the non-compete to play out.

In 1963 Paul Stoddard, a hot-shot salesman for KFWB, was at his wit's end. His relationship with the local Rambler dealer was cooling off and he needed help. In desperation he called Blore. "Can you cook up a promotion for me?" he pleaded.

Blore thought about it for a moment before he responded. Then he told Stoddard he didn't think giving away balloons and hot dogs at a car dealership made people buy cars, which was the state of promotions in '63. "You gotta get them down there to the showroom to see 'em. Sell them on the cars *before* they go!"

"How do I do that?" Stoddard asked.

"Do a good commercial," Blore replied.

Strangely enough the notion of doing a good commercial simply hadn't occurred to the salesman. Blore, however, knew the spoken word was king and that creating compelling audio events, like a good commercial, could bring the keys to the kingdom.

Skeptical, yet somehow relieved, Stoddard went in for the kill. "Uh, Chuck. Would *you* do the commercial?"

Blore agreed. Technically, Blore was no longer a KFWB employee but, when he called the publishing company that held rights to *Beep Beep,* a 1958 hit by The Playmates, the publisher wasn't aware of Blore's employment status and was thrilled to hear from someone at the #1 radio station in Los Angeles.

Blore told him he wanted to use the song in a commercial.

"Yes, yes, yes!" was the publisher's response.

Blore then explained that he wanted to pay for the rights.

"No need to do that," replied the anxious publishing exec.

Blore insisted. "C'mon. I'm going to charge the Rambler dealership."

Five hundred dollars later the song was his to use. "Then, I called Johnny Mann and asked if he could imitate The Playmates."

Blore, along with Mann and his singers, recorded the jingle and put in on the air. The result was that Rambler dealer was happy and Stoddard got to keep the account. And Blore, not thinking much about it, went back to playing golf. "And then I got this telegram," he says:

Congratulations! You've won first place in the Advertising Association of the West.

Two months later, the phone rang with more news. "They told me the spot had won an international broadcast award, that it'd been named the best commercial in the world."

Blore remembers thinking, "Jesus, maybe I can do this."

•

Ted Factor was a big shot at the West Coast branch of Doyle-Dane-Bernbach, the advertising agency that had come up with the "Think Small" campaign for Volkswagen, a breakthrough moment for the Beetle.

Blore, with his Rambler spot in hand, asked for an appointment. "So, I played it for him and he thought it was good," says Blore. He also says he told Factor, "I really don't know anything about doing this."

"Maybe that's why it's good," replied Factor. "You're bringing a different approach to it."

"Well, do you think I could do it?" asked Blore.

"Close the door," Factor answered. For the next four hours Factor lectured Blore on the principles of good advertising and Blore was captivated. In the succeeding weeks the two met two more times — each session lasting four hours — each an opportunity for Blore to soak things up and for Factor to gauge his student. Finally, after twelve intense hours, Factor thought Blore was ready. "We have a client named Rainier Ale," he offered. "Why don't you do a commercial for them?"

"So," says Blore, "I wrote these spots, got Pearl Bailey to record them and, after they put them on the air, my God, you couldn't go anywhere without hearing Pearl singing about Rainier Ale."

Soon Blore was in demand. "Suddenly people were calling me. 'Hey, I want you do my commercials!' I was in business instantly!"

He didn't, however, have a long-term plan. His only thought was he'd do this commercial thing until his non-compete was over and then, go back to radio. But, by the time the date came and went, he was so successful in the advertising game that he just kept floating along.

"I was thinking, 'You know, this is kind of fun. I'll just do it for a little while.' "

That was over forty-five years ago.

•

During the '50s and '60s Stan Freberg made a name for himself writing for radio. His work, including *St. George and The Dragonet, The Yellow Rose Of Texas* and *Green Chritma*, was controversial, comedic and cutting edge. The man was on everyone's A- list.

Blore, the beginner, considered Freberg the man to beat and in a startling move, one that grabbed attention for its audacity, Blore wrote an ad for a trade publication that said:

> **"If you can't get Chuck Blore to do your commercials,
> get Stan Freberg."**

Freberg was furious. "My God, did he hate me for that," Blore says, laughing. "It was great."

By 1965, Blore's plan to return to radio was on permanent hold. "I'd never thought anything could be bigger than radio," he told me, "but I was being invited to speak in every English-speaking country in the world that had commercial broadcasting."

One trip took him to London where he was so famous and in such demand that he was invited to have dinner with the Queen.

Yes, of England.

•

Al Davis, of football fame, and Don Richman got to know each other at the University of Southern California, and the two became partners in a public relations firm. "At first, Don and Al's only client was the University of Southern California," says Blore. "And even though USC football wasn't a big deal to (newspapers like) The L.A. Times, Don and Al did their jobs well."

In the late '50s Barron Hilton (Paris Hilton's grandfather, the one who cut Paris and her cousins out of his will) became President of the Carte Blanche Credit Card Company. At the time he owned a six-million-dollar orange juice company, a jet-leasing business, assorted oil investments, and was also Vice President of the Hilton Hotel Corporation. In 1960, Hilton bought a football franchise in Los Angeles and hired Richman and Davis to do their PR magic. Job one was coming up with a name for the team. "Hilton bought the team because he thought it'd be a great way to promote Carte Blanche with, you know, all the football fans," Blore explains. "So, Don gave the team their name: The Chargers. It had nothing to do with charging down the field. It was, at least in Don's mind, about the card."

In 1961, when The Chargers left L.A. for San Diego, Richman chose not to go with them. Instead, he decided to write for television and, in short order, he wrote "The Farmer's Daughter," "Rat Patrol" and some early "Tarzan" episodes.

"The reason I met him," says Blore, "is he was trying to write at home and his wife would come in and ask, 'Do you want peas or carrots for dinner?' " Because vegetables were the last thing on Richman's mind, he asked Blore to come to his rescue. "Look, I can't deal with peas and carrots and I've got to have someplace else to do my writing. So, just give me a corner of your office here and, whenever I need money, I'll write a television show."

The relationship between these two men lasted for twenty-two years, until Richman's death. Not the least of the reasons the partnership lasted was Richman's claim that he could write just like Blore. "It's the Lord's truth," Blore insists. "We were partners and, God, it was great."

•

Aaron Sorkin, the creator of "Sports Night" and "The West Wing" had a short-lived show on NBC, "Studio 60 on the Sunset Strip." A behind-the-scenes look at a "Saturday Night Live" type program, the show provided a microscopic view of what it takes to conceive, assemble and execute fifty minutes of original sketch programming each week.

This show reminds me of the golden age of radio and of what Chuck Blore was trying to accomplish when he decided to take on the programming job at KIIS-AM/Los Angeles.

By 1974 Blore hadn't been a hands-on programmer for almost ten years, but he had been listening. "With the exception of Robert W. Morgan and Don Steele, my initial take on KHJ was that it was mechanical. It was very slick and I admired it, but my first impression was it didn't have any heart." This comment seems severe considering the august place KHJ holds in our collective memory, but please consider that the conveyance of emotion is everything to Chuck Blore. When he took over KIIS-AM, his first priority wasn't the guys on the air, but the establishment of a creative department that would work behind the scenes. Its job, he says, was to weave the tapestry that would be the heart and soul of the new station. "It was all about what we did between the records," Blore explains. "We did mini-dramas and dramatized intros to records and the audience loved it."

Here's an example of "Kiss-ettes":

> Voice one (adult male): "And the meek shall inherit the earth."
>
> Voice two (a child): "As if we don't have enough problems."

Here's another:

Voice one (adult male): "God is dead — Nietzsche."

Voice two (God with thunder): "Nietzsche is dead — God."

Coming up with ideas and getting them written, produced and on the air was an arduous task. But, the creative output wasn't the only idea that made K   different. Blore also took advantage of audience listening patterns. "People listen at the same time every day — habit patterns — and we know from research that they listen anywhere from nineteen to ninety minutes. So, I concentrated on creating the best and most compelling radio I could, packaged it into two hour programs and played them in rotation all day long. I figured no one would ever hear things twice."

His efforts paid off when the station went from zero (no show) to #6 in its first rating period. And, then, it was over. "They (the station's owners) told me I had $300,000 to do it," says Blore. As it turned out, the owners of KIIS were absolutely broke and the $300,000 actually represented the debt they had to service.

Blore, while slightly disappointed, was, and still is, philosophical about it all. "I think what we did reflected the very up, positive wonderfulness of life that the radio station was supposed to be."

•

Chuck Blore is wrapping up a book on his life and career which is scheduled to be published some time in the near future. It's called "OK, OK, I Wrote The Book" and, in it, you'll find a memo he wrote to the staff at KIIS. His words convey a spirit and point of view that, sadly, is missing in radio today. Read them, please, and see if you don't agree.

Should you disagree — well, I'll find consolation in believing Aaron Sorkin and the fictional writers at "Studio 60" would side with me.

To: All Concerned With KIIS Programming
From: Chuck Blore

What follows here, in addition to being confidential, is an explanation of what this station is about to become. KIIS is about to burst wide open with an unfamiliar, seldom used approach to radio — it's called entertainment. Radio as an entertainment medium — pretty wild idea, huh? Entertaining, not casually, specifically. Not some of the time, all of the time.

Every radio station I have programmed, all of which have dominated the markets they served, were not driven by music. The audience was flawless in choosing the music they wanted to hear — and that was the music we gave them. What made these stations so successful was what happened between the records. The name of that was ... entertainment.

The question is, if it's not specifically music, what constitutes entertainment as it pertains to this radio station? It's what makes the listener smile. It's what makes them think or, at least, think they're thinking. It's what's fascinating, what's compelling, what's relevant to them, what's interesting — other words for entertaining.

This radio station will have a creative department whose job will be to create non-stop entertainment pieces. Much of these entertainments will be pre-produced "smile or thought provokers," which will be programmed three or four times each hour. There will be pre-produced, topical, multi-part dramatizations of topical and/or sensational events. These will be in five parts presented weekly: part one, Monday; part two, Tuesday; etc. We will also produce a series of Mini-Dramas each week. These "audio dramas" will actually be dramatized introductions to records featured on the station.

Although much of what goes on the air will be produced in advance, most of the "entertainment" stuff will be done daily by the live on-air presenters.

The presenters, the on-air personalities, are likable, intelligent, charismatic people who are obviously in love with what they are a part of. What they must do is ask themselves, with everything they prepare, "Does what I am about to do, or say, matter to the audience?" Remember that everything we do is done from the audience's point of view. Everything is a constant, non-stop answer to the audience's non-spoken question, "Why should I listen to this station? What's in it for me?"

And this is not something that can be done part of the time. When a person tunes to the station they should hear the difference at once. When they come back the next time, it should be there again, immediately, positively. While it's not difficult to get people to try your station the first time, once they try it, tire of it and leave, it's almost impossible to re-attract them.

The beauty of what we're talking about is, this interesting stuff, this stuff that's relevant to our audience, is everywhere. All we gotta do is funnel it through to them continuously, relentlessly, unremittingly around-the-clock in an entertaining manner.

Now, I guess we're gonna have to put something on to fill up the holes between the "entertainment" stuff.

I suppose the obvious answer is music, but maybe, not so obvious is … we must not be trapped into a "format," or even a demographic. One of my pet peeves about what has happened to radio today becomes painfully clear when you ask a PD about his radio station. He will probably not describe his station at all, but rather, he'll tell you the kind of music they play, "We're a CHR" or an Oldies or Top 40 or Hard Rock or whatever. I think that's the worst kind of trap you can fall into. A much better idea is to play the stuff that enhances the radio station in the minds of people listening, regardless of what kind of music it is. It's far better done by "feel" than by somebody else's list.

Chuck Blore, 1974

CHAPTER 5

JERRY BOULDING: DR. JOLLY JERRY B.

The good Doctor doesn't blow his own horn, but he should.

In a career stretching over forty years, he's programmed sixteen major market radio stations, developed the first urban format delivered by satellite, SMN's "Heart and Soul," headed a major record label division, consulted more radio stations than you can imagine, and been in charge of programming for one of America's most prominent broadcasting companies, The American Urban Radio Network (AURN).

Jerry Boulding joined AURN in late 1997. His job, according to an announcement in "Jet" magazine, was to "oversee the network's entire entertainment program menu." A few years later, around the millennium, Boulding told me he'd always thought he'd end his career at an African-American company, and that AURN fit the bill. And, it might have happened that way, but it didn't.

Instead, Joel Denver, the publisher of Allaccess.com, invited Boulding to join him in Los Angeles and to share his wealth of knowledge with those coming up in the radio business.

•

Jerry Boulding grew up in Beaver Falls, Pennsylvania, a steel town forty miles northwest of Pittsburgh. "I knew guys who worked in the mills, who made a lot of money, but hated what they did," he says. It wasn't a path he wanted to travel.

In the early '50s, Pittsburgh radio was interesting enough, but it was the late night signals — the big AMs from far away — that grabbed young Boulding's ears. "I listened to WLAC/Nashville and heard 'Hoss Man' Bill Allen and John R, two white guys, playing rhythm and blues." He also listened to artists like Ruth Brown, Lloyd Price, and The Drifters and songs that, for the most part, weren't being played on radio stations in western Pennsylvania.

"I went to where the music was," says Boulding. "The color of the guys presenting it wasn't important."

Although few and far between, some full-time black radio stations were on the air back in the day. "But, they were mostly in the south," says Boulding, "in cities with heavy black populations: Birmingham, Mobile, Miami, Atlanta, and Macon. And in a lot of markets black programming just didn't exist, except for rhythm and blues shows on weekends."

Then things started to change. "A guy at WIXY/Cleveland found a Sam Cooke record and started playing it. The next thing you know Alan Freed heard the song and said, 'Oh, man I'm gonna find all of this music I can.'" Freed, says Boulding, was one of the first to sense the goldmine in rhythm and blues. "Then, he went to New York, where he got big, got caught with payola and died broke." (Freed *did* get big, *did* take payola, and *did* die broke. But, payola *was* legal in the '50s. Freed's problem was not declaring it as income and not paying taxes.)

•

WILY-AM/Pittsburgh made its money selling time to preachers and it was there, on a daytime only signal, that Boulding got his radio start. "The station needed someone to run the (preacher's) tapes and I was lucky if I opened the microphone three times," he says. "Still, I knew if I stuck around long enough, my time would come."

Boulding had already decided the mills were a bad idea. So, when he graduated from high school, he went on to college, earning a bachelor's degree at Pittsburgh's Duquesne University. "I did it so I could have some career options."

After graduation Boulding had ROTC obligations and the army sent him to Korea, where he did get to do a little Armed Forces Radio, but not much. "There were very few blacks in Armed Forces Radio," he observes, dryly. Honorably discharged at Ft. Riley, Kansas, Boulding jumped back into radio at nearby KJCK/Junction City. "It was the perfect transition," he explains, adding that KJCK wasn't an African-American station. "It was one of those places where you got to do everything and I picked up some skills – production and formatics – that I probably wouldn't have gotten if I'd stayed in black radio."

From Junction City he jumped markets, up to WHB/Kansas City. It was there that Dave McNamee, the National PD of Sonderling Broadcasting, found him. Boulding laughs and says he still remembers their first phone conversation. "He asked me if I was black. I told him, 'Yes, I can't fake that.' "

"When I started doing black radio," he continues, "I was told, 'You don't sound black.' " My response was, 'What is black supposed to sound like?' "

Sonderling sent Boulding to Washington D.C., where he went on the air using the name Jolly Jerry B. "I was one of the original soul brothers at WOL," he says. "And I started doing things on the air that made me sound like either the hippest white boy you ever heard or a black guy, who wasn't going to go too far out."

•

A side bar to Boulding's time at WOL involves social activist Petey Greene, recently portrayed by Don Cheadle in the movie "Talk To Me."

Greene was a real person, who died of liver cancer in 1984. He was a high school dropout, discharged from the Army for drug use, and a man who'd been convicted of armed robbery and sent to prison. He was also a man who spoke up against poverty and racism, mostly in the Washington D.C. area, on radio (WOL), on television (Petey Greene's Washington), by doing standup and, according to the movie, on "The Tonight Show." In real life, Greene was also invited to The White House by Jimmy Carter and, when he died, over ten thousand mourners attended his funeral; one count had the number as high as twenty thousand. "Talk To Me" is about the events that happened after prison and before his death. I asked Boulding if the film clung to the facts. "No," he says. "It isn't an accurate depiction of what was going on."

What about Greene? Was his character for real? "Well, he was a 'character,' but he never did mornings at WOL, and the station's morning man never was fired to make room for him, as was depicted in the film. Petey did the weekend Public Affair shows, but he wasn't a disc jockey."

While Greene wasn't a star at WOL, Boulding says the man did have a following and that he represented the wild, outspoken side of the radio station — the "in your face" part of the audience that needed a voice and wanted to be heard. "In those days," he says, "there were a lot of angry groups who got on the air on Sundays to express their views."

"Talk To Me" portrays Dewey Hughes, the man who "discovered" Greene at Lofton Prison, as the Program Director of WOL. Boulding says that's not right either, that Hughes was WOL's Public Affairs Director, not an insignificant job in pre-deregulation radio. "Dewey was very good at what he did. He felt the pulse of the community and made sure the radio station was on top of and reflected the issues that affected the people who were listening to the station."

In the movie, the Hughes character argues with station owner E.G. Sonderling about the need for WOL to have more street credibility. "Did that really happen?" I asked.

"Yes, that part was true," replies Boulding. (In the interest of full disclosure, I think he's talking more about the concept than the actual scene or dialogue itself.)

What the movie does get right is its portrayal of "Nighthawk" Bob Terry, the night jock at WOL. "Terry had huge ratings," says Boulding. Terry also had two Doberman pinschers. "He was crazy. He used to keep the dogs in his convertible, right outside the radio station in Dupont Circle. He'd park by the meter, but never put any money it. And the gimmick was that the police would try to give him a ticket, but never could get close enough because of the dogs. So, between records, Terry would open the third-floor window, yell down to the dogs and command them to sit down. Then, he'd yell down to the cops and dare them to give him a ticket. This kinda thing even got Terry on television," Boulding says.

Yes, the dogs were in the movie.

•

Boulding's success at WOL led to a series of programming jobs along the eastern seaboard — in Roanoke, Richmond and Baltimore — and he was, eventually, invited to rejoin Sonderling as Program Director of WWRL/New York City. "I almost didn't go because I was doing so well in Baltimore," he says. "But, something inside me said, 'You gotta try it.' "

Boulding, like many of his contemporaries, saw society changing around him. By the time he arrived in New York City, he says many black Americans were seeing themselves in a different light. "James Brown had this song out, *Say It Loud, I'm Black and I'm Proud,* and the whole black thing was starting to happen. (But, by then) Martin Luther King, Malcolm and Bobby Kennedy were dead and there was a lot of anger."

From the anger, he says, came recognition of the need to come together. While no longer part of the vernacular today, Boulding remembers that the words "Right On" took on a special meaning in late 1968; that they became an expression of solidarity for the black community and by using them on the air and reflecting their spirit, WWRL became a force to be reckoned with in New York. Boulding and his staff — including Frankie Crocker and Enoch Hawthorn Gregory, aka the Dixie Drifter — created what Boulding calls "Black Boss Radio." "The only difference between WWRL and WABC was we played some songs they didn't. But, the formatics were there."

Boulding decided to leave WWRL to consult. He believed his experience and success positioned him for success, but just as he was gearing up to launch his business, he was drafted by MCA Records to run their black division. He accepted the job, he says, because he wanted to see "how that game worked."

The money was good, but the bloom wasn't on the rose for long. "At some point you have to tell radio to play a record that you know isn't a hit," says Boulding. "I couldn't do that."

He returned to radio and the hands-on chapter of his programming career closed at WBMX/Chicago, before he joined the ranks of Network programmers.

•

Today, Jerry Boulding is concerned that the job of a Program Director has changed too much and that no one's minding the store. "So much of what PDs do now is geared to the bottom line, with one programmer trying to keep his eye on three stations, or even more. No one can watch over three stations and do the job correctly," he insists.

That's not all he has to say.

"Urban Program Directors don't make the decisions they used to make, consultants do. And the problem is that some Urban consultants are light years away from the shallowest black experience." (He is quick to point out exceptions, of course. "Don Kelly, Jerry Clifton and Dean Landsman figured it out.")

When Jerry Boulding looks back at the evolution of contemporary urban radio, it becomes clear he knows his history and has a unique perspective. "The white guys taught us formats," he says, "but we taught them hipness. Beyond the music, it was the hipness that a lot of white folks came to black radio to hear."

When I asked Boulding about the future of radio, he wasn't quick to answer. "I'd like to think about that answer before I give it to you," he said.

After a moment, he spoke. "I believe in what radio is and what I know it can be.

And, that's the short version," says the good Doctor.

Chapter 6

Scotty Brink: The Ultimate Team Player

When Ron Jacobs wrote his book "Inside Boss Radio" he asked Ken Levine to describe the KHJ staff as if they were a major league baseball team. Levine, who describes himself as a writer/director/baseball announcer, wrote this about Scotty Brink.

> "Table setter. The ultimate team player. Traded to the Army then returned. Had big free agent offers elsewhere (WABC/New York) but chose to stay. Professional. Loves to play and it shows. No big headlines but coveted by every major league team for years."

Brink is all these things and more. In the history of American radio he is unique among all the Boss Jocks because he was the only one to do mornings in New York (WNBC), afternoons in Chicago (WLS and WCFL) and nights in Los Angeles (KHJ). He joined the majors at WIBG/Philadelphia, when he was still in his teens, which is a good place to jump into his story.

"I went to sleep every night listening to him," says Elaine Konrad. Konrad was fourteen and remembers record hops, Danny and the Juniors, Bobby Darin and WIBG disc jockey Don L. Brink, on stage, standing between two roaring turntables. "My friend, Elizabeth, and I used to throw our hair around and try to catch his eye," she says.

She also remembers taking Brink home. What she means is she left the dance with an autographed 8" x 10" glossy and taping it on her vanity when she got home. She says he almost never knew.

•

In 1955, when he was only thirteen, Donald L. Brink started a combo called Don Brink and the Stardusters. He liked singing, thought it might lead to something someday, but was also considering the ministry. "That was my main goal until I got into radio."

But, three years later, in 1958, he got a chance to audition at his hometown radio station, WWPA/Williamsport, Pennsylvania. "As green as I was," says Brink, "a wonderful guy, named John Archer, gave me my first radio job, weekends, playing Mantovani." Brink says he gave himself ten years to make it to a major market.

In 1960, he left Williamsport to do the morning show at WLSV/ Wellsville, New York. He was eighteen, a young man on the move and everything was going swimmingly until one day, on a morning after the night before, he overslept. He still remembers what happened. "The PD came and woke me up at nine o'clock, and — I'll *never* forget this – he told me, 'You're *never* gonna make it in this business.' " Of course, it wasn't true, but it scared him all the same.

He was working at WSBA/York, Pennsylvania when he got the call from WIBG, the big Top 40 station in Philadelphia. "Roy Schwartz (PD of WIBG) had driven to Baltimore to listen to a jock and, as he was driving back, he heard me," says Brink. "He was on the phone right after I got off the air."

Brink left York early the next morning. From there to Philly was about eighty-five miles, but he was determined to be on WIBG's doorstep when the station opened for business. He remembers hitting the city, being nervous, but passing the audition and getting the job as the all night man. According to consultant Bob Hamilton, in Philadelphia in 1960, Brink was given a nick name: Don L Brink, the All Night Fink.

"Yeah, it's true," Brink admits, laughing. "That was a Joe Niagra-ism. And, if you call me that, I won't like you."

•

Don L. Brink stayed at WIBG for five years. Then, in 1965, afternoon drive at KYW/Cleveland opened up. "It was my first drive time gig and a big opportunity," he says. "But, and this is convoluted, there was that NBC/Westinghouse swap thing that happened." (For a nine year period, between 1956 and 1965, Westinghouse and NBC swapped stations in Philadelphia and Cleveland. In 1965, the FCC reversed the swap and the call letters, KYW, returned to Philadelphia. The station Brink had gone to work for in Cleveland went all news in September of 1965, with the call letters WYKC. This meant he was out of work.) According to Brink, the whole thing was a surprise to him and everybody at the station. But, as it turned out, Brink had a guardian angel. "Fortunately, at that point I lucked into KHJ," he says.

In October of 1965, Boss Radio, KHJ/Los Angeles, was only six months old. At the time the station already had someone on its staff named Don — The Real Don Steele — so, when Ron Jacobs called Brink about coming to LA, one issue they had to clear up was his first name. "I don't remember why," says Brink, "but we decided on the name Scotty." To this day Brink insists he really doesn't remember the reason. "Maybe because it made a good jingle."

On December 5, 1965, the day the Rolling Stones appeared at the Los Angeles Sports Arena — tickets were only $5.50 — KHJ released the new Boss 30 list. Brink's picture was there and underneath it were these words:

Hear SCOTTY BRINK on 93/KHJ, 9 a.m. to 12 noon.

It was perfect, a Hollywood dream come true until Brink got his draft notice. "I went from being a pampered little disc jockey to a private in the army," he says. And, that's all he says.

Like many who served in Vietnam, Scotty Brink doesn't talk about his time in the Army, or in a war zone. I pushed and he pushed back, finally saying, "I think Vietnam was valuable to my life." Nothing more.

So, when he got out of the army, he went back to KHJ, right?

Nope.

•

It was the law. Veterans were guaranteed their job would be waiting for them when they returned from the service.

Brink, however, had turned in his resignation at KHJ, telling Jacobs he didn't want someone to lose a job just because "some poor guy just came back from Nam."

So, when he returned to civilian life he didn't have anything lined up. He arrived stateside and received some good news: RKO *did* have a slot for him, at WOR-FM/New York, *if* he would agree to use another name. "Bill Drake liked the name J. J. Jordan," says Brink, "and because I wanted to work with Sebastian Stone, I agreed to it."

But, four months later, when KHJ called about him coming back to Los Angeles, the name thing became a matter of contention. "I remember telling Bill Watson, Drake's right hand man, 'If you want Scotty Brink back at KHJ, I'm coming. Otherwise, J. J. Jordan can stay in New York.' "

On October 25, 1968, in an internal memo to the Boss Jocks, Ron Jacobs announced that Brink was returning:

> As you may have heard, Scotty Brink will be replacing Frank Terry. Scotty, who was with us through the spring of '66 when he left to serve in Vietnam, will be doing the same shift: 9 am-noon Monday thru Friday and 9am-3pm Sunday.

Seven months later Jacobs resigned from KHJ and, although Brink stayed at the station until the next summer, he says without Jacobs at the helm KHJ just wasn't the same station.

In July of 1970, Brink went to Chicago to do afternoon drive for WCFL, the station owned by the Chicago Federation of Labor. (On the air he was preceded by Dick Biondi and followed by Larry O'Brien.) Due to his ratings however, he didn't stay very long. When his first Chicago book was released it showed Brink beating his direct competitor, WLS's Larry Lujack. "Shortly thereafter, I got pitched by 'LS," he says. "They moved Lujack to mornings and I went over to WLS to do afternoons."

He was twenty-nine, had been in radio for thirteen years and had already played in Philadelphia, Cleveland, LA, New York and Chicago.

Brink was on the move.

He left Chicago to join KJR/Seattle, where he began a life-long love affair with the Pacific Northwest. But, KJR was a tough adjustment; after KHJ and WLS, KJR was just a little "too" Seattle (my words, not his)and, in the summer of 1971, he signed what he called "an on-site consultancy" deal with KELP/El Paso. It was, in fact, Brink's first programming job.

Once inside the KELP building in Executive Center, Brink began experimenting with programming concepts that emphasized music by (what would later be called AOR) artists like Rod Stewart, Led Zeppelin and The Beatles and de-emphasized teen-oriented acts like Tony Orlando and Dawn and Donny Osmond. In 1971 FM was barely in the game and AM Top 40s were facing an identity crisis that had a lot to do with the disparity between the single and album charts and short and long hair. As a reflection of the direction he was taking the station, Brink's top of the hour ID positioned KELP as "The Voice of Change." It was a preview of what was about to happen.

"About seven months into his employment Scotty told me he'd gotten a call from Bill Drake and they wanted him to fly to Boston to interview for the PD's position at WRKO," remembers Bob Gourley. Gourley, General Manager of KELP in 1971, says as forthright as Brink was about the situation, he knew the station's owner, John Walton, would have a fit. "So, I told Walton Brink's father was sick and that he had to go back to Pennsylvania for a couple days."

Early the next morning Brink hopped a plane for Boston. An hour or two later Walton popped into Gourley's office. "We're going to Boston tomorrow," he told the young manager. "WMEX is for sale and I'm interested in buying it."

The following day Walton, Gourley and Ray Potter, the group's National PD, left El Paso on what Gourley describes as "the first leg of a journey from hell." "Walton's secretary had booked us through Dallas, St. Louis, up through Chicago and then on to Boston," he says. "And, of course, we drank the entire way there."

The three men arrived in Boston at nine o'clock that night and checked into the Copley Hotel. Leading the charge, John Walton asked where the nearest bar was. "The clerk told us that there was only one still open and that it closed in less than an hour," remembers Gourley. "So, we paid a bellboy to take our bags to the room and headed up to the bar. God knows we needed a few more drinks."

The thirsty travelers got off the elevator and walked into what appeared to be an empty lounge. By then, it was closing in on ten o'clock, the end of what was turning into a very long day. "The minute we sat down I looked around the room," says Gourley. "And way back in a corner, I saw these guys talking."

He thought they looked familiar. He remembers flinching, looking again and saying to himself, "No, it's not true; it couldn't be." But, it was. Gourley says he almost fainted. Sitting less than twenty feet away were Bill Drake, Gene Chenault and Scotty Brink. "When I saw them, well, it was probably the first time I'd peed my pants since back in third grade."

Sooner or later Gourley knew Walton would catch on. "So, I got up and went over to their table." To this day Gourley can't or won't find the words to describe the look on Brink's face. What he will say is the rest is history. "WRKO hired Brink, Walton didn't buy WMEX, and the only good thing is he never figured out that I'd known Brink was actually going to Boston, instead of Williamsport, Pennsylvania."

Brink remembers other things. "The very first song I added at WRKO was *Stairway to Heaven.* "Doesn't sound like a big deal now but, back then, the song had never been played on a major AM station."

After Boston, Scotty Brink was invited to program KAUM/Houston but the station's signal limitations got in the way, the promise of an upgrade never came to fruition and KAUM, no matter how good the programming was, could never compete. Once he understood, Brink accepted a programming job at KUPD/Phoenix. He loved the desert, he says, but also recalls that during the middle '70s KUPD went through PDs like there was no tomorrow. By 1977, Brink had had enough management stress to last for a lifetime and decided to accept an offer to do a morning show. The station was WNBC/New York.

Bob Pittman, WNBC's boy wonder PD, had jettisoned Don Imus to Cleveland and, seeking something different, teamed Brink with comedian/actor Richard Belzer to create "The Brink and Belzer Show," a morning partnership that lasted two years. "I really enjoyed it," Belzer told me. "We got into a groove and had a great time. I was amazed by Scotty's encyclopedic knowledge of music."

But, in September of 1979, Pittman and his boss, Bob Sherman, decided Imus had done enough penance and then decided to bring him back to NBC. Brink, acting quickly and trading on his work at WNBC, crossed the street to join PD, Don Kelly, at WXLO-FM. (Belzer returned to comedy, writing and acting. In 1993, he appeared, for the first time, as Detective John Munch on "Homicide: Life On The Street" and "Law & Order: Special Victims Unit." With that role, he's made television history by becoming the first actor to appear as the same fictional character [Munch] in eight different television shows.)

A year later, in 1980, WXLO/New York changed musical direction and, by June of the next year, it was rapidly morphing into the station that would become WRKS, Kiss.

By then, Brink was long gone. He'd relocated to Nashville to be with his family and to realize a life long ambition of owning his own recording studio, which he named *Brink's Production Workshop*. Until the end of the decade he combined recording and production work with occasional radio gigs, at stations that included WLAC. Then, in late 1989, Gannettt President Jay Cook hired him to program KSDO-FM/San Diego.

For Brink, the '90s were like the '70s all over again: lots of stations and lots of cities. But, after a decade in Nashville, despite his stellar resume, he found he had to prove himself all over again. He did mornings at Gannett's KOAI/Dallas (smooth jazz), afternoons on Alliance Broadcasting's KYCW/Seattle (one of the nation's first Young Country stations), and programmed KXGL-FM/San Diego.

In the late '90s Brink returned to Seattle as VP/Programming for New Northwest Broadcasters. For the next five years he traveled Alaska, Montana, Oregon and Washington directing the programming and mentoring programmers and managers. "His depth was astonishing," says KXDD/Yakima's Dewey Boynton. "We seldom faced anything he hadn't dealt with before."

In 2003, Brink moved to Oklahoma City and, from there, on-line, he joined his old WLS cohorts, Larry Lujack and John Gehron, to create WRLL/Real Oldies-1690/Chicago. Today Scotty Brink consults, occasionally fills in on KOMA-FM, and does voice and production work.

•

Oh. Remember Elaine Konrad?

In 1989 she lived in San Diego. One night her phone rang. "Auntie Elaine? It's Scotty Brink calling. Your niece gave me your number..."

"His voice was familiar, but I couldn't quite place it," Konrad told me. When she finally did, she didn't tell him, but she did call her old friend, Elizabeth.

Two years later, Elaine Konrad married Scotty Brink. And today, after more than fifteen years, she still gets to hear his voice.

Every night, just before she falls asleep.

Chapter 7

Kent Burkhart: The Consultant

It wasn't an easy thing to do. Still, he sat down and in longhand scrawled thirty letters to people he knew, people who understood his true love was programming. Suddenly, he had a dozen clients; then thirteen, then fourteen, each paying $1,000 a month. Soon he needed help. He called George Burns, his National PD at Pacific and Southern Broadcasting, but Burns was happy in California. "But," Burns told him, "I read an article in one of the trades written by a young guy who has a great understanding of research and demography."

"What's his name?"

"Lee Abrams."

"Funny," Kent Burkhart replied, "I've gotten two or three letters from him in the past few weeks and he wants to join forces."

The day after their first phone call, Kent Burkhart met Lee Abrams in an airport lounge in Minneapolis. Abrams was still in his teens and Burkhart wasn't, but age didn't matter, because they connected. "It was like instant love," says Burkhart. "He had great big blue innocent eyes and you could just tell he wanted to do well."

The relationship and the company that grew from it, Burkhart/ Abrams, began in the early '70s with a handshake and, by the end of the decade, was the largest and, some say, most influential radio consultancy in the nation. Today, Burkhart still calls their association a perfect partnership. "I couldn't have asked for anything better in my life."

If this were a movie, the screen would get fuzzy now. Colors, once splashy and bright, would turn to black and white and we'd start time-tunneling back towards the past. By the time our journey was over — in the few seconds it would take to fly through time — we'd be in Monterey, Mexico. If you're with me, we're already there. Look around. It's the early 1940s and what you're hearing is a band tuning up.

•

"I was sitting and watching this wonderful orchestra," says Burkhart. "It was the first one I'd ever seen — *ever* — and halfway through the concert the orchestra leader told us they were going to go on the radio and be broadcast throughout all of Mexico."

He was eight years old and the concept of radio, apart from listening to it, was foreign to him. "I pulled on my uncle's sleeve and said, 'Can you get me backstage? I'd like to see how this works.' "

Backstage the young boy sat next to the announcer, who, presumably, spoke in Spanish (although the man, who was the boy, doesn't mention it. What he does say is that the experience changed his life.) "I walked away with the sense that I could be an entertainer, that I could do a credible job entertaining the public by playing records."

A year or so later his uncle – yes, the same one – moved into an office in a building that had a radio station on its bottom floor. On the radio was a man named Ed Keene and, for two weeks, young Burkhart sat in the lobby, staring at him. "Finally, one day he waved me in."

"C'mon in the studio," Keene motioned.

"So, I walked in and he went on the air and said, "We have someone in the studio who's been sitting out in the lobby for the last two weeks during my show, and I'm just curious about who this guy is."

"He brought me up to the microphone, put me in front of it and asked me all these questions," remembers Burkhart. "You know, 'Why was I there? What was I doing?' Little did I know that he was recording it. After the program was over, he played me the tape and I was hooked."

Bay City was, and is, south of Houston. Kent Burkhart was, at the time, south of fourteen, and Johnny Long, a Bay City institution back then, was the owner of a radio station, KIOX.

"I went to see him," says Burkhart. "I said, 'Listen, I'd like to play music for fifteen minutes a day for all the kids. Is that OK?' "

"Sure, when do you want to be on?" Long replied.

He went on the air at 4:15, right after school got out. On his first day, he played "popular" hits — things by artists like Dinah Shore, Nat "King" Cole and Peggy Lee. "I don't remember (exactly what I played)," Burkhart says, "but I do know that when I left the studios and went down to meet my friends at the drugstore, they'd all heard the show, listened to the music and thought it was great."

On his second day, he decided to play jazz. "Again, I went to the drugstore, but this time nobody would talk to me."

The third day, he opted for country and western. "And they wouldn't talk to me again," he says. So, on the fourth, he reverted to pop. "The kids talked to me again," says Burkhart. "I didn't need a ratings service to know what people wanted to hear."

By 1952, when he graduated from high school, Kent Burkhart had been on the air for close to five years. Describing his on-air approach, Texas radio legend, Chuck Dunaway, says it was "laid back," which is to say Burkhart's approach was the opposite of, say, a Dick Biondi. But, Dunaway says, what Burkhart lacked in on-air energy he made up for in pure enthusiasm for the medium itself.

•

Burkhart chose a college away from home, Texas Christian University in Ft. Worth, where, instead of concentrating on his studies, he went to school on KLIF, Gordon McLendon's station in Dallas. "McLendon wanted the jocks to be free and spirited," Burkhart remembers, "like how he'd done his baseball broadcasts. And, there were *certain* disc jockeys, like Jim Randolph, who were allowed to play whatever they wanted."

During the summers, when he headed home to Bay City, Burkhart filled in at McLendon's KLBS/Houston. That's where he first ran into Bill Stewart. "I met him after he left Boston and came to Houston. He wanted to set the market on fire, so he played Stan Freberg's *Dragnet* for twenty-four or forty-eight hours, maybe an entire week, and the whole town went crazy!"

On the strength of what Stewart had done in Houston, McLendon offered Stewart the Program Director slot at KLIF. It was early 1954. "I remember having dinner with him and he asked me if he should take the job," says Burkhart. "I said, 'Of course, it's a great station and a great company.' "

Stewart left for Dallas and Burkhart stayed in school. But, a year and a half later, six months shy of graduation, McLendon offered him a job at WNOE/New Orleans. By then Stewart had been transferred to WNOE and, when Burkhart accepted the job — never completing his degree — Stewart commented that he wasn't particularly impressed with the kid's on air work. "But, he liked my energy and aggressiveness," says Burkhart. Those qualities were enough to make the relationship prosper. Later that year, when Stewart returned to Omaha to rejoin the Storz Organization, he invited Burkhart to accompany him. Burkhart jumped at the change.

He was twenty-two, with nine years of radio under his belt and had already worked for Gordon McLendon. Now he was about to come face to face with Todd Storz, the other Father of Top 40.

•

In 1956 not everyone inside the Storz organization embraced rock 'n' roll. "There was a major league discussion in the entire group about whether or not we should play it," says Burkhart. He remembers that Storz, himself, wasn't in favor of the idea. "But, Bill Stewart and I argued — how the hell can you ignore Elvis Presley?"

They reached a compromise: KOWH would play the softer side of Elvis: *Love Me Tender*, but not *Jailhouse Rock*. But, once the phones went crazy over Presley, the cat was out of the bag and Burkhart says the station began adding more and more rock 'n' roll. "Graduating," he says, "to Gene Vincent."

Two years later, in 1958, Storz sent Burkhart to Miami to clean up a payola mess at WQAM. "The station actually had a payola rate card!" Burkhart says, incredulously. "The GM was oblivious, but the PD and one of the jocks — a big personality with a 40 share — were cashing checks."

Burkhart fired the PD and cleaned up the playlist. Within forty-eight hours a record guy showed up with two henchmen. "I want my records back on the air!" he demanded. "I paid for them."

Burkhart stared him down. "Talk to the guys that made the deal," he said. "Maybe they need to reimburse you." He remembers being scared. "I didn't know if I was going to get knocked out, rubbed out or what."

His WQAM adventure lasted for two years. Then, he got itchy feet to own his own radio station.

He was twenty-six.

•

After searching and doing due diligence — something he'd never even heard of before – Burkhart bought KTXL in San Angelo, TX for $55,000. "Five grand down and $456.10 a month," he says. By doing so he became one of the first programmers to ever venture into ownership. "Most programmers didn't want to get involved in sales," he says. "It's still true today."

As the owner/operator he had to do everything. Up at four AM, on the air at six, out by nine, sell all day, back at the end of the day to write and produce commercials. Then, he had to sweep out the place. You get it, it never stopped. "I remember very distinctly that my major client — the first guy I ever sold — was the General

Manager of Mustang Chevrolet. Well, anyway, every morning at six-thirty, he'd call me and say, 'I want to hear my favorite record.'

And, every morning, I played it for him, breaking format to do it. You had to get along; it was a relationship issue."

He kept at it every day, keeping up the pace for close to a year, but it was starting to wear him down. Finally, totally exhausted, Burkhart started to make a few calls.

"I'm running the Mays stations now," Earl Fletcher told him. "I can use you in Waco and Oklahoma City."

It wasn't a full time job; it was consulting for two hundred dollars a month per station, but Fletcher upped the ante by calling in markers with friends with stations in Little Rock and Lake Charles.

Not big money, Burkhart thought, but it put food on the table and would do the job, even if that meant packing up Pat and the babies (Burkhart had gotten married in 1956), driving hundreds of miles, spending a few weeks in a rundown apartment while praying the checks would catch up before he had to hit the road again. "It was frightening and wasn't going to work very long," he says.

After eight months he realized he needed a real job.

•

"In the spring of 1961 Barry Sherman, "Esquire" magazine's radio guy, told me "Esquire" was going to build a radio group," Burkhart says. Sherman, says Burkhart, told him the plans were all in place, but there was a problem with the first station they'd bought, WQXI/Atlanta. "It's lost half its ratings and half its revenue and we just don't understand."

Burkhart volunteered to help. He flew to Atlanta, parked himself at the old Riviera Hotel and began to listen to WQXI. "It was one of the worst radio stations I'd ever heard," he says. "Total clutter, wrong music and wrong people." Later, all he could do was shake his head, when he discovered that "Esquire" had run a full page newspaper ad stating:

BIG TIME RADIO BY ESQUIRE MAGAZINE FROM
NEW YORK CITY COMES TO ATLANTA

When he got back to Sherman (not a popular name around Atlanta) the man liked what he heard and offered Burkhart $12,000 to become Program Director of WQXI. Burkhart accepted. It was solid, paying employment, he thought, and it might lead to some big things. Then, something no one could have anticipated happened. One day, John Smart, Esquire's Chairman of the Board, arrived in Atlanta and heard a Preparation H commercial on the air at WQXI. Smart's response was to raise hell with everyone involved. He insisted that accepting an advertisement for Preparation H was something Esquire would never do. But, here's the rub: Preparation H was one of WQXI's biggest sponsors.

Within twenty-four hours the station was for sale.

•

Jupiter Broadcasting owned WSAI in Cincinnati and, sensing his employment at WQXI was on a slippery slope, Burkhart applied to the station for work. A few days after he applied a company exec, Harold G. Ross, arrived in Atlanta and gave Burkhart a call. "We won't be needing you at WSAI, after all," he told him. "But, why don't we have dinner?"

That night, over cocktails, Burkhart told Ross the Atlanta story. "It's a southern city on-the-grow with lots of opportunity and great weather."

Three days later Ross called up again. "I'm still here," he told Burkhart. "You know, I like the look of Atlanta and I know the radio station you're working for is for sale. If we buy it, will you stay?"

Jupiter moved quickly to acquire WQXI and, once the sale was announced, Esquire, to no one's surprise, quickly began cutting costs. One of the first jobs to go was the General Manager's. "At that point they made me GM and told me if I didn't leave before the deal closed, I'd get a one year bonus," says Burkhart. He didn't have to think about it for long. "In essence, I had six months to prove I could be a large market manager. It was my test."

During Burkhart's tenure, WQXI's ratings doubled. "At first, we beat WSB in all day parts, except mornings. Then, we — he means he and PD Paul Drew — brought Dr. Don Rose in from Duluth, MN and put him on in mid-days. "One day there were some studio malfunctions," remembers Burkhart, "and, in order to make things work, Don had to ad lib a lot." Burkhart says he still remembers sitting in his office captivated by a talent working without a net. When Rose got off the air Burkhart was waiting. "Don," he said, "you're a pretty funny guy. Let's move you to morning drive."

Whether true or anecdotal, Burkhart says he gave Rose fifty bucks and told him to go out and buy all the joke books he could find. Six months later, when the next ratings were released, WQXI had gone from a 10.0 to a 20.0 per share and sales went through the roof. Burkhart attributes the revenue gain to increased ratings and the efforts of his new Sales Manager, Jerry Blum.

With WQXI's success, Jupiter bought an FM station for $80,000. The money came from WQXI-AM's profits. When the next ratings results arrived, WQXI-AM was #1 and the FM was #2. Burkhart says he was never so delighted.

In 1967, in recognition of his accomplishments, Kent Burkhart was named President of Pacific and Southern Broadcasting.

•

His job was to acquire new stations and, in quick succession, he bought KIMN/Denver, KYXI/Portland and KRHM-FM/Los Angeles — the station that would become KIIS-FM. Burkhart says one of the highlights of the LA acquisition "was handing that guy a check for $800,000."

Since money was available and the company now had a Los Angeles presence, the Chairman of the Board of the parent company — a much larger entity than the broadcasting division — decided the corporation also needed a station in New York. His choice, for six million dollars, was WJRZ/Newark, NJ.

Burkhart was skeptical about the price and the station's coverage. When he shared his concerns with the Chairman, he was challenged.

"Are you sure?" asked the Chairman.

"Let me come up and drive the signal," responded Burkhart.

After driving around New York, he returned to the office and explained that he'd discovered the signal was lousy. "In essence, it's a daytimer," he told his boss. "No one will be able to hear it at night."

"Well, I guess that does it," said the Chairman. "We won't buy it."

Then, much to Burkhart's surprise, he got another call ordering him to prepare budgets for a New York radio station. Yes, for WJRZ , the station he'd said would be a bad acquisition. When he submitted figures — he sent both an operating budget and a sales forecast — the Chairman and his minions thought Burkhart was crazy. New York, he'd written, was a fifty-million dollar market and would grow to eighty-million within five years. This meant money could be made assuming conditions were right. But, because New York was a union town, and because of the problem with the night time signal, he projected WJRZ would lose money. Again, he said, buying the station was a bad idea.

His bosses didn't listen and the acquisition was made. When the radio station started losing money, as Burkhart had projected, it was he who was blamed.

"We came to blows," he told me, "and even though the radio division (as a whole) was making a pot load of money, the board elected to say goodbye to me. The next day I was jobless."

•

As President of a broadcasting company in a highly regulated era Burkhart had spent half his time wrestling with FCC, FTC and SEC issues. "I was dealing with regulatory problems and didn't like it. I was a radio guy and it just wasn't any fun."

This was an important realization. For a while, he entertained an offer to run NBC's group of stations, but the more he thought about it, the more he realized he wanted to get back to where the thought he belonged — programming. And that brings us back to when he sat down to write his letters, and to when he and Abrams began their consulting business.

At its height Burkhart/Abrams had close to 80% of the programming consultant business in America; at least, that's the claim. But, after Abrams left in 1988, and later, when Don Benson went to Jefferson-Pilot (now Lincoln Financial), Burkhart began to see the writing on the wall. "I was smelling consolidation," he says, "and the question I kept asking myself was, 'Why would radio need consultants, at $4,000 a station, when they could hire one guy for $300,000?' "

So, in 1995, after twenty-three years, he sold his firm (his baby) to Mike McVay.

•

An observant writer (his blog is at radiodailynews.com), an informed consultant and an enthusiastic station owner, Burkhart is still active and bullish about radio today, but not naively so. "Some consolidated groups run very fine radio stations and some don't; those who don't have found their ratings have decreased and, as a result, they've lost money. But, that's the way it's always been."

How about internet and satellite radio? Will they impact terrestrial radio?

"Internet radio is still in its infancy," he says." Satellite is doing OK and those who subscribe to it seem to love it. But, expenses are tremendous and losses are huge." (We talked before XM and Sirius Satellite merged.)

What about the deregulation and consolidation of the radio industry? Has that impacted what listeners hear?

"My ears tell me it ain't as good as it used to be," says Burkhart. "And, there are a lot of veteran programmers and announcers, sitting on the sidelines, hoping for a chance to get back in."

That, of course, would require a government act — one that would reduce or slow deregulation down.

"That's what it might take to get entrepreneurs to move back into radio," says Burkhart.

"Stand by. It just may happen."

CHAPTER 8

AL CASEY: "TO KNOW HIM WAS TO LOVE HIM..."

My friend, Al Casey, died of cancer here on Bainbridge Island in 2004.

Sadly, in the years since, his face isn't as clear in my mind's eye as it used to be. But, there are things about him I'll never forget. Al was smart, although he never really thought of himself that way and he was the kindest man I ever met. Yes, I told him while he was still here.

Here's how Al made his name: He jocked at WNOE/New Orleans and KYNO/Fresno in the '60s and then, over the next three decades, he programmed some of America's most influential radio stations, including WHBQ/Memphis, WMYQ/Miami, WDRQ/Detroit, KSLQ/St. Louis, WXLO/New York, KCMO and WHB/Kansas City, KOGO/San Diego, WPGC/Washington, and WYCD/Detroit. At a time when Top 40 was new to FM, Al was the National Program Director for Charter Broadcasting during a period that saw the entire industry watching the group's every move.

"Al understood radio better than anyone I've ever met," says consultant Bill Tanner. "He did everything from Top 40 to Country and his stations always sizzled."

"It's because he was great with people," says his long time friend, Rick Torcasso, a partner at Point-To-Point Marketing.

"To know Al was to love him."

I said that.

•

In 1962, on the day he won five dollars from his hometown station, KAOK/Lake Charles, Al Casey says he decided there must be money in radio. Two years later he was a player and no longer a beginner.

By 1964, Casey had jocked in Lake Charles, Midland-Odessa and even up in the panhandle — in Andrews, TX. On top of that, he'd gone to Elkins Institute to get his First Class Radiotelephone License. (AM radio stations with directional signals used to require an engineer with a First Class license be on duty at night. Ambitious disc jockeys, eager to do whatever it took to get and keep a job, took courses in engineering so they could pass the test. In 1980 the FCC abolished the requirement.)

And, there was one more thing: Casey was even thinking he might like to own a radio station one day. That, by the way, was why he was back home in Lake Charles studying business at a local college.

So, he was going to school, doing part-time radio and, from time to time, he helped his father out, as the older man drove his route. "My dad had gumball machines throughout southern Louisiana and I'd go with him to help fill them up," he explained one day. Then he told me about one particular time he remembered. "It was dusk and Pop and I were driving home and listening to WNOE/ New Orleans."

Suddenly, perhaps inspired by what he was hearing, the younger man turned to his father and said, "Pop, you know, I'm going to work there one day."

Always supportive, his father simply nodded. "Okay, son."

"Well, anyway," Casey said, "I sent a tape to WNOE and got hired to do all-nights." But, get this: On his first night, WNOE PD Greg Mason told him that he didn't like the name Al Casey. "So, just do the format, play the records, and don't use a name," Mason instructed.

Four hours later WNOE morning man Dan Diamond walked in, sat down and said to his audience, "Did you hear him? HIM sounded pretty good."

"So, it stuck," laughed Casey. "They even got me jingles that sang – 'HIM — the pronoun sound of the Crescent town.' "

And, that's what Bill Drake heard the night he was listening.

•

"Drake didn't like my name, either," Casey said, "So, at KYNO, I became Bob Taylor."

By now it was 1966 and Casey (that's the name we'll use from now on) was at KYNO/Fresno, the station Gene Chenault owned, where Bill Drake got his consulting chops together a few years before signing KGB/San Diego, KHJ/Los Angeles and the rest of the RKO stations.

"The Drake format was so different," Casey said.

Different from what? I asked.

"Well, Southern radio was so garbaged up! In New Orleans, we talked between every element!" What he meant was the adjustment to the more streamlined Drake format took some time to get used to. "I was terrible at first, because I had that Southern thing in my voice."

Accent aside, within a year Casey was named Music Director and, when the Program Director of KYNO was on vacation, he got his first taste of programming. "I really enjoyed it," he said. "Then Drake called and offered me the programming job at WHBQ Memphis."

The call flipped him out. First-time programmers don't ever get shots like this, he thought.

•

Casey arrived in Memphis determined to be successful. He worked hard and around the clock to make the station sound as good as it possibly could. "Still," he says, "I got my butt kicked by WMPS."

There were, however, two bright sides to Memphis: One was meeting fellow RKO PD, Buzz Bennett, which led to programming WMYQ/Miami; the other was meeting Janie, his wife of over thirty years. "We did thirteen major moves, coast to coast, border to border and several places in between," she says. "We had the time of our lives.

But, I would tell young women, 'If you need to be close to your family, don't get involved in radio.' " The newlyweds arrived in Miami on February 14, 1971. Two weeks later, the station, WMYQ, flipped its format to Top 40. "If I'm not mistaken, we were the first FM Top 40 station in the country," Casey told me.

WMYQ exploded, but not without some controversy. "People called saying, 'You can't play Top 40 music on FM!' " said Casey, "And we said, 'Well, we're doing it!' "

And, when they weren't doing it at the station, the boys and girls of WMYQ were at The Q-House, in Coconut Grove. "That's where Lee (Abrams), Robert (W. Walker) and I lived," said Casey, with a laugh. "It was a party place. I remember waking up one morning and finding Buzz Bennett asleep in a tree."

•

Over the years millions of Americans heard Al Casey's work and were touched by it. Torcasso says it was because Casey's radio stations were always about real people, and listeners, even though they were on the outside, could hear it.

Inside the radio station, at work, Casey was about humanity and dignity. "He was able to see the talent within people that others didn't see. Al's the guy who taught me that people come to work wanting to do a good job," says Torcasso.

Paul Drew says it's true. "Al was a good man and a good programmer."

As the cancer started to hit hard, Casey became more reflective. "I've had some great jobs," he told me. "Some really great jobs."

"Why were the good ones good?" I asked.

"Because the stations were product driven and we had the tools to do the job."

"And that's important?"

He just looked at me.

"It's more than important," he said. "It's all that matters."

And that's the gospel. According to HIM.

(In 2004, five months after he died, The Midwest Conclave recognized Al Casey by awarding him the prestigious "Rockwell Award." The Rockwell, first awarded in 1989, is a lifetime achievement tribute to those who have contributed to the radio and record industries through achievement, inspiration and mentoring. Al's widow, Janie, and his daughter, Kelli, were there to accept it for him. Yes, I was there too.)

CHAPTER 9

RON CHAPMAN: "DAMN IT, THE LISTENERS PAY ATTENTION..."

Ron Chapman doesn't live here anymore.

It's unlikely this message ever appeared on KVIL/Dallas's website but, when Chapman moved down the dial to KLUV-FM in September of 2000, it was surely hidden between the lines. At the time KVIL's PD, Bill Curtis, put a positive spin on Ron's departure, as did Ron himself. But, the most revealing comment may have come from former KVIL PD, Michael Hedges. "If Mel Karmizan was righteous, he'd have retired the call letters."

This was also unlikely to happen. Even more unlikely was that Chapman would move to KLUV and, effectively, take his audience with him.

As it turns out KVIL, without Ron Chapman, would be like the Rolling Stones without Mick Jagger. They'd keep playing songs, but the lead voice would be missing.

•

Ron Chapman came to Dallas from Haverhill, Massachusetts in 1959. He'd been hired to do the all night show on Gordon McLendon's flagship station, KLIF. He says he learned his on-air name was going to be "Irving Harrigan" while listening to the station the day he drove into town. He also says he didn't do the all night show for very long, because KLIF teamed him with Jack Wood (aka Charlie Brown) and "The Charlie and Harrigan Morning Show" was born. "Ron was the spark that drove the engine," says KLIF alumnus, Chuck Dunaway. "What comes to mind is the intensity with which he prepared for that show."

According to Ken Dowe, Executive VP of KKDA/Dallas and one of McLendon's protégés, Chapman had impact on more than just his show. "Ron was extremely involved in all the success KLIF was having, not just on the air, but from a programming point of view, too."

In 1965, still calling himself Irving Harrigan, Chapman left KLIF to do a local television show. WFAA/Channel 8, the Dallas ABC affiliate, gave him a daily teen dance program called "Sump'n Else" (one of the teen dancers was actress, Morgan Fairchild) and, in short order, he became "the Dick Clark of Dallas." But, not without a glitch.

It seemed McLendon wasn't happy about his morning star leaving. Word came from KLIF that his name, Irving Harrigan (a KLIF "house" name, they said), belonged to them. The search for a new name began quickly. WFAA's producers opted to use his real last name — Chapman — but, according to Dallas oldies expert Bud Buschardt, they took a while to come up with his new first name. "They played around calling him Rock or Rob," he says, "and finally settled on Ron. By then the story was out and made the paper."

The headline was pretty straight forward:

IRVING HARRIGAN BECOMES RON CHAPMAN

"The audience caught on right away," remembers Dowe. "To who he was and what he was doing. Irving Harrigan literally 'died' overnight and Ron Chapman was resurrected in his place."

•

Chapman joined KVIL-AM/FM in 1968 and stayed for the next thirty-two years.

Yes, there were a multitude of job offers, particularly when KVIL became hugely successful, but Chapman opted to stay put. "He told me the secret of success in this business is to stay in one place as long as you can," says film executive and former record promotion man Don Sundeen.

By 1976, KVIL was the #1 radio station in Dallas/Ft Worth, and that's where it stayed through much of the '80s. The station was female-centric because Chapman believed women were more loyal listeners, and it was one of the first in the nation to adopt the musical position that would, eventually, be labeled Adult Contemporary.

Under Chapman's leadership, KVIL was both a Dallas and a Ft. Worth station, an unusual move given the long held animosity between Big D and Cowtown. "Chapman was the first Dallas broadcast voice to drop the Dallas-Ft Worth hyphen and the cowpile jokes," wrote Bud Kennedy in "The Ft. Worth Star-Telegram." "He gave Ft. Worth equal standing and respect, and we gave him back our loyalty for a generation. And our ears."

The magic of KVIL was in its attention to detail. Former ABC exec Phil Hall says Chapman watched over the station like a parent. "Hell, he made love to the antenna and transmitter to make that baby. He nurtured it, held it and even disciplined it when necessary."

One of the biggest areas Chapman fixated on was promotion. KVIL promotions were always bigger than life, a lesson Chapman picked up from McLendon. Chapman challenged afternoon drive jock, Mike Selden, to a race around the world, each calling in from different ports of call. Ron won. He decided it would be fun to parachute out of an airplane in the middle of morning drive, so he made the arrangements and then — live on the air — he made the jump, never mentioning that the landing wasn't quite as easy as it sounded on the radio.

"He was all about bigness," says Hedges. "He understood it and knew what it sounded like."

In 1988, Chapman asked his listeners to send him $20. He didn't say why and they didn't ask. Within three days, over $240,000 arrived in the mail.

In the end, Chapman gave the money to various charities but, in the beginning, there wasn't much of a plan in place. "I don't think he knew what he was going to do with it," says Sundeen. Everybody speculated (about his motivation), but what he was really doing was demonstrating the power of the radio station."

•

Chapman's first shift at KLUV-FM was the day after Labor Day, 2000.

From the very first he sounded right at home; truth be told, he sounded better and more himself than he had in his last seasons at KVIL. And, to say he took KLUV to new heights doesn't do his accomplishment justice.

Five years later, Chapman announced his retirement. At the time, it was widely assumed that he'd hung up his spurs. According to friends, he left Dallas, sold his home in Naples, FL and went on a world-wide cruise. But, then, something unexpected happened; actually two things.

First, on March 20, 2008, Chapman showed up on the ABC Radio Network subbing for Paul Harvey. According to the Dallas Morning News, he'd gotten a call from Citadel Broadcasting CEO Farid Suleman. "He asked if I'd try sitting in for a couple of days for Paul Harvey," says Chapman. "I've studied Paul all my radio life and have patterned many things I do after him. He's my radio hero. So my answer was, 'What time, where, and what do I wear?' "

Then, on June 30, 2008, Citadel announced Chapman would come out of retirement to assist in the creation of a new Dallas radio station to be called Platinum 96.7. Chapman, commenting to Reuter's News Service, said, "The opportunity to play architect and create a new station in the Metroplex from the ground up is a new and exciting challenge for me."

Mr. Chapman already has three Dallas notches on his belt: KLIF, KVIL and KLUV.

Whatever happens next will be interesting to watch.

CHAPTER 10
DICK CLARK: THE OLDEST TEENAGER

In 1949, after eighteen years on the air, Fred Allen's long running network radio show was canceled. Allen blamed television and was widely quoted at the time, when he said, "Television is a device that permits people who haven't anything to do to watch people who can't do anything."

Allen may have been too old to get it, but Dick Clark wasn't. By the summer of 1956, which is when Clark took over a local Philadelphia teen dance show, he'd already been around radio and television for ten years, even if his acquaintance with rock 'n' roll was less than intimate. "I was young, naïve and very innocent," he says. "I didn't know about politics or big business and didn't know there was a concerted effort to kill the music."

What Clark *did* know was that rock 'n' roll was wildly popular to the youth of America, even if he didn't realize that one day he'd have to fight for its legitimacy before Congress, or that the music and its presentation on television would be the foundation for his career.

On July 9, 1956, George Koehler, General Manager of WFIL-TV in Philadelphia, announced that Dick Clark would replace popular local DJ, Bob Horn, and become the new host of the station's afternoon TV dance show, "Bandstand." (Horn had originated the show in October of 1952, but after a DUI arrest in 1956, along with allegations involving statutory rape charges, he lost the show.) In his book, "Dick Clark's American Bandstand," Clark tells of being met outside the studio that day by picketers "furiously waving their signs."

He says he began to speak to them, by introducing himself and telling them about his new job. He wrote that the crowd stayed silent and, not knowing what to do, he simply said, "I've got to get to work now. If you want to come in, please do." With only two minutes to air time, the picketers caved and ran into the studio. Clark says relief swept over him. "I dreamed of doing the show," he told me. "It was the opportunity of a lifetime."

What it was, was a ticket to ride.

•

"**When I was** thirteen," Clark says, "I saw a radio show done by Garry Moore and Jimmy Durante and decided that's what I wanted to do."

Utica, New York, is near Rome, about two hundred and fifty miles northwest of New York City and today, among other things, it's the home of the Boilermaker, the largest fifteen-kilometer road race in the nation.

In 1946, when Dick Clark was sixteen, his uncle, the owner of a local newspaper, was in a race with time to get a new radio station, WRUN, on the air, and he needed help. He turned to Clark's father. Dick Clark, the father — think the two George Bushes — had been in the cosmetic business for over a quarter of a century. But broadcasting appealed to him and, in fact, he remained in radio until he retired. (Interestingly enough, the Rock 'n' Roll Hall of Fame's bio on our Dick Clark says that *he* was WRUN's Sales Manager, not his Dad. This mistake, particularly when I referenced it, almost derailed my interview with him. You may infer, as I did, that Clark is not amused about historical inaccuracies.)

So, to set the record straight, Dick Clark didn't break into radio as a sales executive; instead, he got his foot in the door by way of the mailroom. But, it wasn't too long before he opened a mic. "I was sixteen," he says, "and was on the FM station. Which, of course, nobody listened to in those days."

After high school, Clark raced west to Syracuse University. "I went to study radio, but they didn't have a course in it."

So, and this won't surprise you, he studied business administration, labeled radio an "extra curricular activity," and found time to work at a local two hundred and fifty watt station, WOLF. "Prior to the well known guys, McLendon and Storz," says Clark, "there was a guy named Sherm Marshall who hired kids from the college at a dollar an hour." Clark did a country show called "The WOLF Buckaroos" and hosted "The Sandman Serenade," the all night Top 40 show.

•

One day the phone rang at WRUN. Dick Clark, the elder, answered it. "WRUN."

"Dick," said the manager of WKTV Television, "I need a newscaster. Would you mind if I hire your son?"

The younger Clark had graduated from college, returned home and agreed to work for his father. Still, he was ambitious and, fortunately, his father was supportive. Television, they both agreed, was the perfect next step and WKTV was a good place to pay his dues. "So, I did the six and eleven o'clock news and probably did it pretty well because I started getting job offers," says Clark.

But, did he leave for greener pastures? No, not yet, because WKTV wouldn't release him. "The manager of the station," says Clark, "would call the guy offering me a job and say, 'You can't take this kid away.' "

So, Dick Clay (he used an air name early on, reasoning that his father was the Dick Clark everyone in Utica knew) stayed put at WKTV. But, he continued to send out tapes. "Like all disc jockeys do, although I was in TV, I said to myself, 'You need to get into a bigger market.' " His tapes went out to Albany/Schenectady and to stations in Philadelphia. When nothing happened, his father made a phone call to the Station Manager at WFIL-TV. "I've got this kid. Would you have somebody look at him?"

Now Clark had a shot, but he had to perform.

"The way I won the audition was unique," he says. "They gave me a ream of copy and said, 'OK, we're going to the control room and we'll call you after you've had a chance to look it over. Just read into the camera.' " For most young auditioning performers hitting the copy cold would have caused a problem but it wasn't for Clark because, in Utica, he'd discovered a secret. "We recorded the copy onto audio tape and then fed the recording into my ear. That way I could spit it back at the camera." And he could do it while looking into the camera. In other words — eye contact!

They called down from the booth. "Are you ready?"

"Yeah, I said," remembers Clark. "Then I read it back to them, absolutely verbatim. They were flabbergasted because there wasn't a teleprompter or cue cards. And, that's how I got into television in Philly."

Well, almost. In truth, WFIL TV thought he looked too young, so they gave him a radio show instead, and allowed him to do occasional TV fill in work. One of the shows he subbed on was called "Bandstand."

•

On August 5, 1957 "American Bandstand" went national. "ABC gave us a seven week trial," says Clark. Within four weeks the show was the #1 daytime TV program in America. From a 21st Century perspective, Bandstand, particularly the shows from the '50s, seems very old school. But, at the time, it was cutting edge music television and over the years — 1957 to 1989 — acts that appeared on its stage include Frankie Avalon, Aerosmith, The Animals, The Beach Boys, Chuck Berry, James Brown, Bon Jovi, The Carpenters, Johnny Cash, The Doors, Van Morrison, Otis Redding, Run-D.M.C., Roy Rogers, "Weird Al" Yankovic, and even Rick Dees. In 1963, after six years of doing the show for five days a week, Clark turned it into a weekly show and a year later, he moved its production from Philadelphia to Hollywood.

Once in California, Clark began to build a production empire that grew to include "Where The Action Is," "Pyramid," "TV Bloopers and Practical Jokes," "The American Music Awards" and, perhaps most famously, "Dick Clark's New Year's Rockin' Eve." For radio, Clark developed "The Dick Clark National Music Survey" for the Mutual Broadcasting System (1981) and "Dick Clark's Rock, Roll and Remember" for his own company, United Stations (1982).

•

On December 8, 2004, Dick Clark suffered a stroke. Initial reports called it "minor," but a week later his company announced that for the first time since 1972, Clark wouldn't be hosting his New Year's Eve television show. (He did return the next year and, in recent years, has been joined by Ryan Seacrest.) Behind the scenes Clark is still active, though not as much as he'd like, but his businesses, including restaurants licensed under Bandstand inspired names, continue to flourish.

Over fifty years ago, when rock 'n' roll scared the hell out of adults (and almost anyone over thirty) it was Dick Clark who stood up to promote and defend it. While it's true that "American Bandstand" brought him glory, wealth and fame, it's also true that he was blamed for perpetuating what many non-believers referred to as "raw, insidious music."

In 1990 Dick Clark was inducted into the Radio Hall of Fame. This recognition — just one of dozens, if not hundreds, of awards and accolades he's received over the years — was well deserved.

Dick Clark's legacy comes down to one thing, and it's that he brought teens and music to television, and by doing so, redefined and caused a cosmic shift that impacted the entire culture.

CHAPTER 11

FRANK CODY: THE FATHER OF SMOOTH JAZZ

Frank Cody is the father of Smooth Jazz. OK, maybe that overstates it. Cody argues that credit should go to the entire team that developed the format, underline the word TEAM. In fact, when I called to talk about his story, he was embarrassed. "Jeez, Bob, don't you think I've gotten enough ink?"

The truth is Cody *has* gotten a lot of press over the last twenty years, but not much has focused on his pre-smooth jazz contributions. Given that he was a cog in the AOR (Album Oriented Rock) wheel, when that was really something to be proud of and also part of another innovative team that re-invented network radio in the early '80s, I thought there might be more to his story than you know.

•

Cody's first radio job was at KLOS; no, not KLOS/Los Angeles, KLOS/Albuquerque. "It's one of those famous sets of call letters that's listed in two cities," he explains.

The station wasn't well defined — a little this, a little that — but, when it played jazz, Cody was captivated. "I'd call the woman on the air to ask what the songs were." He turned his love for music into ambition. "I figured the fastest way to get into show business was to become a disc jockey," he says.

By the time Cody was sixteen, he had an early morning shift at KDEF/Albuquerque. One morning — blame it on caffeine or the crazy wings of youth — he pre-taped thirty minutes of his show, flew from the studio, pausing to lock the station's front door, and jumped into his Austin Healey Sprite. Then, he cruised around listening to himself on the air. "I wanted to experience it. The danger never occurred to me."

So, this was a one time thing, right?

Well...no.

By 1970, Cody had worked all over Albuquerque: KLOS, KDEF, the night shift on 50,000 watt KOB ("I'd get calls from L.A....") and then, back to KDEF, where he programmed for the first time. Then he quit and went to Europe. "I traveled everywhere," he says. "I visited radio stations in Holland and Sweden, zipped down to Tangiers and hitchhiked around Morocco."

Arriving back in London, he decided to interview with the BBC. But, not being a British subject yanked his chances of employment there and, when the money ran out, he headed back to the United States.

He applied for work at KFML/Denver, the city's progressive FM station. When he was told 'No,' he spent a few weeks camping out on a friend's couch and then decided to pitch a programming job in Colorado Springs. "I put together a presentation about what I thought a progressive station could be," he says, remembering that it was "heady and very trippy."

He had flip charts with colorful graphics and three face types. The goal was to paint a picture for the station's owner. "It's not about the music," he told the exec, "it's about the culture. When radio clicks, it reaches out to people because it's greater than the sum of its parts."

It's a vision he still believes in today. Yes, he got the job, but he didn't stay long. Colorado Springs, he thought, was fine for working out the kinks, but Denver was a stepping stone to the big time. Cody wanted to climb. He stopped briefly at KBPI/Denver — eventually he'd program the station three times — but he had itchy feet and wanted to work for a big radio company in a big city.

His dream came true, but was short lived. "I had a short run at KLOS/Los Angeles," Cody admits. He dismisses the experience quickly, except to say that LA is where he met Jeff Pollack, today the Chairman of Pollack Media. What he doesn't say is he was young and in over his head. He chalked it all up to experience and

he and Pollock left LA together, heading to Albuquerque to start
KMYR-FM. "*That* was a truly progressive rock station," Cody told
me. "We played everything from Steeleye Span to Steely Dan."

•

In late 1977, after a second stop at KPBI/Denver, Cody got a
call asking him to return to KLOS/Los Angeles.

By the late '70s rock 'n' roll was big business and FM radio
was its delivery system of choice. In Los Angeles, the album rock
radio battle was being fought by Metromedia's KMET and KLOS
(Frank's station, owned by ABC). KMET, "The Mighty Met," was
considered the "hip" station and KLOS was fighting an uphill battle
that wasn't helped when ABC execs in New York decided to add
their two bits. KLOS, they suggested, was an album station and so
they couldn't understand why it wasn't playing "Saturday Night
Fever," the biggest selling album of all time. Cody says he was
caught between rock and corporate politics. "In my heart, I knew
there were two different cultures and that disco was anathema to
rock. But, I caved."

He says he agreed to play the Bee Gees on KLOS because he wanted
to keep his job. "But, it was a terrible mistake." Several years later,
Allen Shaw, ABC's head of FM Programming, admitted that forcing
Cody to add the Bee Gees at KLOS had been the wrong thing to
do. Cody leaves it this way. "I didn't follow my best instincts and
it was a big lesson," he says.

•

He returned to Denver to rock the Rockies. He'd been hired to
program KBPI again. "When KBPI was #1(12+) we were playing
a mix of the best music we could find at that specific moment in
time: The Eagles, Pink Floyd, Led Zeppelin, Fleetwood Mac, and
Tom Petty. We realized there was a huge bulge in the demographics
and we went after them."

In New York, a group of NBC executives, including Dick Verne,
Willard Lockridge and Ellen Ambrose, were sensing the same

demographic and cultural opportunities. They understood old line network programming didn't fit on FM radio. Cody agreed. "Most traditional network programming sounded too corny for stations like KBPI." When NBC, to his surprise, pitched him on the idea of a network that would provide news that was relevant to the demo, along with specials and concerts, Cody went for it in a big way. The NBC folks told him they were going to call the new network "The Source" and invited him to join the young network's advisory board. "I badgered them," recalls Cody. "Do a health feature, do concerts; no — don't do *that*!"

To no one's surprise, NBC offered Cody a job. "Frank started as in-house consultant," says Andy Denemark, Vice President of Programming for United Stations.

As part of the team at "The Source," Cody was involved in the re-invention of network radio. For the first time news and programming were designed for a specific demo and lifestyle set, i.e. FM rock stations. "It was great fun," he says. But, by 1986, when General Electric bought NBC and decided that radio didn't fit into their business plan, Cody was ready to move on. He says the idea that pointed him in his new direction was something suggested by Denemark at a celebration lunch.

That idea became "The Jazz Show with David Sanborn."

•

By the beginning of 1987 KMET/Los Angeles, long the darling of album rock circles, was dead on arrival.

Cody, hired to revive the station, arrived in Los Angeles ready to do whatever was necessary to revive the patient — that is, if it could be done. But, just in case, a decision was made to conduct a search for a new format.

Cody says it was a challenge. What do you do with a legendary radio station on its last legs? Do you fix it, or blow it up? The question they faced was — what format would work in LA in the late '80s? How about full time Spanish? What about extending the

KMET rock mindset and turning the station into a 24-hour live music experience? (The working title for this idea was "Rock 'n' Roll Adventure.") How about a station that engaged in full time sex talk? Another idea the company tested had the code name "The Malibu Suite," and it's the one that won out. On Valentines Day, 1987, playing what was then labeled "New Age" music (and would later be called "Smooth Jazz") KMET changed format and became "94-7, The Wave."

Within the radio industry the response was immediate and, virtually overnight, the format was quickly copied with Cody singled out as the format's guru. This recognition led to consulting — he advised the syndicated "Wave" format developed by the Satellite Music Network – and the consulting suggested other opportunities.

In 1989, Cody left Metropolitan Broadcasting to join Owen Leach to form the Smooth Jazz consulting firm Broadcast Architecture. (By the way, Cody says the term "smooth Jazz" came right out of a focus group in Chicago, conducted for WNUA. When a woman was asked to describe the music the station played, she replied, "It's jazz. No, no, no, it's uh, smooth. Yeah, that's it. It's smooth jazz." Cody says everyone on the station side of the glass looked at each other and said, "That's it.")

In 2002, Cody left Broadcast Architecture and returned to Los Angeles to form a media company and music label, Rendezvous Records, with long time friends, Dave Koz and Hyman Katz. Since its birth the company has directed the careers of Praful, Marc Antoine and Michael Lington. Cody says that the company has achieved the kind of success the partners dreamed about when they laid out their goals. "The plan was to *be* good and do good work," he says.

From the outside, it appears as if things are working out just fine.

CHAPTER 12
LARRY DANIELS: ARIZONA'S COUNTRY GENTLEMAN

Research and marketing? He was into it earlier than most of his peers. Music scheduling? That, too, and he wrote his own software. Success? You betcha: close to twenty years of #1 ratings. It all began, he told me, with one question, "Do you know how I can get into radio?"

His teacher looked up, thought a moment and replied, "Why don't you go to a radio station and ask?"

The programming at KGEN-AM, a daytime only station in Tulare, California, was all over the road, but the station was only a few blocks away. The young man was jazzed. When the bell sounded for lunch, he marched over to the station, walked in and asked to see the manager. "I'm willing to file records, sweep the floors; whatever you need — if, in return, you'll teach me about radio," he told the bemused exec.

He also said he'd do it for free.

Larry Daniels started in radio the next day.

•

Country radio didn't always have the muscle it has today. In fact, in 1961, the Country Music Association only reported eighty-one full time country stations. Over the next ten years, the number of stations would increase dramatically. But, back then, by anyone's standards, country wasn't cool. (Sorry.)

Back in Tulare, Larry Daniels had graduated from high school. He was still working at KGEN, not quite sure what to do next with his life, but damn sure he wasn't going to play country music, which was the plan the station's new owners had. "You can do it without me," he told them.

He found a job across town playing the rock 'n' roll he and his friends liked. But, Daniels had been raised to do the right thing, so he worked out his notice. "As we got closer to the format change, they started bringing in the records and my upbringing took over," he says. "I started thinking, 'I *know* all these artists. I know who they are. I can't leave.' "

Less than a week after the format changed, just as Daniels was signing off the station, the phone rang. "Larry?" a voice said. "I just heard you on the radio. My name is Buck Owens."

At the time, Owens had a few hits, but Larry knew him from his Bakersfield TV show. "So, you guys started playing country music," Owens said.

"Yes, sir. This is our first week."

"Well, I've got a little time. Do you mind if I drop by to say, 'Hi'?"

The two men ended up spending an hour together and, over time, they became telephone buddies. (On the day they met Owens pulled out a 45 — a record, not a gun — handed it to Daniels and mentioned he thought the singer was going to be a star. Daniels believed him and became one of the first disc jockeys in the country to play *I'm a Honky Tonk Girl* by Loretta Lynn.)

Daniels, recalling his early days with Owens, says one of his most vivid memories is when he finally mustered up the courage to do an on-air interview with Buck. "I fumbled around and had no idea what to ask," he says. "Buck came to my rescue and ended up asking all the questions."

As it happens, it wouldn't be the first time Owens interviewed him.

•

Merle and Larry were (and still are) close to the same age. Within six months of each other, both arrived in Bakersfield, full of hope for a better, more fulfilling life. Larry'd driven down from Tulare to take a new job at KUZZ (a station Buck Owens would buy a few years later) and Merle arrived, probably by bus, after serving three years of a ten year sentence for burglary at San Quentin.

What they had in common was the music.

One night in 1962 Daniels was overseeing a station remote from a club called "The Blackboard," when he heard the announcer say, "Well, here's a guy who just got back into town, a great singer, Merle Haggard." Daniels didn't know who Haggard was, but liked what he heard and says the two became fast friends. "He'd come down to the station and hang out while I was doing the morning show," says Daniels. "I remember he particularly liked Jimmie Rodgers."

Playing records on the radio is one thing and playing music live in front of an audience is another. Daniels says he got to do both and it began because, one night, Owens invited him up to sing. "I'm not a bad singer," Daniels says, with a grin.

Then Owens asked him to form a band to fill a Saturday night slot at a dance hall he owned. Daniels did and the music career grew from there, lasting for almost seven years. He says he'd play music until two in the morning, take a short middle-of-the-night nap and wake up to do the morning show at KUZZ. Eventually, it got old, but not before he had a chance to open for Haggard in Pasa Robles, CA. "He pleaded nervousness that night and convinced me to go out and sing the first song."

•

KMAK/Fresno had been a Top 40 "laboratory" for years. In the early '60s it was home to Ron Jacobs and Robert W. Morgan, before they landed in LA at KHJ. But, by 1968, the year Daniels became the station's music director, KMAK was a country station and it was there that Daniels says he learned about programming formats from the station's Program Director, Bobby Martin. Daniels stayed in Fresno for a year and half. But, after an unexpected plane ride with Buck Owens, he accepted a programming job at one of Buck's stations, KTUF-AM, in Phoenix. It was 1970, Daniels was just shy of his thirtieth birthday and the population of Phoenix was about eight hundred thousand. When Daniels arrived, he took stock of the situation. Including KTUF, an AM daytimer that went off the air at sundown, Phoenix had two other country stations, KHAT and KRDS. What it didn't have, however, was an FM country station; not that many places did. Along with KTUF, Owens Broadcasting also owned a little Phoenix FM, KNIX, which was playing a mish-mash of rock 'n' roll.

Daniels, after careful thought and study, pulled the General Manager aside and quietly made a suggestion. He told him he wanted KNIX to play country. "You know," he said, "our only chance is to, somehow, look to the FM for our future."

•

Most radio people don't get a chance to plant roots, but Larry Daniels did. His stint at KTUF/KNIX lasted twenty-eight and a half years — almost a lifetime. But, in 1999, a few months after the stations were sold to Clear Channel, he announced the formation of his consultancy, Daniels Country Radio Resources. It was a move friends had encouraged him to make for years. Why? Consider this: Under his stewardship KNIX, in 1989, became the first station to win the NAB's Marconi award in two categories: Major Market Station and Country Station of the Year. During the same period, the Country Music Association named KNIX Radio Station of the Year five times!

RJ Curtis, Country Editor at "Radio and Records," says Daniels is one of a kind. "He's a master strategist, a determined and fierce competitor and an incredible manager. He's been a mentor to a ton of guys in this business, including me."

Country consultant Rusty Walker concurs. "I've worked with just about everybody in country radio, but I've never worked with anyone more considerate, more open to new ideas, more caring about those around him, and with a more gentle spirit than Larry Daniels!"

In 2007, Daniels was elected to the Country Radio Hall of Fame, recognition that coincided with his 50th anniversary in radio.

Buck Owens, sadly, wasn't around to see it but what he told me, in March of 2001, still speaks volumes. "There's no one better or more diligent than Larry," he said. "You'd have thought KNIX belonged to him, not to me."

CHAPTER 13

RICK DEES: THE RADIO STAR WHO KISSED HOLLYWOOD

•

Put the money, the accolades, the Billboard Awards, the Radio Hall of Fame and the star on Hollywood Boulevard aside. Now, put yourself in his shoes. No matter what kind of face he put on it, you'd have to imagine that staring in the bathroom mirror that morning, February 10, 2004, must have been shattering.

After twenty-two years, one of the longest runs in the history of LA morning radio, Rick Dees was being replaced. It wasn't on his terms and the way it was coming down, most likely, wasn't the way he'd ever imagined his time at KIIS-FM would end. The sadness in his voice was palpable to those listening that morning. "It's been decided I will no longer be doing the daily morning show on Kiss-FM," he told his long-time audience.

Twenty months later, it's clear he's had a lot of time to think about it. "You can't make decisions like they did with me and our show without planning it at least a year in advance," he says.

At the end of 2004, Dee's contract with Kiss was coming up for renewal and industry scuttlebutt suggested that talks weren't going well. Dees had even made an on-the-air-off-the-cuff comment about an upcoming "life-changing" announcement. Still, he says, he wasn't fully aware of what was going on behind the scenes. "They, basically, took my show and all that I created and the people I trained. Well, it cut deep."

Dees, however, is a realist. "When a company owns twelve hundred radio stations you have to deal with them. It's just that (now) we all know what we're dealing with.

That's fine. It was nothing personal."

•

It was the day before the Ides of March, March 14, 1950. The 45-

RPM record was only a year old, Hank Williams, Nat Cole and Ivory Joe Hunter were playing on the radio, and rock 'n' roll wasn't anyone's concern. No, not yet. It was on that day, in Jacksonville, Florida, that Rigdon Osmond Dees was born and named after his father and his grandfather.

Dees spent his first eight years in Florida and then, because his father wanted to be closer to his family, they moved to Greensboro, North Carolina, which is where Dees grew up.

Like many, he first connected with radio in high school. "There was a guy named Paul Allen in my history class and he'd go off and do the school announcements," Dee remembers. In person, Allen's southern drawl was like molasses pouring from an old jelly jar, but once he hit the PA, a polished announcer's voice emerged. When Allen returned to the classroom, Dees says he looked at him and said, "You weren't in there; it was some other guy, a guy from a radio station."

Allen tucked his chin down and, in his best announcer voice, said, "No, Rick. That was me."

Dees recalls laughing out loud and then, quickly, doing his best imitation of Allen's radio voice, which embarrassed Allen, who then challenged Dees to try to do it himself.

And, that's how the whole thing started.

•

His first job was playing religious tapes on Sunday mornings at WGBG/Greensboro. He only opened the microphone to identify the station, at the top and bottom of each hour. His voice hadn't fully changed and he says he was "beyond awful," but he wasn't dissuaded.

In 1967 Dees immersed himself in the business. He fantasized about a future at WLS/Chicago or WABC/New York but was only ready for a shot in Raleigh-Durham. "The first big test was to be on WKIX, the flamethrowin' behemoth,' " he says.

By the time Dees was twenty-one, and in his last year of college, he was hired by WKIX to do the evening shift. He says he didn't really take any of it seriously. "I loved being on the air — performing, acting — and I loved to make people laugh. But, what I really wanted to do was become a psychiatrist," he reveals.

This isn't as far fetched as you may think. "My grandfather was a surgeon," Dees explains, "and my father should have been one, too. My dad was really smart, a Phi Beta Kappa at Davidson College University in the Carolinas, and then attended Jefferson Medical School. But, then, something happened."

This part of our conversation wasn't easy for Dees. According to what his uncle told him, his father got to med school and figured that he'd slide through. Instead, he flunked out. "It was the worst thing that ever happened to him," says Dees, "and it affected his whole life."

His father's failure was something Dees wouldn't come to understand until he was older. What he did get was that all of his father's subsequent career pursuits — sales for Johnson & Johnson, furniture sales and, finally, owning an equipment company that sold forklifts and the like — never seemed to work out or make him happy. "As brilliant as he was," Dees told me, "he never finished anything. So, it was like a fire burning inside me. I wanted to finish things and accomplish something. It didn't matter whether I was successful or not. I just wanted to finish."

•

In March of 1973, Dees was offered, and accepted, afternoon drive at WSGN/Birmingham, a Southern Broadcasting station. As he was motoring south, Glen Powers, WSGN's PD, reached him on the road with word that the morning man had just quit. "So," Powers asked. "Would you like to do the show?"

Dees jumped at the chance and began a life-long habit of doing morning shows and getting up very early. "I've never taken a nap in the afternoon and I've always been tired. I've just used the adrenalin. I get up in the morning about four and it's never light and never fun. But, once I get on the air, I'm one of the quickest people to wake up you'll ever see. I'm there, I'm present, I can't wait."

In radio, Dees believes we learn by doing and by listening. "There was a guy named Joe Rumore who really influenced me. He *was* Birmingham. He talked about the teams, he talked to his daughter about smoking, he talked about planting these tomato seeds and how they were coming along. As a listener, you were compelled to follow his show every day because it was like a soap opera."

Something else happened in Birmingham that caught his ear. "Just after I started at WSGN, another station started up called WERC that was AM and FM. And they brought in a guy to help run it named Scott Shannon."

Dees says Shannon did a great job selling the benefits of playing more music by using the slogan "WERC plays less commercials." "People were beginning to discover FM and I realized that it wasn't going to be a pretty sight," he says today. "I just barely escaped when I went to Memphis and WMPS."

It was 1974, the year the Hues Corporation released *Rock the Boat,* a song many consider the first disco record.

•

Memphis: the cradle of the blues, the home of Sun and Stax Records and the city where Elvis once drove a truck for the Crown Electric Company. Another thing about the city is that it's where Rick Dees, with the help of The Memphis Horns, recorded a novelty record called *Disco Duck.*

In 1976, two years after segueing from Birmingham to Memphis to do mornings at WMPS, Dees was doing just fine, thank you very much. The morning gig paid $15,000 a year, but the perks — personal appearances, hops, etc. — threw him into the low six figures and made him a local celebrity. "I was appearing at clubs all around town when disco hit," he says.

The idea of doing novelty songs was nothing new. Dees had done many for his radio show and had even signed a development deal with Fretone Records, a label started by Estelle Axton (the AX of Stax Records) after Stax fell apart. "I wrote one called *The National Wet Off* — about a wet T-shirt contest. It was fun to do, but it didn't amount to much and I was getting ready to be thrown off the label."

One night Dees was playing records at a Memphis nightclub when he noticed how people responded to certain songs, including *Gimme Some* by an artist named Jimmy Bullhorn. It got him thinking. "So," says Dees, "I listened to the beat, wrote a melody and then hummed it to a guy named Bobby Manuel (one of the Stax session men), who did a great arrangement. Then, I took the idea to Estelle Axton and told her what I wanted to do."

Axton reluctantly agreed. "We don't have a budget for you," she told him. "But, I'll tell you what. I've got the Memphis Horns and a string section coming in for a Catherine Chase session and if you can cut a rhythm track and use the horns and strings, I'll give you $800 to do it."

On the day of the session Dees says he told the players he was looking for a 4/4 stomp beat. "You know — bump, bahmp, bump, bahmp." The drummer, more practiced than Dees, added a twist to the drum pattern and Dees got excited. Then the bass line hit: "Dood it, dood it, dood it, dood it, dood it." Instantly, Dees knew they were onto something; that is, if he could get the storyline right. He decided to do a parody of disco, where a guy goes to a club, does this dance and in the middle of it all, starts flapping his arms and clucking. "And he calls himself," says Dees, laughing, "the disco duck."

As a final touch, Dees decided to throw in a duck voice. He had a guy from the morning show who could do it.

"So, lo and behold, we laid it down. I sang the melody, got the duck voice in there, added horns and strings and then we did the mix down."

When the song was done and he listened back to it, Dees says it occurred to him that *Disco Duck* might actually turn into something. The next job was to get WMPS, his radio station, to play it.

But they wouldn't. Yep, you read that right.

Dees sent a copy of the record out to all the major record companies and they all passed, except for one. "I sent a 45 to Al Coury at RSO," remembers Dees. "He took it home to his kids in Woodland Hills and they went crazy laughing and wanted to hear it again."

The next day Coury called Dees and Axton and said RSO would like to buy the master for $3,500, plus a penny to Dees for each record sold. Dees says he knew it wasn't the best deal in the world, but when RSO's owner, Robert Stigwood, heard the song and told his promotion staff to "make it number one," Dees began to suspect that things would work out fine.

Coury and Stigwood would not be denied. *Disco Duck* entered the Top 40 on September 4, 1976 and, by the time it was number five with a bullet, Dees was getting ready to go on the road to promote it. Just before leaving town, he opened his WMPS mic and said to his audience, "Can you believe this? I'm getting ready to go to California to appear on "American Bandstand" and "The Midnight Special" with a song I've written and performed called *Disco Duck*. And this station isn't even playing it!" (In all fairness, none of the radio stations in Memphis were playing the record.)

"Channel 5 heard about it and came by with their camera crew," says Dees. "It hit the news all over town."

•

He was the #1 morning man in Memphis with a top five national hit record. One might think the management at WMPS would be thrilled. "Nope," says Dees, "the GM was pissed."

The day after he mentioned the record on the air Dees walked into the GM's office.

"Well, Rick," said the un-named GM, "You know, we're going to have to part ways."

"Yeah," Dees replied. "I'm going to California to do these two TV shows, but I'm only going to take one day off, be back on Tuesday."

"No," explained the GM. "You're being terminated. You're fired."

"Whhaaat?" Dees replied. "Whadda ya mean?"

"We consider it a conflict of interest for you to have talked about your song on the air."

"Conflict of interest!?! It's a conflict of interest if I played the song and didn't say it was me!"

"It's a conflict," replied the GM, with finality. "That's what we think. We're a drug company and we can't take any chances."

Exasperated, all Dees could say was, "C'mon!"

And that might have been the last word, except that it wasn't. His contract with WMPS had a forty-five-day no-compete but, before it was over, RKO's WHBQ called, offered him more money (than he was making) and told him that by doing the morning show for them, he'd get his needed revenge.

By the time he started the new show, *Disco Duck* was the #1 song in the nation and after the dust settled The Rick Dees Morning Show became the #1 morning show in Memphis. Again. This time on WHBQ.

By the way, WMPS was eventually forced to change format.

•

Had it been ten years earlier, the LA real estate agent's comment would have been different. But it wasn't. It was 1979.

"So, you said radio? Is that what you said?"

"Yeah," replied Dees. "I'm doing a morning show on KHJ."

"Isn't that AM?" the agent asked.

"Uh, huh," Dees nodded.

"Why wouldn't you be on FM?" the agent asked, adding, "the station that's really hot, the one everyone listens to, is KMET."

In September of 1980, after fifteen years as one of America's most talked about Top 40 radio stations, KHJ went country, and Rick Dees, after only a year and half in the chair where Robert W. Morgan once sat, got the shock of his life. "It was my wife's birthday," he says, "and I was supposed to meet with Neil Rockoff, KHJ's General Manager, to sign a new contract."

But, when Dees got to the office, Rockoff wasn't there. His secretary, the queen of diplomacy, told Mr. and Mrs. Dees the station had decided not to finalize the deal. "We've decided to just, well, move on," she told them.

"Rick," asked Julie Dees. "What does she mean?"

Dees says he was too upset to answer the question immediately. Later, when they were alone, he explained that he'd been fired.

Happy birthday, baby.

•

Dees was off the air for almost a year. "I don't know what the deal was, but no one would hire me."

During his down time he took some acting lessons, got the hives, and did some voice work. He was one of three voiceover guys on CBS TV.

He remembers being very frustrated. He talked to MTV about becoming a VJ — no, it didn't work out — and finally, just as he was about to accept a $28,000 offer from Drake Chenault to do some syndicated projects, the PD of KIIS-FM, Don Benson, called.

"They were thinking about taking the station Hot AC (Hot Adult Contemporary). I didn't know what that was and told them I didn't want to do it," says Dees. Another option the station was considering was straight ahead Top 40, an idea Dees thought was the right move. "So, we had a meeting and Don told me they could only pay me $45,000 to $50,000, but they were going to put a great bonus package together."

I'd like to tell you Dees got excited because he'd done his homework and knew Gannett was a killer radio company. It'd also be great to tell you he understood that FM was the name of the game and that Kiss could be his home forever, and take him to lofty heights he could only have dreamt of. But, it's just not so.

He was petulant. "Well, if you make the bonuses great, because I was making two hundred thousand at KHJ, and..."

Benson interrupted him. "I know, I know."

And that was that.

•

"When I went on," says Dees, "Kiss had this rag tag bunch. I grabbed this girl named Liz Fulton and started calling her Liz 'Rug Burns' Fulton. And, a guy on the AM doing news, Charlie Wright — I called him 'Coach' Charlie Wright."

With nothing to lose, Dees resurrected all the characters he'd done in Memphis, but this time around he cast them as Mexicans, instead of trailer-park southerners.

When Dees started at KIIS-FM in 1981, the station was a two point seven share radio station. By 1998, it had a ten share, and Dees, remarkably, posted a twenty point six share among 18 to 34-year-olds — something that hadn't been done in Los Angeles since the heyday of Boss Radio. In the blink of an eye he was back and surrounded by a publicity campaign built around the question — "Did you hear what Rick Dees said this morning?"

Next Kiss launched a million dollar promotion that put Dees's face on virtually every bus and billboard in Southern California.

It was the start of an LA ride that would last for years.

•

Dees has his fingers in lots of pies, just as he always has. He hosted "Solid Gold," had his own late night TV show, "Into The Night" (he says God told him that even He didn't watch it), has appeared in countless movies and TV shows and, since 1983, has been the host of "The Weekly Top 40," a countdown show heard on over three hundred and fifty stations in the United States and in one hundred and twenty-five countries around the world. He has his own star on the Hollywood Walk of Fame, has received the People's Choice Award, was inducted into The Radio Hall of Fame and was named Billboard Personality of The Year ten years in a row.

In August of 2005, Dees announced the launch of "Rick.Com" — a website designed for those who want to "explore music, videos and entertainment" – and Dees is also an equity partner in the cable channel, "Fine Living."

Then, in August 2006, two and a half years after leaving Kiss-FM, he was named the morning man at KMVN-FM/Los Angeles, a station owned by Emmis Communications. Dees says he's thrilled to be doing morning radio in Los Angeles again. He also says getting up every morning still isn't easy, but that he greets each new day with the question — "God, what have you got for me today?" and a pledge to "stay positive and work hard."

(The Orange County Register, April 14, 2009.
Reported by Gary Lycan)

> On April 14, 2009. Emmis announced that KMVN-FM was changing format. KMVN, known as "Movin 93.9" FM, is moving on out April 14, and so is Rick Dees. The Emmis Communications-owned station is switching to a Spanish format on April 15. Advertisers and others were notified by the station

Friday after Emmis announced it had signed a local marketing agreement with Mexican radio company, Grupo Radio Centro, which will take over programming and ad sales.

"Buenos Tardes," Dees said in a phone call Friday afternoon. He said he applauded the company decision, saying, "It's the way business is right now."

On the same day, this message was posted on Rick.com.

This is absolutely ridiculous. You are the only morning show I have ever listened to. After kiss fm switched from steak (you) to a wiener (rs), I listened to nothing until you came back on 93.9. When I turned on my radio, I thought my radio was malfunctioning, then I thought it was one of your pranks...but no it wasn't. So once again, no more morning show for me.....until you come back again!!!!!

Sincerely,
Nanette

The fat lady hasn't sung yet.

CHAPTER 14

TOM DONAHUE: THE FATHER OF PROGRESSIVE RADIO

"My name is Tom Donahue, and I play phonograph records." Yes, that's what he said and it's what he did, but there's more to it.

Bigger than life, both literally and figuratively, Donahue was no kid when he and a group of friends started an FM radio revolution in San Francisco. It was 1967 — yes, that storied year — and Donahue was thirty-nine. A few years before, he'd left a successful Top 40 career to start a record label, Autumn Records (featuring Bobby Freeman [*C'mon and Swim* — Billboard #5 July 1964] and The Beau Brummels [*Laugh, Laugh* — Billboard #8 May 1965), and to do concert promotion. By the time the "Summer of Love" arrived, Donahue had had it with radio.

With no radio station signal to express his views, Donahue took his voice to the pages of "Rolling Stone," where he wrote an article headlined, "AM Radio Is Dead and Its Rotting Corpse Is Stinking Up the Airwaves."

"He'd had enough (of Top 40)," says his widow, Raechel Donahue. "He knew that it wasn't the kind of music that people were listening to and it certainly wasn't what he wanted to be playing."

•

Tom "Big Daddy" Donahue's radio career began at WTIP/ Charleston, SC, in 1949. In 1961, after ten years at WIBG/ Philadelphia, he joined KYA/San Francisco — where he famously promised to "blow minds and clear pimply faces" — before he tired of the music, Top 40 antics and the adolescent audience.

One evening in the first few months of 1967 Donahue and a group of friends were playing cards (it may have been backgammon, mah jong or cribbage; I don't know) and listening to a test pressing of The Doors's first album. "I wonder why nobody's playing music like this on the radio," Donahue is said to have asked.

The next morning he hit the phones, making calls to every FM radio station listed in the San Francisco phone book. He reasoned that a station with a disconnected phone line might be in financial trouble and, therefore, open to a new idea. The radio station he found was KMPX, where Italian and Chinese immigrants bought airtime and where owner Leon Crosby was having trouble making it.

At six p.m. on April 7, 1967, two months before the Monterey Pop Festival and three months before the release of "Sgt. Pepper's Lonely Hearts Club Band," the FM rock 'n' roll revolution began. Tom and Raechel Donahue were both there, along with an assortment of friends, including actor Howard Hesseman, aka TV's Dr. Johnny Fever. The music they played that night came from their personal collections.

It's only a guess, but I suspect KMPX's signal had no processing and the mic had no echo. For sure, there were no jingles and no hype — none of the accoutrements of Top 40. It was just Donahue and his phonograph records.

It must have been, to borrow a phrase, "far out." The phones at the station started ringing, remembers Ms. Donahue — older Koreans and Italians demanding to know what was going on and young folks, too, who couldn't believe what they were hearing.

•

It didn't take long for word about KMPX to spread throughout the Bay Area. Today, we'd call it viral. With no marketing and no promotion, certainly no television proclamations about a "new radio station" because no one even thought of selling radio on TV back then, KMPX became a mini-success.

Donahue and all the DJs played their songs in sets, segregated by themes, sounds, musical idioms, even contrasts. They didn't stop between the records and didn't talk over the intros. And, when

Donahue declared that the station would serve as an "open bulletin board" for the city's hip community and promised that the station would be honest and direct with its audience, he was believed.

But, good deeds don't go unpunished.

Before long, KMPX's owner, Leon Crosby, forgot how bad things had been. Reveling in his success, he decided the station should start playing music his wife liked; she, one assumes, had the ears of someone who would know what was and wasn't great rock 'n' roll.

Next, and equally as offensive to Donahue and company, was the dress code Crosby established for station personnel. All free spirits, they took exception to the man's edicts and, in more than one word, said no. In protest, Donahue resigned and the staff went on strike. They took themselves seriously — well, kinda, sorta. They named themselves "The Amalgamated American International FM Workers of the World" and hired an old-time mining attorney to represent them. They set up a picket line, where they were joined by members of The Grateful Dead, Blue Cheer and Credence Clearwater Revival, and that was only the beginning. "The longshoremen down on the waterfront went on the picket line with us," says Raechel Donahue. "They were quite willing to bash heads, if necessary, but we told them not to." The strike lasted eight weeks, ending on May 13, 1968.

Under Donahue, the experiment that was KMPX lasted a little more than a year and, while the station would continue under new leadership, it was never the same. For those who heard it live and in real time, the station was unique, soulful and, with a little help from whatever they were smoking, real and unembellished.

(In the interest of full disclosure, I have to tell you that I've only heard tapes and only from thirty years away. Go to the Internet and listen yourself.) In hindsight, it's clear that, at a specific point in time, KMPX was able to touch people's lives. There is, for example, the story of a guy in jail who, with only one call to make, decided to call the station.

When asked why, he replied, "It's my only friend."

•

When the strike ended at KMPX, Donahue and his band of merry record spinners were replaced by a new staff, led by Tom Yates, who called himself Tom Swift. (Years later, Yates became Program Director of KLOS/Los Angeles). Then, on May 21st, Donahue and friends resurfaced across town at KSAN, a classical station owned by Metromedia Broadcasting. Within days, the station rolled Beethoven over and began rocking.

While all of this was happening in San Francisco, Metromedia began to shake things up in Los Angeles, too. The company hired KPPC/Pasadena staffers (KPPC was KMPX's sister station and had also been programmed by Donahue) and moved them over to their Los Angeles property, KMET. The new format on both stations was labeled free-form. Think of this as anti-Selector and "think of Donahue," says Mike Harrison, Publisher of "Talkers" magazine, "as the first corporate VP with a pony tail."

•

There were only a handful of stations doing anything like KSAN. In Boston, there was WBCN; in New York, WNEW, and Philly had WMMR. The thing to remember is that it all happened before ABC's progressive rock experiments, Harrison's AOR and the Burkhart/Abrams Superstars format.

KSAN wasn't formatted and, consequently, it could take you anywhere. "You might hear a classical piece (segue) into some rock 'n' roll thing and then into a jazz piece," says Bonnie Simmons, who was with the station for over ten years. "And the whole set could end with a country song. It was up to each jock to decide what to do and how to do it."

KSAN, like KMPX before it, was more than music, and, as Donahue had promised, it stayed connected to its listeners. "We were always our audience. We weren't these rarified disc jockey creatures sitting in a glass room," says Simmons.

Like its listeners, the station was anti-Nixon, anti-Vietnam and pro-pot. In 1974, when the Symbionese Liberation Army kidnapped heiress Patty Hearst, it was KSAN they chose to communicate their message and demands.

When Simmons and I chatted several years ago, she told me about a long-standing KSAN holiday tradition. "We did this thing called the Turkey Exchange. People would call or send us notes saying, 'I'm in town this week and don't know anybody,' or 'Eight of us are having Thanksgiving dinner and have room for four more.' So, we'd give out phone numbers and perfect strangers would go to perfect strangers' houses and have Thanksgiving."

Simmons says that in the eight years that KSAN did The Turkey Exchange they never had a problem. "But, we wouldn't do it today," she says.

•

Tom Donahue died of a heart attack on April 28, 1975 and KSAN, as a rock 'n' roll station, only lasted another five years before falling victim to the "Urban Cowboy" craze of 1980, and changing format to country.

"Having worked with a lot of people," reflects Simmons," I realize how larger than life he was. I haven't experienced *that* since."

"My perceptions of Donahue inspired me to make great radio through orchestrated anarchy," says former WNEW PD, Charlie Kendall.

In 1996, because of his contributions to FM radio, Tom "Big Daddy" Donahue was inducted in the Rock 'n' Roll Hall of Fame. For a radio man, this honor is a big deal, one only shared by Alan Freed.

"If he were alive today," says Raechel Donahue, "I think he'd say it's time for another revolution."

CHAPTER 15
KEN DOWE: UNDERSTANDING
GORDON MCLENDON

The crucifixion took place over dinner. "Change the call letters," said the consultant. "Blow up the format! The station will never come back!"

Hyman Childs, the owner of KKDA-FM/Dallas, lost his appetite. He turned to his friend, Ken Dowe. "Do you think it's true, Ken?" he asked. "Is this what's going to happen?"

Dowe, who knew all about station ownership, replied, "No, I don't think so. I don't think you'll have to do all that."

But, KKDA-FM (K-104) *was* in trouble. Its direct urban competitor, Summit's KJMZ-FM, was hipper, hotter, and the acknowledged flavor of the month. To add insult to injury, all the research confirmed K-104's vulnerability. But, Dowe wasn't concerned. In September of 1992, he took over K-104's programming and methodically went about applying the lessons thirty years of radio had taught him: focus on mornings, make the station bigger than life, become part of the community.

Two years after Dowe rolled up his sleeves and began to actively compete with KJMZ-FM, the station left the format. Today, K-104 is consistently on top of the ratings in Dallas — Ft. Worth.

"Ken's always had great instincts about local programming," says Dan Mason, President of CBS Radio. "People talk about his radio stations."

Somewhere, Gordon McLendon is smiling.

•

Ken Dowe spent his Sunday mornings haggling with preachers. "If you don't have the money, Brother Smith," he'd say, "I just can't let you on."

He was "working" at his hometown radio station, WGBM/Greenville, Mississippi. His job was to hang out, get coffee for whoever wanted it, and to not ask too many questions. Some afternoons, after they got used to seeing him, he'd show up to watch Eddie Williams play rhythm and blues records. He says he'd just sit there quietly and think to himself, "You know, I could do that."

One obstacle, however, was his voice. "It came out like Jimmy Carter's," Dowe admits. "Way up in the top of my throat." There was also that Mississippi accent, something he decided he had to lose, so he started going to movie matinees — not for the stars or stories, but for the voices. Then he'd go home and practice in front of the mirror. "One day I woke up and didn't talk like a Mississippi puker anymore," he says. "I was ever so grateful."

•

His first full time job was in Hattiesburg, one hundred and seventy-seven miles from home.

He'd no sooner arrived when the owner named him Program Director. Of course, he had no idea what that meant or what he should do, but inspiration was on the air less than a hundred miles away. "I could hear WNOE/New Orleans like it was local. Listening to it made me to want to do radio for the rest of my life."

He says that now and he means it, but back then, at age nineteen, he was worried radio might not be his ticket to fame and fortune. So, he decided to become a fighter pilot. Really. Don't laugh. You see, during high school Dowe had been a page in the Mississippi House of Representatives and, as unlikely as it seems, he was able to pull some strings and get accepted for training at Kessler Air Force Base.

So, he was ready to sail off into the wild blue yonder; except, at the last minute, he heard about a radio job and decided to junk his fly-boy plans. Instead, he flew across the border to Alabama, landing a job at WABB/Mobile, a station owned by Bernie Dittman. His life was about to change. "A guy named Jim Taber was there," Dowe recalls, fondly. "Jim was from Dallas and played me airchecks of KLIF and KBOX and I went nuts."

Now we go to warp speed.

Before the year was out, Dowe met the love of his life, eloped, accepted a job at KDEO/San Diego and headed for California, where, with little experience, he somehow ended up doing the morning show. "There was a guy on the air at KCBQ named Happy Hare," Dowe says. "I was the first to ever beat him."

That's when he heard from Chuck Dunaway, the PD of KBOX/ Dallas.

•

In 1961, KBOX and KLIF were fighting a Top 40 war in Dallas. KBOX, owned by Balaban Broadcasting, called itself "The Dallas Tiger" and though the station never did beat Gordon McLendon's KLIF, it did give KLIF a run for its money. Dowe believes KBOX sounded better.

One day, only nine months after he arrived, one of Dowe's heroes, KOMA/Oklahoma City's "Hot Rod" Roddy (the announcer on The Price Is Right — "Come on down!!!!") blasted through the station's door. "I'm on my way to WQXI/Atlanta," he told Dowe. "When I get there, I'm going to get Kent Burkhart to call you."

Roddy did as promised and Burkhart called with an offer for Dowe to come to Atlanta, which Dowe accepted. At first, he says, it was about the money. But, as he settled in at WQXI, he realized something else was going on. "Kent was the first person to give me the confidence to really be somebody on the radio," says Dowe.

A year passed and then he heard from KLIF again. McLendon, based on positive comments from his morning man, Ron Chapman (at the time, his air name was still Irving Harrigan), wanted Dowe to return to Dallas. "So, I did mid-days at KLIF for a few heartbeats and then afternoons for, maybe, two and half years," Dowe says. "I loved everything about it."

Well, maybe not everything.

Dowe wanted to become a program director, but McLendon thought he was too valuable on the air. Frustrated, Dowe took matters into his own hands. "Pat O'Day just called from Seattle," he told his wife, Dottie. "He and Les Smith are putting on a new station in Cincinnati."

At twenty-five, Dowe joined WUBE/Cincinnati, but early on it became clear the move was a mistake. "It was the biggest downturn of my entire career," he says. He loved O'Day, but the station ate him up; union hassles, personnel problems and endless stress. Where was the magic? he wondered. When an opportunity arose to join WNOX/ Knoxville, Dowe grabbed at it. But, just as he was getting settled in at his new job, McLendon reached out to him again.

"We want you to come back to Dallas and do the morning show, Ken."

•

Bill Stewart, KLIF's PD, had his demons, but the man knew his business. "Why'd you do that there? What happened during that break?"

"He was like a nasty history professor," says Dowe, remembering how Stewart tore into him. "But, he taught me how to do a morning show."

"Ken was a non-traditional disc jockey, a real person," says Michael O'Shea of *All Comedy Radio*. "He also had an alter-ego, eighty-six-year old Granny Emma."

"Dallas listeners thought she was real," Burkhart confides. "When they discovered it was really Ken, the city was dumbfounded."

Ken and Granny grabbed 38% of the Dallas' listeners and any observer might have thought the show would last for years. Instead, in a surprise move, McLendon took Dowe off the air. "We sat down in my house talking until three or four in the morning," says Dowe, "and Gordon told me he needed someone to run his radio stations."

At the time, McClendon Broadcasting was the largest independent group in America, with stations in Buffalo, Chicago, Dallas, Detroit, Los Angeles and San Francisco. This new job sounded like he was being given the keys to the kingdom. "Well, I was his number-one guy," Dowe laughs, "but he never told me my name was McLendon."

What he did do was name Dowe the first Executive Vice President of McLendon Broadcasting.

•

In 1972, Gordon McLendon sold KLIF to Fairchild Aircraft for ten million dollars, at the time the largest amount of money ever paid for a stand alone radio station. During a last minute meeting with Fairchild executives McLendon, off-handedly, offered to sell KNUS-FM for an additional $150,000. Fairchild declined the offer. On the way back to the office McLendon asked Dowe what he thought they ought to do with the FM. The next morning Dowe delivered a memo outlining his plan and McLendon agreed to it. Within 15 months KNUS-FM was the #1 station in Dallas.

But, by the middle '70s, McLendon had decided to divest himself of his stations and Dowe found himself looking for a new challenge. In 1975, he joined KTSA-KTFM/San Antonio and, in quick order, turned KTSA around and established KTFM as a major San Antonio player. At this point, after close to ten years of running stations and groups for others, Dowe set his sights on ownership.

•

Clint Murchison Jr. had an Electrical Engineering degree from Duke University and a master's degree in mathematics from MIT. His father, Clint Murchison Sr., was a Texas oil man and the son followed in his father's footsteps by starting a company that produced methane gas. In 1960, Murchison attracted attention when he and his partner, Bedford Wynne, acquired a National Football League franchise and founded the Dallas Cowboys. The following year, Murchison and Gordon McLendon invested in *Radio Nord*, a short-lived pirate radio station moored in the Stockholm archipelago. On June 30, 1962, the Swedish government closed the station down, but Murchison maintained an interest in radio and, when Dowe approached him, in late 1979, about investing in a group he wanted to start, Murchison agreed.

The first station they acquired was in Oklahoma City, and Dowe and his Program Director, Dan Mason, applied for the call letters KLTE-FM and nicknamed the station *K-lite*. Over the next ten years Dowe grew the group and, by 1990, it included five stations, in Texas, California and Louisiana. But, Dowe saw consolidation of the radio industry coming and sensing it was time to get out, he put his group of stations on the block, sold them, and returned to Dallas where he counted his earnings. The following year, returning to on-air work, Dowe signed on to host the morning show at KODZ-FM/Dallas. It was a return to his roots, but within the year the station was sold to Alliance Broadcasting.

Shortly thereafter, Dowe had a fateful dinner meeting with Hyman Childs and an unidentified consultant and joined KKDA-FM.

•

"**There were two** people who had remarkable relationships with Gordon McLendon," says O'Shea — "Don Keyes and Ken — and I think Ken understood Gordon's philosophy better than anyone."

Close to forty years ago McLendon wrote Dowe a letter. In it were these words: "**I respect you as a creator and an innovator.**"

Ken Dowe is still smiling.

CHAPTER 16
BILL DRAKE: THE ZEN MASTER

Except for the sound of what's being broadcast, most radio stations are quiet at night. Lights are off, doors are locked and visitors are discouraged. But, there was a night, over forty-four years ago, when two men working the night shift at KHJ/Los Angeles noticed two other men walking through the building. The way it's been described makes it sound like a religious experience.

"I'm sitting in the recording studio," says Bill Mouzis, "and he walked through — this big, tall man. He took one look to the right, looked at me and then looked at the equipment. He was walking with somebody else, I think it was Gene Chenault, and they walked through the room. And then, just like that, he was gone."

Bill Mouzis was a tape editor, a man good with a razor blade. He'd had to be to hold onto a job for fifteen years in a radio station that had changed formats as often as KHJ.

"So, this guy I'm working with says, 'You know who that was, don't you?' "

Mouzis says he shook his head, "No."

"That's Bill Drake," said the other man. "And those are the guys that are gonna come in and rock 'n' roll this place."

"Really," Mouzis replied. "How well do you know them?"

"Pretty well," the other man claimed. "You know, they did a lot of great things out in some small markets."

"How good is he?" asked Mouzis.

"Very good. If anybody takes Bill Drake lightly, they're crazy."

•

KHJ had been the second station to go on the air in Los Angeles, when it signed on in 1922, and many famous entertainers got their start there, including George Burns, Gracie Allen and Eddie Cantor. In the mid '30s, Bing Crosby broadcast from KHJ's studios every evening for fifteen minutes and, in the '40s, before jumping to television, Steve Allen did a morning show on KHJ called "Smile Time." (A reincarnation of that program was on the station in 1965, the year Drake took the station over and launched Boss Radio.)

By the following spring KHJ was the #1 rock 'n' roll station in Los Angeles. "KHJ changed the way Los Angeles listened to radio, the way a generation of Program Directors programmed, the way copy writers copied and djs jocked," said Robert W. Morgan, in 1990. "It was the most talked about, air-checked and emulated radio station in America. No station, before or since, has had the national impact that's even come close to that of 93-KHJ."

He wasn't exaggerating.

•

In 1955, a teenager named Phillip Yarbrough got a job at WMGR-AM/Bainbridge, Georgia, a radio station twenty or so miles north of his hometown of Donalsonville, Georgia. Yarborough had a big voice, one people always seemed to notice, but pro basketball, not voice work, was his plan and he was good enough on the court to earn a scholarship to Georgia Teachers College, upstate, Statesboro.

But, almost before he began, he blew out his knee, which blew his dream to smithereens. That's when Yarborough turned his sights on radio.

In 1961, he went to work for Bartell Broadcasting at WAKE/Atlanta. One of the first suggestions station executives offered was that he change his name to one that would rhyme with *wake*. They came up with Blake, but young Mr. Yarbrough opted for his mother's maiden name instead. The name he chose was Drake.

In 1962 Bartell Broadcasting sold the station and transferred the newly named Mr. Drake to San Francisco to program KYA. Very quickly the Georgia native realized the distance between Atlanta and San Francisco was more than geographical. "He took a lot of grief from people in San Francisco because they thought he was a hillbilly," says Tom Rounds. "He didn't like it very much."

Another thing Drake didn't like much was the size of KYA's sixty-record (new music) playlist. San Francisco writer, Ben Fong-Torres, in his book "The Hits Just Keep on Coming," says Drake found the number of songs so "unwieldy" that he cut the size of the music library in half. Fong-Torres wrote that this move "resulted in increased ratings."

Drake's success at KYA brought him to the attention of Gene Chenault, who hired him to do his magic and science at KYNO/Fresno and KSTN/Stockton. When both stations hit #1 – KYNO earned fifty-two percent of the available audience in its listening area – Chenault told friends he'd seen the future of radio and, in short order, he and Drake formed Drake-Chenault Enterprises.

The two men, like modern day evangelists, began to tell Drake's "more music, less talk" story to all who would listen. One who did was Willet Brown, the owner of KGB/San Diego. In 1964, he gave Drake a shot. In less than three months KGB's ratings skyrocketed from #14 to #1, and it was this success that led Drake to Tom O'Neal, Chairman of the Board of General Tire — the company that owned RKO General Broadcasting and KHJ/Los Angeles.

•

The new KHJ, Boss Radio, was born in Hollywood on May 3, 1965. "All of the disc jockeys that came into KHJ had been program directors," says Rounds. "So, this was actually the most easily managed group of guys in the world. It was a dream job for Jacobs." (Ron Jacobs, KHJ's first rock 'n' roll Program Director, may or may not agree with Round's assessment. What we do know is that if Drake was KHJ's architect, it was Jacobs who built it.)

With KHJ's success, Drake was asked to consult some of the other stations in the RKO chain, including KFRC/San Francisco,

WOR/New York, WRKO/Boston, WHBQ/Memphis, and CKLW/ Windsor-Detroit. The agreement with RKO wasn't an exclusive arrangement and Drake and his team were free to work with stations owned by other companies, as long as they weren't in markets where RKO had stations. By 1967, Drake was being touted as the next big thing in the radio industry and several national magazines, including "Time," "Newsweek," "True," "Look" and "Entertainment World" wrote stories that described him sitting by his Hollywood swimming pool monitoring radio stations in cities all across the country.

"The Drake sound," wrote "Newsweek," "is a deliberately bland, smoothly modulated mixture of pop favorites, and has been so successful in capturing mass audiences that, within the trade, its creator's name is now used generically, like cellophane and aspirin."

The Drake-Chenault consultants," says Mel Phillips, who pro- grammed WRKO/Boston, "were more than just the names on the masthead. There were people working for Drake — Bill Watson, chief among them — who were connected to him and connected to the local PDs at each radio station." KAKC's Lee Bayley agrees that that's the way it was. "Watson," he says, "was to Drake what a prime minister is to a king."

Chenault and Drake decided to expand their business by creating a syndication company. Bayley, by then in Canoga Park at Drake- Chenault, says, "The whole thing came about because RKO said, 'You guys are doing such a good job with the AM stations. What can you do with our FMs?' Drake's response was, 'Well, we don't want to do any live stuff. So, let's try this automation thing?' "

By 1978 Drake-Chenault had over 320 client stations running their automated formats.

•

In 1983, after a twenty-one-year partnership with Gene Chenault, Drake sold his interest in the company. A few years later, a New Mexico based entrepreneur, Bill Sanders, bought Drake-Chenault and the programming division of TM Communications, its biggest competitor, took both companies to Albuquerque, set them up on two different floors of the same building and told them to continue to compete. It wasn't a good idea. Today, what remains of Drake-Chenault and TM — including shows like "The History of Rock 'n' Roll" — is owned by the Triton Media Group.

As for Bill Drake, aside from a false start in the '90s at First Broadcasting in Dallas (an attempt to create an oldies format for satellite distribution that never got off the ground), he retired to Los Angeles.

•

So, Bill Drake's biggest successes occurred over forty years ago and they just aren't relevant anymore. Right?

"Not so," says Steve Rivers. "I'm a student of his work and the airchecks of those great RKO stations taught me a lot of the basics that I still use today."

"Drake and his associates understood the needs of the young adult listener — more hit music, hip DJs, fun audience involvement — and packaged it in a tightly produced, forward-moving continuous flow," says Bob Henabery. "They executed that vision masterfully and put post-TV radio back on track all by themselves."

"Drake realized that if a station is programmed as a single, strategic entity, it's less vulnerable to attack. "His is a strategy that's been copied by other media, including MTV," says consultant Walter Sabo."

Ok, but who was he? Was Bill Drake really more myth than man? Former WRKO PD Mel Phillips answers the question this way: "It was like you couldn't believe all of this great stuff was coming from a guy who was as plain and simple and laid back as he was. I never saw him where he wasn't in control of the situation."

•

On May 9, 1990 there was a celebration in Century City, CA. It was KHJ's 25th Anniversary, held on the opening night of that year's Radio and Record's convention, and everybody who was anybody in Boss Radio history was there.

On stage, in his element, Robert W. Morgan was nostalgic. "Bill's the guy who, along with Mr. Gene Chenault, hijacked KHJ from RKO, hired us all and let us do our thing. As long as our thing wasn't longer than six seconds. (The crowd howled.) He's the tallest guy in this room tonight and, since 1965, he's been the tallest guy in radio." (Again, the crowd went wild.)

"By the way," added Morgan, "he's the only programmer who didn't have to copy the Drake format."

In July of 1996, Bill Drake was inducted into the California Broadcasters Association Radio Hall of Fame and Georgia gave him the same honor in 2007. As of this writing; however, (December of 2008) the National Association of Broadcasters has yet to recognize the man.

John Rook says it's a shame. "Bill Drake's contribution to radio ranked with that of Gordon McLendon. Isn't it about time we make a concentrated effort to make sure Bill's inducted into the NAB Radio Hall of Fame?"

•

Bill Drake died in Los Angeles on November 29, 2008. He was seventy-one.

As with both Robert W. Morgan and The Real Don Steele, the two disc jockeys he and Jacobs built KHJ around, the cause of death was lung cancer.

"He was the Zen Master," says Tom Rounds. "Words weren't his tool. Rather, one gained enlightenment by just being in the presence of his powerful intuitiveness. It was then up to you to figure out how to turn his all-seeing knowingness into action. The Drake format was so powerful it was scary. We were the acolytes. Drake was the source."

Sounds kinda religious, doesn't it?

CHAPTER 17
PAUL DREW: THE BUTTONED-DOWN MIND

Yoko Ono had already called six times.

"When I called her back," says Paul Drew, "she told me the call was confidential, a secret."

"You can't tell anybody," Yoko had whispered down the line.

Once he agreed mum was the word, Yoko confided that she and John Lennon wanted to make a new record, but didn't have a manager.

"So, she asked me to help them," Drew explains.

That Drew would get a call from Lennon's camp isn't as off the wall as it may seem. First of all, he'd traveled with the Beatles in the mid '60s, when he was at WQXI/Atlanta. Then, in the late '70s, after his stint as VP of Programming for RKO Radio, Drew journeyed to Japan regularly and, by chance, ended up at the same hotel as the Lennons. "One night I heard someone call out my name," Drew recalls.

He says he turned around to find John and Yoko standing there. "So, we went into the restaurant and talked for about three hours. It was a beautiful experience. They checked out the next morning, but John left me a lovely handwritten note."

So, Drew was back on the phone with Yoko. "Are you familiar with my music?" she asked.

"Not all of it," he answered, tactfully.

"So, I spent an evening listening to Yoko Ono," he told me. "Can you imagine what that was like?"

The record John and Yoko made, "Double Fantasy," was finished in the fall of 1980, but still there was no record deal.

"Yoko called and said, 'We have all these offers and don't know what to do. Can you come to New York and help us?"

Drew flew up on his own dime, checked into the Waldorf and joined the Lennons for dinner. "We went to a restaurant where they had a private room stacked with letters and telegrams." One inquiry was from David Geffen.

"I told them to sign with David," Drew says. "When they asked me why, I said, 'David will care about your music because his name is on every record pressed.' "

"At one point, Yoko asked if I would consider managing them." Then, says Drew, she asked him for a bunch of numbers. He didn't know why. Two days later Yoko called back to say the numbers – dates, times, astrology related stuff – hadn't checked out.

"I didn't want to say 'No,' " Drew admits today. "But, fate helped me out."

It wasn't the first time.

•

It was a Saturday night in 1957.

Drew was freshly out of Wayne State University/Detroit and in the middle of an odyssey through Pennsylvania and Ohio that he hoped would land him a radio job. That evening he was in Cincinnati sitting at his uncle's kitchen table. "He had a copy of "Fortune" magazine and the cover had a picture of Atlanta," says Drew.

"You know," his uncle said, pointing his finger towards the picture of the Georgia skyline, "If I was a young guy like you, this is where I'd go for a future."

"Me, too," thought Drew.

Adrenalin racing, he bolted out the door, jumped into the car he'd borrowed from his mother, gunned the engine and aimed south. Down through Kentucky he went, across Tennessee and into Georgia — two lane highways all the way. "Eventually I ended up in Atlanta and went straight to WQXI," says Drew. "But, they didn't have a job, so I went over to WGST and discovered they'd just fired somebody. I got hired."

Job in hand, Drew drove home to Detroit, packed his stuff, bought a car and hit the road again. Heading towards Atlanta, Drew flashed on something he'd heard from his college professor, Lee Dreyfus — a man who, in later years, would become the Governor of Wisconsin. "If you keep knocking on doors," Dreyfus had coached, "someone will hire you. That's how it works in radio."

So he was right, thought Drew. You just have to keep knocking on doors.

•

Atlanta wasn't the city it is today. In 1957, the year Drew took over the night shift at WGST, its population was under a million and traffic, a nightmare today, wasn't an overriding concern. In fact, Atlanta's first parking meter had only been in business for five years.

Playing rock 'n' roll on the radio and riding the wave of "American Bandstand" quickly made Drew one of the top three night time personalities in Atlanta. "It was all about timing," he says. WGST was across town from WAKE, where Bill Drake was the Program Director, and Drake himself was living in an apartment, across the pool, in the complex where Drew lived. "So, one day he and I were having breakfast and he said, 'Isn't it about time that you became a WAKE Hit Parader?' "

Drew says he looked over and agreed the timing was about right. "I'd been at WGST for close to four years and was looking for a place to go where I could be better."

So, Drew made the move to WAKE, but when Drake was transferred to KYA/San Francisco the following year, he didn't stick around for long. In 1963, he crossed Atlanta's streets again to join WQXI. Three years later, on June 6, 1966, Kent Burkhart, the General

Manager of WQXI, wrote a memo announcing that Drew had been appointed the station's new Program Director. But, the job didn't last very long.

On December 1, after only five and a half months as PD of WQXI/Atlanta, Drew resigned. He said he was going to San Francisco, to KYA.

Drew had been in Atlanta nine years. He'd been there when Martin Luther King Jr. preached, when JFK died, when The Beatles arrived, and as the Vietnam War escalated. He'd even turned thirty there. (Unlike many of his peers in the mid '60s, Drew was white-shirt, business-suit serious. "I wanted everyone to understand that radio is a business and should be taken seriously," he says.)

His start date at KYA was supposed to be January 1, but a call from Perry Ury, GM of WRKO/Boston, changed his plans. Ury wanted to know if Drew might be interested in programming CKLW/Detroit. "I told him about the job at KYA but, because I was from Detroit, I agreed to talk." After the conversation with Ury, Drew started calling around to see what he might be getting into. What he got was an earful about how awful the manager in Detroit was. "So, I went to meet Bob Buss, CKLW's GM, and told him, straight out, that I'd heard he was a buttinsky."

This frontal assault apparently didn't bruise Buss; at the end of the meeting he offered Drew $25,000 and the autonomy he'd demanded. "There was one more thing," says Drew. "I told him I'd only do the job for twelve months." His rationale was that he wasn't experienced enough to stay for the long haul. "I mean, who was I trying to fool? I've always told myself that it's important to know what I don't know."

Drew had been at CKLW for only four months when RKO, the station's parent company, signed a chain-wide deal with Drake-Chenault Enterprises to "advise" their stations. Drew says he wasn't concerned. "I was told I didn't have to do anything I didn't want to do."

But, that didn't mean he wasn't going to learn whatever he could. "I got exposed to the architecture of KHJ and to the genius of Ron Jacobs," says Drew. "Of all the Top 40 or popular music stations I've heard in my lifetime, the best one of all, by fifty touchdowns, was Ron's KHJ. KHJ *was* Ron Jacobs," he says, "but he didn't get the glory or the money."

After twelve months, just as he'd promised, Paul Drew resigned from CKLW.

●

W-I-B-G stood for Why I Believe in God. The call letters had been chosen by Dr. Theodore Elsner when he applied for the station license, in 1925. WIBG (pronounced *wibbage*, like cribbage) had been Philadelphia's only Top 40 station for ten years with no competition until 1966, when WFIL took up the format. By the time Drew arrived at the station, in 1968, WFIL had the advantage. "WFIL kicked my ass," says Drew. "Jim Hilliard had a better signal, was a better programmer, and he had (morning man) Dr. Don Rose."

Drew's Philadelphia story didn't end happily and, by 1969, he was back in Detroit, acting as a caretaker for CKLW, as it was being prepared to sell. (The Canadian government was forcing RKO to give up the station; Drew's job was to keep the station strong and viable until the last, get-the-cash-in-the-door, moment). He says minding the store didn't bother him because he and RKO had come to an understanding: after CKLW was sold Drew would have his pick of either KHJ/Los Angeles or KFRC/San Francisco. When the time came, Drew went to San Francisco.

"I was very happy at KFRC," he told me. One of the reasons may have been that, early on, he realized that San Francisco wasn't what it appeared to be. During his first weekend in town he attended a 49er's game at Kezar Stadium and a Raiders game in Oakland. Being out amongst the people made him realize that the market wasn't full of elitists. "I saw that San Francisco wasn't Nob Hill, it was Milwaukee," says Drew. This realization helped him get a handle on what he thought KFRC would need to do in the early '70s, and had a lot to do with Dr. Don Rose being hired for mornings in 1973.

By then; however, Drew and KFRC had parted company.

It began with a call from Ross Taber, RKO's Vice President/Radio, asking Drew to come to New York for a meeting. Taber got to the point quickly. "I'd like you to meet with Bob Forker, GM of WGMS in Washington," he told Drew. "You'll be the guy to flip the station to Top 40."

Washington D.C. Top 40! Great!

But, changing WGMS from classical to Top 40 would prove to be a hurdle the company couldn't jump. RKO never anticipated how much opposition they'd face. When the smoke cleared, WGMS was still classical, the company was pretty shaken and Drew, who'd opted to stay in D.C. after the whole thing fell apart, was independently consulting.

Not long after that RKO offered him a deal in LA he couldn't refuse.

•

Bill Drake's RKO days were over. The relationship between Drake-Chenault and RKO had lasted eight years but, by 1973, Bruce Johnson, RKO's President, felt Drake's loyalties were with Drake-Chenault, not RKO.

In anticipation of what might happen if he terminated the agreement with Drake, Johnson called Drew. "Bruce hired me for KHJ," explains Drew. "But, the deal was that after some indeterminate time I would become VP of Programming." Drew knew which way the wind blew, but today he insists he told Johnson that he wasn't accepting the job to grease the steps for Drake. "I promised to work with Drake and I wanted to. But, three months later, he was gone."

As Vice President of Programming for RKO, Drew was on the road eighty percent of the time — always working, always listening. It wasn't unusual for him to hit a town, call a PD late Saturday night and ask for a Sunday morning meeting, an early meeting. He told his programmers, a group that included Les Garland, Michael Spears, Jerry Clifton, Bob Hamilton, Don Kelly, John Long, Dave Martin and Al Casey, that preparation was everything, and he had notes to prove it.

After leaving RKO, Paul Drew became a full time media consultant. In 1979, he discovered a Japanese duo, two twenty-one-year old girls called Pink Lady, who'd sold over seventeen million records in their homeland. Convinced they'd succeed in the United States, Drew arranged for them to be signed to Elektra/Curb Records and even got them a short-lived television show on NBC. But, despite his best efforts, Pink Lady didn't catch on. Not speaking English may have been a problem.

In 1981, the Reagan administration called Mr. Drew to Washington and asked him to help fix some problems with Radio Marti, the monster U.S. created radio signal aimed at Cuba. Drew rolled up his sleeves and got the job done. Today, Paul Drew is retired and living in Georgia, where he occasionally takes on consulting projects.

A few years ago he campaigned to become CEO of the National Academy of Recording and Sciences. In the end, he didn't get the job, but, perhaps, he did get the last word. "Michael Greene would have been a hard act to follow," said Paul Drew. "But then again, in radio, I followed Bill Drake."

CHAPTER 18

CHUCK DUNAWAY: THE ROUND MOUND
OF SOUND

Chuck Dunaway thinks radio people have gone crazy. "Back then," he says, "it was war. Today I hear stories about program directors that hang out with their competition. What's that about?" By back then Dunaway means the '50s and early '60s. "Disc Jockeys were stars and the audience cared about us. It was just a different game."

For Dunaway the game began when he was seventeen. "A friend of mine had a '46 Plymouth and we took off from Houston and stopped in every town that had a radio station. We'd check the phone book, drive over and I'd audition for a job." He passed the audition at KBST/Big Spring, Texas, where he says the most important part of the job was making sure the commercials got played. "We had so many spots to cram into a thirty minute segment that we'd play half a record, stop it, play the spots, then finish playing the record. "It was stupid," he laughs, "but that's the way we were taught to do it."

KBST only paid sixty cents an hour, so part of Dunaway's ambition was focused on money. He says he left Big Spring and went to Galveston for a fifteen cent raise, was off to Freeport for twenty-five cents more, and then KXOL/ Ft. Worth called and offered him eighty dollars a week.

"A pretty good wage," he says.

•

Ft. Worth was about forty miles west of Dallas, but it was a world away. How far? Well, there's an old joke about it being noon in Dallas and 11:55 in Ft. Worth. KXOL wasn't KLIF/Dallas, but it was still a place to be discovered, and Dunaway got noticed quickly. "Chuck was extraordinarily good," says Kent Burkhart, founder of Burkhart/Abrams. "He had some sort of communication deal with his audience. You know what that's like. You've heard it."

Whatever *it* was, it got ratings which brought Dunaway to the attention of Gordon McLendon's boys at KLIF. He took their call but, as it turned out, they didn't want him for KLIF, they wanted him for WRIT/Milwaukee. Or, more to the point, they wanted to get him out of town.

Dunaway accepted the job. "Within thirty days we beat WOKY/Milwaukee with our Top 40 concept," he remembers. "We played a tight list, which was a brand new concept at the time."

His name and what he was doing on the air began to be talked about within the industry. In 1958 he was hired by Danny Williams at WKY/Oklahoma City, and his horizons expanded. "Besides radio, they allowed me to do television, too," he says. The TV show was an after school cowboy affair and Dunaway, playing the part of Hog Waller, quickly became a celebrity to the under-ten set. But, it was the radio show that got him noticed in New York City. An 86.7 Hooper rating! "That's when WABC found out who I was," says Dunaway.

The journey from Oklahoma City to The Big Apple began with a call from WABC's in-house consultant, Mike Joseph. "We've been listening to your show," Joseph told him. "We're interested in bringing you to WABC, to fill the 7:15 to 10 p.m. time slot."

Dunaway believed he was happy at WKY. More than that, if asked, he might have said he'd be happy to stay in Oklahoma till his dying day. But, the WABC overture changed everything. "Sounds good to me," he told Joseph. "Let's talk." Within a week or so, not a bit shy, he'd told everyone at WKY about the ABC offer. "I said it loud and many times and thought nothing of it," he says.

But, when it came time to hit the air, the WABC offer was all he thought about. He convinced himself they were listening to everything he did on the air.

So, when he walked into the studio one day, put on his headphones and discovered he couldn't hear anything, he got angry. "I messed up the first intro on my show," Dunaway says. He called for an engineer, but was forced to do two or three more breaks without working headphones. He started to see red.

Mad as hell, he put a record on and stormed into William's office to complain. "Someone turned off my cans!" he exclaimed. Jerry Kunkle, one of the other WKY jocks, was sitting in front of William's desk. He stood up, looked at Dunaway and said, "I did it."

Dunaway exploded. "I hit him in the face as hard as I could and then turned and went back to the control room."

Shortly thereafter, he was relieved from his shift and told to report to the General Manager's office. Danny Williams was there waiting. "I'm sorry, Chuck," Williams told him, "but you can't do things like that. I'm going to have to let you go."

In his book, "The Way I Remember It," Dunaway says there was no further discussion. "I left the best job I ever had, working for people I truly had affection for. It was the saddest day of my career." ——

But, he had WABC in his back pocket.

At least, that's what he thought.

•

Dunaway had a family to support and, since nothing with WABC was carved in stone, he called WKY's competition, KOMA. He thought they might be interested in him. The PD and Manager of KOMA agreed to meet with him and suggested he get in touch with Bud Armstrong, the Manager of WHB/Kansas City. "WHB," says Dunaway, "was to the Storz organization what KLIF/Dallas was to McLendon."

A dominant #1 in Kansas City, WHB was interested in Dunaway, even after he told them about his talks with WABC. Armstrong told him New York wouldn't be a good move and, by the end of the meeting, Dunaway agreed, verbally, to a five year contract with WHB. But, as he was walking out of the meeting, he got a message to call his wife at home immediately. When they connected he discovered Mike Joseph was flying to Kansas City that day.

"I met his plane," says Dunaway, "and we headed to the coffee shop, where he asked me if I'd signed anything. I told him, "No."

Joseph had a firm offer from WABC and Dunaway accepted "because New York City was where every disc jockey in America wanted to be." But, it wasn't over yet. Dunaway called Armstrong and told him he'd changed his mind and had decided to go to New York after all. Armstrong responded firmly. "No, a contract is a contract, and this one is enforceable. Welcome to WHB."

Dunaway was confused and conflicted. He jumped in his car and drove home to Oklahoma City, where he collected his wife and family, packed some bags and headed back to Kansas City and WHB. The next morning he and the entire family were sitting in the waiting room for an audience with Armstrong. "We looked pretty pathetic," Dunaway remembers.

Finally he was summoned. Armstrong told Dunaway he was willing to let him out of the deal, but there were a few hitches. "We'll tear up the contract, but you have to go back to Oklahoma City and record some promos saying KOMA is the best station in town. Then, I want you to sign a new piece of paper that says you won't work in any market with a Storz station for five years."

Dunaway had no choice. He says he signed the paper and drove back to Oklahoma City, where he recorded the promos for KOMA. Then, he got on airplane for New York. On the day he arrived, the weather forecast called for twenty-two inches of snow.

The job was to replace Alan Freed.

The new WABC staff included Herb Oscar Anderson, Charlie Greer, Jack Carney, Dunaway and Scott Muni. Dunaway remembers the WABC playlist was huge. "We were playing seventy-seven records, plus album cuts. It was silly," he says. "I'd been with McLendon and Jack had been with Storz and we knew the magic number was forty! We did go up 250% in one rating period, but the station didn't really kick in until we pared the playlist down."

Dunaway never liked like New York and, from day one, was homesick for the southwest. (Think the line about taking the boy out of the country.) After nine months he gave WABC his notice. "At age twenty-four," he wrote, "New York wasn't my cup of tea. I wanted to work at a station with a tight playlist, with listeners who could call me on the phone and request a song that I could *actually* play for them." He headed back to Oklahoma City — to WKY — but this time around it didn't work out. Sadly, he says, the job only lasted four months. From there, it was back to Texas and to a litany of impressive call letters, including KBOX, KLIF, and KILT.

He got disc jockey famous and, on the air, he called himself "The Round Mound of Sound," a name he'd started using at WABC. Now, laugh if you'd like, but this was all very cool, until it wasn't. By the late '60s Top 40 DJ antics didn't play as well as they had in earlier years. Maybe it was the war. Or, perhaps, it was the difference between early '60s rock 'n' roll and the progressive rock of the late '60s. Regardless, Dunaway says, "When Tom Donahue got the idea to play album cuts, it started messing around with Top 40."

In 1971, when he was programming WIXY/Cleveland, Dunaway spoke at a programming conference in San Juan, Puerto Rico. "I said, 'You know folks, if you don't realize it AM Radio is in trouble. FM is about to kick our ass!' "

Later he explained that he didn't mean that radio was over. He just meant that there was now a new place to do it.

•

Dunaway and KCBQ/San Diego PD, Buzz Bennett, decided to do some research. "We put people in these "egg-shell" things with speakers in them and played tapes of radio shows, complete with commercials," he explains. "When the jock came on, they lost interest and when spots came on, their interest went down further. And, the more commercials we played, the more they didn't give a shit."

"But then," he says, "when the music started again, the listeners started to pay attention again."

Based on this information Bennett and Dunaway decided that in order for a radio station to get credit for the music it played (and to report the name of the station to the ratings companies) the call letters should be the first thing a disc jockey said out of music and the last thing he or she said when the music began. They figured if a station was playing great music it'd be a good idea to get credit for it.

•

In the years that followed, Chuck Dunaway programmed stations in Tucson (KIKX), Phoenix (KUPD) and Dallas (KAFM). During the late '70s he took some side trips into record promotion and magazine publishing but, by the early '80s, he was back managing stations in Austin, Corpus Christi, Nashville and in the Carolinas. Burkhart says when Dunaway became a General Manager all his experience and talent came together. "His enthusiasm in the administrative and sales side was really as good as his programming, and you very rarely find that."

In 1998, after close to fifty years in the radio business, Dunaway and his partners sold a cluster of stations he'd been managing in Joplin, Missouri, and he and his wife retired to Houston. (By the way, the cluster he built was the fifth highest rated station cluster in the United States.)

Today Dunaway is still listening to radio.

"The formats haven't changed in all these years – it's just the music that changes," he says. "I still hear the stop sets falling in the same places and we're still playing and programming to Arbitron, and not to the listener."

Hmmmmm. You can take the boy out of radio...

CHAPTER 19

BILL FIGENSHU: CONSOLIDATION'S POSTER CHILD

Roll this around your brain for a moment.

"When I hear radio stations that have the same structure as they did twenty or thirty years ago, even going back to the old KHJ days," says Bill Figenshu, "I wonder, why somebody hasn't tried to think about this differently."

Figenshu, who was a baby DJ in Atlantic City forty years ago, and a corporate titan in Manhattan at the height of radio consolidation, knows a thing or two. "Imagine you own Coca-Cola and then buy Pepsi and the first thing you do is change it. Why would you do that? It's counterintuitive. It seems to me that if you buy your competitor, you'd want to crank them both up. You'd raise the promotion budget on both stations and have them compete with each other."

But, that's not how it is, is it? In the cluster culture, one-time fierce competitors are expected to treat each other like siblings. But, who wins and who loses? Figenshu doesn't miss a beat. "The big loser is the audience because they didn't get the memo about 'kumbaya.' They sense when a station's not totally on its game. All they know is there were two stations that were going at it, working hard to get the concerts and promotions, and, all of a sudden they're not working so hard anymore."

He pauses. "Remember, I was the poster boy for consolidation, so I've been through this with Clear Channel, Chancellor, AM-FM, Infinity, ARS, and CBS. And, what really happens is the station that gets bought is the one that gets beat up. We bought our competitor, flushed the place out and immediately stopped the marketing. And, generally what happens is the big station gets everything and the other station gets used as a flanker."

"I'm not saying that consolidation is bad," Figenshu continues, "but I am saying the execution of consolidation could have been better. I believe the concept of buying your competitors, stripping out the station, cutting expenses and running eighteen commercials an hour, just because you can and just because you're not competing any more, is not necessarily a good thing."

One gets the sense that Figenshu is torn. He recalls the days when radio and television — with ownership caps at seven AMs, seven FMs and seven TV stations — was a mom and pop business. He was also there when Wall Street embraced the radio industry. "It was a party every day. We couldn't raise the rates fast enough."

"But, don't blame Wall Street," he says. "They didn't make us raise our spot loads, overpay for radio stations, or cut our marketing budgets. Wall Street said, "If you deliver a bottom line, you'll be rewarded.""

"In my opinion," Figenshu says, "we were seduced."

•

Anyone who ever aspired to be a disc jockey was seduced by the music, the lifestyle and the notion of fame — such as it was. Bill Figenshu was no exception.

In 1968, when he was eighteen, he opened his first microphone at WMID/Atlantic City. It was an AM Top 40 station and the music being played was like a casino smorgasbord — everything from Jeannie C. Riley's *Harper Valley P.T.A.* to *Hello, I Love You* by The Doors.

In the late '60s gambling hadn't arrived in Atlantic City yet, but sun lovers from big east coast cities did show up and during the summer months the Jersey Shore's population mushroomed. "There were people everywhere you looked," says Figenshu. "And while my friends were flipping hamburgers on the boardwalk, I was 'pumpin' the wattage into your cottage' on WMID."

By September, Atlantic City was a ghost town, but young Figenshu stayed right where he was, because he'd fallen in love with radio. "The station was my wife," he says with dedication, "and the people who worked there were my family."

I suggested this doesn't happen today. "Not so," Figenshu insists. "There are still kids as passionate about the radio business as we were. They live at the radio station, they love doing production and they go to all the remotes. They're doing it because they love it and because they believe there's an opportunity to succeed."

"I hope so," I said.

•

The road to success meant packing the car and driving towards the sound of opportunity, wherever it might be. In 1971, twenty-one-year-old Bill Figenshu was in McKeesport, Pennsylvania working for WIXI-AM and rooming with the station's morning man, Jeff Christy. He says they shared an apartment, but most of their waking hours were spent at the station. "I can't tell you what we did on the weekends other than hang out in the production room and figure out ways to edit records."

Christy, who'd eventually give up his air name in favor of the one his parents gave him, Rush Limbaugh, couldn't have known what the future held for him, but Figenshu says there were some hints early on. "I recall he always seemed to be in trouble because he was talking too damn much."

By the early '70s, FM was starting to rear its head. "I had an FM converter in my car," says Figenshu. Once he started listening to FM — no, he didn't mention what he heard — Figenshu says he started to think there might be something to it. So, he quit his AM Top 40 job and aimed his car south. "While my friends stayed on the AM dial making good money, like a dope, I quit to go work at, what is today, WKDF-FM/Nashville."

The station's format was album rock. Along with Fig, there was Ron Huntsman and Dave Walton, all three committed to the new vision.

(Huntsman, who'd gained some notoriety doing nights at KOMA/ Oklahoma City, later managed Charlie Daniels, and Walton became half of the morning team, Walton and Johnson.) "I was working nights, seven to midnight," says Fig, "and talking like this...(he lowers his voice to a whisper and does his very best underground DJ imitation). Across the street, at WMAK, in the same timeslot, was one very young Scott Shannon. WMAK didn't have much of a night signal, but Scott raised the modulation just by screaming. So, anyway, I'm in Nashville playing album rock," Figenshu continues, "but, I really wanted to go home to Philadelphia."

He found work in Philly at General Cinema's WIFI-FM. Programmed by Jerry Del Colliano (of Inside Radio fame) the station's format was described as *progressive alternative* and probably wasn't much different than what he'd been doing in Nashville, though maybe a little hipper. All Figenshu remembers is they segued a lot of records.

Then one day a new PD, named Steve Young, arrived from Shreveport and things changed quickly. "He blew in and asked if I could do Top 40."

"Well, I'm no dope!" says Fig, "I said, 'Hell, yes! Give me those little records.' "

So, it was back to Top 40, but this time it was FM Top 40. He was also back to staying in one place for a while. He remembers that it was then that he began to think about the future. "At some point, about 1974, I had this notion that I could actually program a radio station," he says.

•

In the days before FM broke out of the box Sonderling Broadcasting was best known for its AM soul stations in San Francisco, Chicago, New York and Washington D.C. The company's FMs, and this wasn't unusual at the time, were treated like second class citizens. "WOL, in D.C., was the big soul station with a twelve share and their FM station, WMOD, was doing automated oldies," explains Fig.

He'd been given a chance to program and, along with the PD stripes, came the morning show. What Figenshu would do with the station would set the stage for the next five or six years of his career. But, it was what happened during his first two days on the air that established his "bona fides" as a critical thinker; albeit one with a sense of humor.

During his first eight years on the radio Figenshu had gone by many on-air names. "I was Bill Foster, Bill Steele and even Chuck McCartney," he says. But, by the time he applied for the job at WMOD, he'd decided that his real name, Figenshu, was pretty memorable and he thought listeners would get it. Besides, there was some parental pressure. "My father said, 'Jeez, are you ever going to use your real name?'"

So, his first morning on the air at WMOD-FM, he identified himself as Bill Figenshu. "At the end of my first show the General Manager walked into the studio and said, 'You know, that name of yours isn't a very good air name. I want you to change it.' "

"No problem," Fig told him.

The next morning he signed on with a new name.

"Good morning, it's seven o'clock and *I'm* FRED Figenshu."

•

There were at least two men in Washington D.C. interested in country music.

One was the sitting President, Jimmy Carter, who knew enough to invite the Charlie Daniels Band to play on the White House lawn and maybe not so much about letting Willie Nelson wander the White House alone. (Nelson, allegedly, smoked marijuana on the mansion's roof in 1978.) The other man was Bill Figenshu, who didn't know anything about country music but had noticed that a lot of people seemed to like it, which had led him to think that might be successful if it became the first FM country station in Washington D.C.

Demographically, Figenshu knew that D.C. proper didn't hold a lot of promise for country, but he thought there was an audience for it in suburban Maryland and Virginia. Country music wasn't entirely foreign to Sonderling Broadcasting — a few of their FMs were already doing the format.

But, when Figenshu asked for some money to research the idea, the company said, "No." Instead, they suggested he get on a plane, fly to Chicago, park himself in a hotel room and listen to WMAQ, the station that called itself "America's Most Listened To Country Station." So, he did.

"I stayed at the O'Hare Hilton for a few days and listened and then I came back and we (changed the call letters and) launched WMZQ. "It was great fun," Fig told me. "I discovered this whole new world with Willie and Waylon and the boys."

•

After WMZQ registered some success, Figenshu was transferred to KIKK/Houston, one of WMZQ's sister stations. Figenshu — Bill again, not Fred — had done wonders in D.C., but country music and Texas go together like whiskey and a shot and KIKK's management was a bit skeptical about this Yankee carpetbagger, regardless of what he'd accomplished in D.C.

That said, KIKK's ratings, a two point nine share, were nothing to boast about. "I mean, this thing was in the toilet," says Fig. "So, I blew into town and we had our first meeting."

"'What you gonna do, boy?' " they asked.

"I said, 'I don't know. I have to scope things out.' So, I didn't do anything for three months except sit there and listen."

He focused his attention on things that were new to him: Gilley's, line dancing and even how to say "Howdy." Three months later, he launched the "Hot Rockin', Flame Throwin' KICK 96 FM." According to Fig (and Arbitron) "the station went from a two point nine to a ten point five, in eighteen months."

Behind the scenes, however, something more important than a wild riding country station was going on. Sonderling Broadcasting was being sold.

The buyer was a television company called Viacom.

•

"In the late '70s," says Figenshu, "Viacom was a company that ran nothing but a bunch of old re-runs on TV."

At the time, Mel Karmizan was still running WNEW-FM/New York (he'd join Infinity Broadcasting in 1981 and Viacom in 2000) and Sumner Redstone was a half-dozen years away from acquiring a majority stake in the company.

Fifteen months after Viacom bought Sonderling, KIKK's ratings hit, and Figenshu and his GM, Al Greenfield, quickly became the company's fair-haired radio boys. "I didn't know these Viacom guys," Fig explains, "but because Kick was so hot, Greenfield got the job as President of the Company."

One day Figenshu says he knocked on Greenfield's door at KIKK. "You know, this Texas thing is really fun," he told the older man. "But, it sure would be fun to go to New York."

Shortly thereafter he was named National Program Director of Viacom Radio, with responsibility for stations in Houston, D.C., San Francisco, Chicago and New York. He says he didn't have a clue, and to prove the point he talks about the decision he made for New York, the one he lived to regret. "Well, country is a lifestyle in Texas," he begins, "but it's not a lifestyle in New York."

That's easy to say now, but back in the day, given his success in Washington and Houston and the national attention that was being showered on country music by the movie, "Urban Cowboy," Greenfield and Figenshu thought Viacom's New York jazz station, WRVR, might be a perfect home for country in New York City.

"So, we launched WKHK and it bombed," admits Fig. "I tanked badly."

His confidence shaken, he began to question whether he really knew what he was doing. "There's nothing like a good failure to make you smarter." (This seemed like a good time to ask why country radio has never been wildly successful in New York. "People ask me that all the time and the answer is really in the Arbitron diaries," replies Figenshu. "In New Jersey and Pennsylvania country is big. But, in the boroughs, you've got to program to the 'ees', you know — Vinnie, Louie and Tony, and these guys just aren't buying it; it's not in their DNA.")

After eighteen months it was clear that WKHK didn't have the strength to survive. Looking for a new direction for the station, Figenshu dug into the research. What he found was eye-opening. "At the time," he says, "Viacom had an easy listening station in Chicago, WLAK, which had a five point share (12+) and a fifty point share (55+)."

With such unbalanced ratings the obvious question was: How could WLAK attract younger listeners? On the national front Bonneville, a leading easy listening syndicator, responded by playing instrumental versions of contemporary hits. "So, rather than play the original hit," Figenshu says, "they'd play the 101 Strings doing their version of *Karma Chameleon*." Figenshu says he thought that was stupid.

"Then somebody said to me, 'Why don't you just play the original versions?' And I'm like, 'Yeah, why DON'T we just play the originals?' "

He approached Viacom Corporate with his idea. "I said, 'It's an easy listening format, but we're going to take out all the instrumentals.' "

Corporate was skeptical and, in true radio fashion, asked, "Who's doing it?"

"Nobody," Fig responded.

With that, corporate nixed the idea. "No," they told him. "We can't risk a Chicago station on an unproven idea."

Fig, however, was determined. Besides, he thought, the guys in the carpeted offices wouldn't know what he'd done until it was done. "So, I de-emphasized the instrumentals. All of them," he says. "I think we played *Chariots of Fire* and *Classical Gas*, but the rest of the songs were vocals."

Somewhere in the transition the station changed its call letters from WLAK to WLIT and on the air became "Lite FM." Success came overnight.

"It was a very quick hit and, so, we took the idea to New York and launched Lite FM there, too," Figenshu says.

•

In 1984, the year WLTW-Lite FM/New York went on the air, adult contemporary was a hot radio format, but there were two schools of thought on how it should be executed. One model, represented by stations like KVIL/Dallas and WYNY/New York, was personality based and presented by energized disc jockeys, all with a lot to say. The other model, the one used at Viacom's Lite FMs and stations like them, had its roots in easy listening and its personalities were very low key. "Lite FM and stations like it had a sensibility about them and played a lot of songs without a lot of talk," says Figenshu, "and that was true in morning drive, too. We actually fought the notion of putting on a big morning show because we knew what the station wasn't."

•

In 1986, when he was thirty-six, Bill Figenshu was named President of Viacom Radio. He wasn't the only one from the programming side given the reigns of a major broadcasting corporation. "Dan Mason, John Gehron, Jay Meyers, Randy Michaels and me — we were all given jobs beyond our years. We were all programmers, and it was the most fun ever. But, when Wall Street started to pay attention to radio, it became more of a financial play and the corporations were turned over to the financial folks, who didn't understand the value of local content. As a consequence many radio stations, particularly those owned by large groups, sought to cut costs and localism and being part of a community became a luxury; it didn't happen everywhere, but it happened in lots of town and cities."

Figenshu acknowledges that it hasn't been a good thing for radio or its listeners.

"OK, so where do you go from here?" I asked. "If you could do anything you wanted, what would it be?"

"I would probably start an HD division and go out and hire kids who have nothing to do with AM and FM broadcasting today," he says.

Ok, Fig, rub your crystal ball and tell me what's going to happen tomorrow.

"I don't think radio stations are willing to invest in music programming as much as they did before, so what they're going to do is invest in people, which is a good thing."

He stops to think for a moment. "If Robert W. Morgan or the Real Don Steele were around today, assuming they were in their thirties, they would probably consider FM talk."

•

On June 22, 2005, Figenshu announced the formation of Fig Media, a company focused on media innovation. "It's like when I had to go work at an FM station," he says. "There's too much stuff going on now and I've got one more ride in me. I want to take it."

This entrepreneurial move led him to join forces with some kids (his word, not mine) that he'd done some work with while he was President of the Western Region for Citadel. "These guys are in their thirties and I helped them get funding." The money raised was for a company named Softwave where Fig was "the resident adult, whose job is to make the trains run on time."

In 2007, Figenshu resigned from Softwave to take charge of Peak Broadcasting, "a new generation" broadcasting company, formed in 2006, to serve local, growing communities. This move is in line with his goals for Fig Media — to offer guidance and strategic planning in cluster and station operations, broadcast branding, talent development, and company creation. More importantly, it takes him back to the day to day of radio, where his heart's been for the last four decades.

"I've known Fig since we were jocks together at WIFI in the '70s," says Steve Rivers, "and he's never been a shrinking violet. He's knowledgeable, opinionated, and passionate about the business. He came up through the ranks: as a Jock, a Programmer, a General Manager and as President of a Radio Company, and he truly knows the business from all sides. He's a great strategist and excellent at seeing opportunities and solving problems."

"Fig has one of the most prolific minds and quickest wits anywhere," says Kurt Johnson, a Dallas based CBS VP. "You won't have trouble finding a long list of people whose careers he's profoundly helped. Radio owes a lot to him."

CHAPTER 20

ALAN FREED: MR. ROCK 'N' ROLL

Rock 'n' Roll was a verb, not a noun.

In the beginning, close to sixty years ago, the words didn't describe a type of music. Instead, in the black community, they were used as a euphemism for sex. In 1951, The Dominoes, with Clyde McPhatter singing lead, recorded *Sixty Minute Man* and, according to rock mythology, it was in the song's suggestive lyrics that Freed first heard the words rock 'n' roll. What he did with them rocked the world.

Radio wasn't Freed's first love or even an early attraction, but he did have a jones for music. He was born in Johnstown, PA in 1921 and, in 1933 his family moved to Salem, OH. It was during high school, in the mid '30s – when Benny Goodman's band was hotter than a pistol – that Freed picked up the trombone and formed a combo he called The Sultans of Swing. From the start he saw himself as a band leader. He thought it a glamorous role and, onstage and off, he adopted a certain swagger that might have lasted years had it not been for an ear infection, which abruptly shattered his music-making dreams. Bad news, yes, but the silver lining was it kept him out of the Army. (Freed's twentieth birthday was a week after the attack on Pearl Harbor).

In his late teens Freed traded his trombone for a microphone and, by 1946, when he hit twenty-five, he'd already worked at WKST/New Castle, Pennsylvania, and at WAKR/Akron—as an announcer, newsman and sportscaster — generally a jock of all trades.

At twenty-eight, Freed left Akron for the big city and a television job at WXEL-TV in Cleveland. He had nine years radio experience under his belt and had been hired to do a "disc jockey" show on TV. At the time, Freed wasn't thinking about playing records on the tube; he thought that was a dead-duck approach and that's what he told the local paper. "I'd like to do away with records and depend entirely on live acts."

But, it was television that got him noticed. "Friendliness makes more friends and that's the ticket in television," he said. (By the way, as a TV personality, Freed still spelled his first name with two "ls" and one "e" — Allen.)

Freed's fling with television was short-lived and, in 1951, he returned to radio, landing a late night job playing classical music at WJW/Cleveland. In his book "The Fifties," historian David Halberstam describes Freed as being "somewhat of a vagabond" and suggests that classical music was hardly Freed's first love; this was just another way of saying the job was all about the money.

Then, along came record store owner Leo Mintz.

Halberstam tells what happened this way: "Young white kids with more money than one might expect were coming into his store and buying what had been considered exclusively Negro music just a year or two before."

What Halberstam meant was the lilywhite world of Cleveland, if not the entire United States, was about to be rocked on its axis.

Mintz convinced Freed that something new was happening and Freed agreed. The two men then convinced WJW management to give Freed a new show featuring this new music. Freed was excited about the idea and management was swayed by the money Mintz was willing to pay for sponsorship.

Freed decided to call the program "Moondog's Rock 'n' Roll Party" and he proclaimed himself "The Moondog." On July 11, 1951 the show hit the air. In his new persona, Freed sided with the kids, professed his love for the music, and though he probably didn't realize it — at least, initially — he began to lead a revolution. "An entire generation of young white kids had been waiting for someone to catch up with them," wrote Halberstam.

Nine months into the show's run Freed decided he wanted to

reward his loyal listeners – and, perhaps, put a little money in his pocket — so, he organized (what has since been identified as) the first live rock 'n' roll show, "The Moondog Coronation Ball." Freed booked the top black acts in the country into the Cleveland Arena, a facility that held ten thousand, and sold tickets for less than two dollars a piece. Then, he held his breath.

On May 21, 1952, twenty thousand kids, white and black, showed up at the arena ready to party. The energy level was high and so was the body count — acerbated by hundreds of counterfeited tickets. It was, truly, a night to behold. The concert began. But, after only one song, fire authorities shut it down. Still, a statement had been made: rock 'n' roll was here to stay.

•

Two years later, in the fall of 1954, Freed's radio show debuted in New York on 1010/WINS and, within months, it was the #1 radio program in New York.

WINS paid him $75,000 a year (about $450,000 in today's dollars) and he added to his earnings by throwing live concerts at The Brooklyn Paramount. The following year Hollywood caught on (to the discretionary money teenagers had to spend) and Freed, the Pied Piper, appeared in a series of low-budget rock 'n' roll movies, including "Don't Knock The Rock," "Rock Around The Clock" and "Rock, Rock, Rock." Then, in 1957, The ABC Television Network gave Freed his own national TV show.

Things began well enough, but when young Frankie Lymon, an African-American (*Why Do Fools Fall In Love* — 1956), was seen dancing with a white girl, affiliates in the South went ballistic and the show was quickly canceled.

This was the beginning of the end.

The next year, WINS opted not to renew Freed's contract. The reason, they said, was Freed's indictment for inciting a riot at a Boston concert. Out at WINS, Freed crossed the street and joined competitor WABC. But, when he refused to sign a letter stating that he'd never accepted payola — he said it was a matter of principal – WABC fired him, too.

•

What happened to Freed next is essentially the tale of a career and a life in a tail-spin.

Because he was so visible and so personified the music, a New York grand jury, convened in 1960 to look into irregularities in the record business, charged him with income tax evasion. (Before 1960, payola *wasn't* illegal. But not reporting the payments as income *was*.) With no radio work to be found in New York, Freed moved to Los Angeles to work for KDAY, but the job didn't last long and, dejected, he settled in Miami, where his career ended.

I could continue to focus this story on nasty little details that don't paint a very positive picture of Mr. Freed, but I won't, because they don't matter. What does is that Alan Freed, in the face of a racially divided society, chose to play and champion rhythm and blues records. By doing so, he helped to usher in the dawn of the first rock age. No, he didn't invent rock 'n' roll, but he was the first to use the term in the context we use it today.

There have been several movies made about Freed, most notably "American Hot Wax" and "Mr. Rock 'n' Roll," but neither pays much attention to the facts and, from our perspective here in the 21st Century, that may be acceptable. Why? Because the spirit of Freed's accomplishments transcend the details and he should be remembered — not for his failures — but for his successes and for what he did right.

In 1986, for his contributions to American culture, to rock 'n' roll, and to the radio industry, Alan Freed was inducted into the Rock 'n' Roll Hall of Fame.

It happened in Cleveland. Where it all began and as it should be.

Chapter 21

Jack Gale: A Character Voice

Jack Gale hears voices. Please file that in the back of your mind.

In 1944, when Gale started in radio, electronic transcriptions (very large records with instrumental music) and scripts were regularly delivered to radio stations where announcers, Gale included, were expected to simply read the words written for them. "Back then, we didn't ad lib a thing and disc jockeys didn't exist," he says. "I tell people that today and they don't believe me."

By the end of the '40s most radio performers worth their salt understood that to compete with television they'd have to do something special. Gale says he worked hard to figure out who he was going to be on the air. But, he says, what he became wasn't planned. "My thing was voices and funny stuff and that came by accident."

Just like lots of thing in life.

•

It was 1948 and Gale was working at WTBO/ Cumberland, Maryland. "I wanted to develop a style," he told me.

He knew it was sink or swim time. One day he flubbed a commercial and covered his mistake by faking another voice. The idea wasn't planned, nor was the voice that came out of his mouth, but it started him to think. Gale remembered the great Fred Allen and his slamming doors, ringing phones, skits and characters. And, there was also a show WBTO carried called "The Johnson Family" that intrigued him. "A guy named Jimmy Scribner played all the parts and I thought if he could do it, well, maybe I could, too."

Gale started experimenting with voices and laying them down to tape. He figured out how to breathe during a phrase instead of between characters, and he decided to give each character a name.

"That's how "The Jack Gale Show" was born," he says.

The show began to create talk and listeners started calling him "that crazy guy on the radio." Before long they were even calling in to the station asking to talk to his characters.

Then, as a prank, Gale decided to tell his audience that every day was his birthday. Soon he was getting cakes in the mail. And, not much later, he started to get calls from radio execs in bigger markets, offering bigger jobs and more money. Some of them, however, were skeptical about his ability to do all the voices himself. So, they made him audition in front of them.

Don't you wish you'd been a fly on the wall?

•

By 1964, Gale was a twenty year broadcast veteran. He'd climbed markets — from Cumberland to Cleveland, Charleston to Baltimore — and now was at WMEX/Boston calling himself "Fenway in the Morning." (Fenway was a WMEX house name.)

Besides radio, Gale also started his own record label, Triple A Records, and become the manager and legal guardian of Johnny Cymbal, whose hit, *Mr. Bass Man*, was in the top twenty in March of 1963. But, now it was almost 1965.

Stan Kaplan was the flamboyant Sales Manager of WMEX. One day he pulled Gale aside and told him a secret. "I'm going to quit this job to marry a woman with millions of dollars and, then, I'm going to buy a radio station. And," Kaplan continued, "I want you to run it and become an owner."

"Yep," thought Gale, "I've heard that one before."

Gale, however, was unhappy at WMEX. The main reason was the station's owner, Mac Richmond. According to Gale's book, "Same Time, Same Station," there were times when Richmond would walk around the station on payday with checks hanging out of his pocket and if Gale or anyone else asked whether checks were ready, Richmond would reply, "Your check will be on your desk at 11:55 p.m. Friday lasts until midnight."

So, by the time Kaplan called him from Charlotte, Gale was ready to get out of the cold and out of Richmond's way. When Jack Gale accepted the job programming at WAYS/Charlotte, he didn't even ask Kaplan about the money. He says his gut told him it was the right thing to do.

•

The invasion of Charlotte was as intense as any you've ever read about. Kaplan ordered fifty-six billboards to promote the station and WAYS vaulted to #1 in less than ninety days. But, there were some in the city that didn't take kindly to Kaplan's carpet-bagging ways. One group was the Charlotte Junior Chamber Of Commerce, who refused to let WAYS join their parade.

"So, Stan and I went to a junkyard and bought an old Olds and painted BIG WAYS in colors all over it," says Gale. With all the jocks piled in the car, they snuck their way into the parade and then, per Kaplan's instructions, stalled the Oldsmobile right in the middle of the road, stopping the parade in its tracks.

The cops freaked. "Get that wreck outta here!!"

Gale says the order was ignored. Instead, the DJs jumped out of the car, tore open the trunk and started handing out BIG WAYS T-shirts to a crowd that Gale says numbered 100,000. Yes, it made the front page of the paper.

The station's popularity grew in leaps and bounds and it became known as Carolina's Friendly Radio Giant. Although Gale was a big part of its success — his show was #1 in thirty-six North and South Carolina counties — he insists that it was the station's events: "The Money Matchbook Game," "The Big Ways Turkey Shoot," "The Challenge Cup Playoff" and "The Big Ways Halloween Trick or Treat Game" that turned WAYS into the southern radio legend it became.

In 1969 "The Gavin Report" named Jack Gale Program Director of the Year and in 1970 Billboard presented him with their first Disc Jockey of The Year award. Gale calls these awards his "accolades and orchids." But, wait — there's more to his story.

Gale owned both radio stations and record companies. For over fifteen years, he regularly traveled to Nashville to produce recording artists you know: Johnny Cash, Jeannie C. Riley, Charlie Daniels, Waylon and Willie, and even George Jones. (Ask Jack about Tiny Tim.) Today, Gale has a voice-over studio in Florida. No, it's not just something to fritter his time away, it's a going concern.

And, when Jack Gale's not working he still hears voices. One says, "If I had to do it all over again, I'd do it the same way. Be nice to your radio, because the voice coming out of it may be mine. And, always remember, whether you have your own teeth or not, keep smiling."

The other voice says, "I don't listen to the radio much anymore."

This admission prompted me to ask why.

"Well, today," he says, "a dj plays six records in a row followed by six commercials, gives his name, the time, and calls *that* a show."

Gale sounds disappointed. "What does the term *show* mean these days?" he wonders aloud.

I tell him I think time has changed things.

He sighs.

It's his way of voicing concern.

LEE ABRAMS

JACK ARMSTRONG

WITH MILTON BERLE (L).

DICK BIONDI

Courtesy National Radio Hall of Fame

CHUCK BLORE

ALL PHOTOS COURTESY OF RADIO & RECORDS UNLESS OTHERWISE NOTED

JERRY BOULDING

BUZZ BENNETT

SCOTTY
BRINK

KENT BURKHART

AL CASEY WITH HIS DAUGHTER, KELLI CASEY

DICK CLARK
WITH MICHAEL
JACKSON, 2002.

FRANK CODY

DICK CLARK

Ron Chapman

Tom Donahue

Rick Dees

Ken Dowe

Larry Daniels

Bill Drake

All photos courtesy of Radio & Records unless otherwise noted

PAUL DREW

CHUCK DUNAWAY

JACK CARNEY, CHUCK DUNAWAY, HERB OSCAR ANDERSON, BILL OWEN, SCOTT MUNI AND CHARLIE GREER, RIDING FOR WABC

Courtesy of Fig.Media.

BILL FIGENSHU (TOP), WITH FRITZ COLEMAN (LEFT)

Courtesy of Fig.Media.

BILL FIGENSHU

BOB HENABERY

ALAN FREED

Courtesy of commons.wikimedia.org

JACK GALE

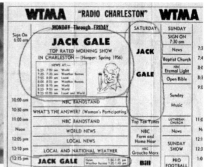

LES GARLAND

RON JACOBS

RINGO STARR,
WITH CAROL
SCHULSTAD AND
BOB SHANNON

ALL PHOTOS COURTESY OF RADIO & RECORDS UNLESS OTHERWISE NOTED

DAN INGRAM

DON IMUS

MURRAY "THE K" KAUFMAN

Courtesy National Radio Hall of Fame

TOM JOYNER

CHAPTER 22

LES GARLAND: "I WANT MY MTV!"

On August 1, 1981, in Tulsa, one of Les Garland's friends loaded up a VCR and recorded the first twenty-four hours of MTV. When he was finished recording, the friend boxed up the tapes and put them in the mail. As unlikely as it may sound, Tulsa was one of MTV's earliest adopters. Garland found that interesting because he'd worked there and knew the city's back story. If MTV worked in Tulsa, he thought, it could work anywhere. He watched the tapes for a few days and jotted down some notes. When he was ready to talk, he called Bob Pittman.

The discussion between the two young men had begun a year earlier when Pittman had queried Garland about music videos. At the time Garland ran west coast operations for Atlantic Records. "How many videos does Atlantic produce?" Pittman asked. "What does the label do with them? What was it that determined if an act did a video or not?"

Several months later, in the spring of 1981, Pittman and Garland talked again. "Bob told me the board of Warner-Amex had signed off on the idea and that he was moving forward with a twenty-four-hour music video channel for cable." The conversation was over dinner and, before the check came, Pittman cut to the chase. "Are you going to renew your contract with Atlantic, or would you like to join the fledgling network?"

•

George Lois was a legend in advertising.

In 1959 he joined Doyle- Dane-Bernbach, the agency that gave birth to "Big Idea Thinking" — what many call the beginning of modern advertising. The next year he went out on his own. "I've always understood concept," Lois told The American Institute of Graphic Designers in 1998. "Everything I did was looking for the big idea." Lois came up with Volkswagen's 1960's campaign, "Think Small," and put Andy Warhol on the cover of "Esquire" drowning in a can of Campbell's Soup. And, it was Lois who came up with the name, "Lean Cuisine." "You have to think in words," he said. "Then you can make one plus one equal three."

Today MTV is one of the world's most successful brands. But, in the beginning, the advertising community didn't support it because viewers weren't offered the channel in Los Angeles, New York or Chicago — markets advertisers demanded. "But, we weren't like anything on television," says Garland. "We had music twenty-four hours a day, amazing graphics, incredible contests, and those great original VJs."

Eventually it became obvious MTV had to get on cable systems in the nation's largest markets if it was to survive.

•

The phone in Garland's office rang. George Lois was on the line and wanted a meeting. ASAP. Garland made some calls and, a few hours later, Lois walked in. He had noting on paper, no design, just some thoughts. "I'm going to do a commercial," said Lois.

The young MTV execs nodded. "Yep. What we want to do is advertise to the cable operators," they said.

"Forget the cable operators," said Lois. "They turned you down." (Lois told this part of the story to M. Bruce Abbott at the University of Texas/Austin.) What Lois wanted to do was to go directly to the audience. He laid out his plan. He was going to take the MTV logo, add shocking, attention-getting visuals inside the logo and, at the end of the spot, have a voice-over saying, "If you don't get MTV where you live, pick up the phone, dial your local cable operator and say..."

He paused for effect.

And then he said, "I would get Mick Jagger, or somebody like that, to pick up the phone and say, 'I Want My MTV.' "

(In 1956, an advertising agency, Fletcher, Richards, Calkins
& Holden, created a television commercial designed to create
demand for a maple flavored breakfast cereal called Maypo. In
the spot a frustrated father tries to get his son to eat. "Nope,"
says the kid. Undeterred, the dad tries again. "Tell you what," he
says, "I'll be an airplane, you be the hanger. Open the doors, here
it comes... (Whrrrrrrr!) loaded with delicious... (Whrrrrrrr!)
maple-flavored... (Whrrrrrrr!) Maypo!" Just as the spoon reaches
the boy's mouth the kid snaps it shut. Frustrated and without
thinking, the father puts the spoonful of Maypo in *his* mouth.
Immediately, the young boy screams, "I want my MAYPO!")

Within days, Garland was on a plane to Paris and, with the help
of his assistant, Joan Myers, who'd once worked with The Stones,
he connected with Jagger, who agreed to do the cameo. Once the
spot was produced, MTV bought limited time on the national
networks and lots of time on the local cable systems. The payoff was
instantaneous. "An advertising guy in New York went home one
night and found his kids and their friends gathered around the TV
set. They weren't watching a show, they were watching a channel."

Garland says the ad exec saw MTV for what is was. "Bingo." The
next morning he was on the phone with money to advertise. At
the same time, avid and motivated viewers responded to the call
for action and bombarded their local cable companies. You know
what they said, don't you?

Within six months, "I Want My MTV" was on the cover of
"Time."

•

In the beginning, MTV was all about music videos. But, every
once and a while the channel went off format to do what Garland
calls his "stunts." Case in point: "Reefer Madness," which ran
every Sunday night for thirteen weeks. When the smoke cleared,
ratings data proved the quintessential anti-pot movie had touched
a nerve with MTV's audience. "We ran the very same movie for

each of those weeks," says Garland. "But, every Monday morning we'd start with a bunch of new promos that ran all week long and the audience kept getting larger and larger."

As the buzz about MTV grew, Garland and a team of close to 150 of the brightest television and music people in America continued to pull off more stunts: "Spring Break," "The Basement Tapes," "Live Aid," and the New Year's Eve events — the world premier of Prince's *Purple Rain* and KISS taking off their makeup.

And, contrary to stories that suggest otherwise, Garland insists MTV was all over Michael Jackson's *Billie Jean* within moments of its release. "I called Pittman, who was on the west coast that Thursday, and said, "Have you seen this Michael Jackson video? It's amazing." Within twenty-four hours the video was electrifying Music Television viewers all over the United States.

Looking back, Garland describes his run at MTV, from 1981 to 1988, as wicked fun. "We didn't leave the music format very often, but when we did, when we did our 'stunts', our concept was to simply allow the event to happen and to capture it on MTV, like a sporting event."

As a result of his contributions and innovations at MTV during the '80s, Garland was named one of the "Music Industry's Heavy 100" by "Rolling Stone," and "Billboard" called him "The Innovator of The Year."

Not too bad for a long-haired kid from Springfield, Missouri who aspired to do something in the music business.

•

"Southern Missouri, where I grew up," says Garland, "had quite a little music scene and I'd gotten my feet wet hanging out with a band that was known as Granny's Bath Water. Later they changed their name to The Ozark Mountain Daredevils."

By the time he was thirteen, he'd discovered radio. "I'd skip around the dial at night and pick up WLS/Chicago, KAAY/Little Rock or

WABC/New York, and I could visualize a really cool jock sitting on a stool in a dimly lit room with little spotlights on him, and he'd introduce a band like The Fuzzy Snakes (he chuckles again) and they'd actually come out and perform. Really!"

He arrived in Dallas in 1965, enrolled at Southern Methodist University and found "gopher" work at KLIF, helping night-time disc jockey, Jimmy Rabbit, who'd broken his leg and couldn't get around. He went to Elkins institute to earn his Third Class Radio Telephone license — with a broadcast endorsement.

Before long SMU was no longer part of the plan and, with a freshly printed FCC certificate, Garland found a job at KSWM/Aurora, Missouri. With a population of about five thousand, Aurora was an all-American-one-horse-town with a radio station where Garland could learn to do everything. He took transmitter readings, read the news, sold advertising and did on-air work that included reading obituaries and announcing the pet patrol.

It was the middle '60s, a simpler time in media, when a kid with ambition and smarts could move up.

•

KELI/Tulsa. Its direct Top 40 competition was KAKC, one of the few stations outside the RKO chain consulted by Bill Drake and, like KYNO/Fresno and WHBQ/Memphis, KAKC was considered by many to be a stepping stone for aspiring boss jocks with their sights set on the RKO organization.

Garland had gone to work at KELI, but he spent countless hours monitoring KAKC, studying the station's execution and formatics. He was beginning to think about the art of programming or, as he describes it, "learning how to manage the creative process." One day he knew he'd become a Program Director. But first, he had to go to Milwaukee with Mike Joseph.

•

Mike Joseph was a broadcasting legend by the time the two men met at WZUU-FM, the station that was going to become the market's first FM rocker. Fastidious to a fault, Joseph did the format by the book, running dry runs for three months. (Garland reveals that when the format finally launched, what they did on the air bore no resemblance to what they'd been practicing.) "I knew Mike wanted to build the cume up as fast as we could and I understood that it meant playing the same songs over and over. But, my God, we signed on with a playlist of seventeen, maybe, nineteen records. No oldies, no re-currents. I mean, how many times can you play *Long Cool Woman* in a three-hour shift?!?"

Garland says Joseph's plan wasn't a good fit for him and, thinking back on it, even suggests his hair was too long for the format. (You'd have to have been there.) So, for the first time in his career, Garland sent out airchecks. When a call came in from KYNO/ Fresno, the station where Bill Drake and Gene Chenault had first joined forces to compete against Ron Jacobs and Robert W. Morgan, Garland was floored. "I was incredibly excited and moved to Fresno to do mid-days. Within a year I was named PD."

Under Garland the Drake-consulted station vaulted into double digits. As a result, he was invited to visit Bill Drake's hideaway in Beverly Hills. "Drake was like Elvis, man," says Garland, "and when he mentored me I hung onto his every word. He was, after all, the most important man in pop radio."

•

It was an odd beginning. "Drake was in a robe when he called down and invited me to join him in his bathroom," recalls Garland.

The young man went upstairs, took a seat on the only sitting area in the room (you know what I mean, don't you?), and was floored when Drake, with shaving cream lathered on his face, offered him the reins of K-100/Los Angeles.

"I accepted the job at once," says Garland. "Here I was, this small town Missouri kid, and I was never so flattered."

But, blinded by ambition and the lure of Tinsel Town, he didn't notice that his salary was never discussed. "There I was in Los

Angeles and still working on the same financial terms I'd had in Fresno," he says. Negotiations began, but he was insulted by management's offer. "I felt that I'd been hand-picked by the most successful guy in the business and should be rewarded for what I was doing. Bill supported my position, but nothing happened."

One night, over drinks, Garland told his friend, Eric Chase, that he was probably going to do something "very crazy." The next morning at 9 o'clock, he walked into the General Manager's office to deliver the news. "I'm out of here," he said.

Pat Shaughnessy, K-100's GM, stared at him and asked, "Where are you going?"

"I don't know," responded Garland, "but I'm leaving."

Today Garland says he's long past passing judgment, but still believes standing his ground was something he had to do. "I left, and thank God I did," he says. "It was the dignified thing to do. If only for myself."

•

He escaped to the mountains to clear his head. It wasn't a Moses thing, but he did come up with some ideas. "Great radio stations," he decided, "all have a great soul that's shared by the people inside. And, if that soul doesn't exist, the station is doomed."

In his mind's eye he saw that compelling radio stations were those that reflected a mix of art and science and that those stations were a direct reflection of the Program Director's personality.

He came down from the mountain and met Paul Drew. "Paul called and asked me to meet with him at his home in LA." The two men clicked and Drew invited Garland to program WAVZ/ New Haven, and to help him out with some of the other stations he was consulting. (In 2004 Garland told "Disc and Dat" magazine, "Radio itself is an art and both Drake and Drew were holding paint brushes and taught me how to put the paint to canvas.")

Garland was in New Haven for less than a year when Drew sent him, first, to CKLW/Detroit and, then, to WRKO/Boston. "One of the first things I did at WRKO," says Garland, "was stage The Spring Fever Festival." He got city permits and told the Mayor's office that he only expected 20,000 people to show up. But, on the day of the event — "the most perfect spring day you've ever seen," he recalls, close to 200,000 New Englanders showed up.

Trouble! The Mayor's office got flummoxed and, believe it or not, requested the music be turned down. It wasn't. The next day the front page of "The Boston Globe" showed a picture of the concert shot from a helicopter. Yes, WRKO's call letters were big and prominent, and Drew later told Garland, "It was one of the greatest radio events ever."

Garland remembers the Mayor's office was "totally pissed and wanted to railroad me out of town. Try to imagine how much I really cared."

•

When the call came from Pat Norman, the General Manager of KFRC/San Francisco, Drew objected. "KFRC is already #1 with nowhere to go but down," he told Garland.

Garland disagreed. "No, Paul, it's only the #1 *music* station."

Looking back, he's jubilant. "KFRC was the top of the mountain and my time there was as magical as the city of San Francisco itself. Dr. Don Rose did mornings, Dave Sholin was the MD — Dave has some of the best pop ears in the business! — and Pat Norman was the coolest GM I ever worked with. And, like all RKO stations, programming ruled."

KFRC's promotions were gigantic: "The KFRC Long Run with the Eagles," "The KFRC SuperWalk with Robin Williams" — who, by helicopter, dropped into thirteen locations around the Bay Area, and, "The KFRC Skylab Promotion," which came about when a piece of the Skylab crashed to earth in western Australia. "We actually smuggled this three-thousand pound piece of metal into

San Francisco and held a press conference," says Garland. Later, in a stroke of money-making genius, Garland sold pieces of the space craft to other radio stations for $1000 an inch. The final touch memorializing the moment came when John Belushi did a skit on "Saturday Night Live" about it.

But, the '70s were coming to an end.

•

In 1979, Garland left radio to join Atlantic Records.

"Those were incredibly fun times," he says. "We all loved music: the artistry of making it and the business of tastefully exposing it. When you think about it today, MTV was the next logical step."

After MTV, he and Bob Pittman formed Quantum Media, a company that produced the short-lived-but-sensational Morton Downey Jr. Show, launched a record label and dabbled in national radio programming with Lee Abrams by creating "Radio Lisa," an idea Garland admits "may have been have a few beats ahead of its time."

Then, he took some time off to pursue another passion — golf. "I wanted to experience big time golf and improve my own game," he says. Through a series of serendipitous events, Garland got a shot to go out on the PGA Tour with his friend, Tommy Armour. "If I ever write a book," Garland promises, "those experiences alone will fill a chapter."

The next year, in 1990, Garland became an executive at "The Box," the nation's first interactive music channel. "Between 1990 and '97, we rolled into twenty-five million homes in the United States. Internationally, we added another twenty-five mil to the mix."

Sadly, as the millennium approached, tragedy hit. While vacationing in Jamaica, Garland was involved in a horrendous car accident. Air-lifted back to Miami, he spent six months in the hospital recuperating. It gave him time to think about what the new century might mean and led to the formation of "AfterPlay Entertainment," a multi-faceted venture which included the development of "The College Television Network," a music and lifestyle channel available to twenty-five hundred colleges across America. "I like to put music on television," Garland says, "and I don't believe those who say it won't work."

Until recently Garland's energies and talents were being applied to "The Tube Music Network." As he told "Disc and Dat" in 2004, "The Tube is honest, has integrity in music, is simple, intelligent and slightly irreverent."

("The Tube" ceased operations on October 1, 2007. The last song it played was A3's "Woke Up This Morning," which ended at exactly midnight, when the network's screen went black.")

•

Les Garland has a set of beliefs that may inspire you. "Be aware of your passions and apply them to ALL that you do: family, friends, hobbies, career, principles and beliefs. Trust and remain true to yourself. Be honest, credible and maintain your integrity. Be loyal, while appreciating and rewarding loyalty in return and constantly re-examine short and long term goals, and then set the bar higher than you actually think you can jump."

"You must chase your dreams," he says. "You never want to look back and say, 'I wish I'd done that.' "

Any thoughts on the future? I asked.

"There is more opportunity in media today than there's ever been," Garland replies. "The digital age has created incredible opportunities for change, which is a good thing and should never be feared."

CHAPTER 23
BOB HENABERY: THE KING OF DISCO

"Bob Henabery invents formats," says Charlie Colombo, Executive Vice President of United Stations.

That's what great programmers do, of course, but Henabery has always been in a class by himself. What formats, you ask? For starters, Rock 'N Stereo for ABC, Disco for WKYS (Disco 93) in Washington D.C. and the Magic format for Greater Media. (In hindsight, Henabery acknowledges that Lite is probably a much better word for it.) Henabery even executed the Drake format at an RKO station, without Drake.

"He's one of the most charismatic guys in our business and a pioneer," says Jeff Smulyan, CEO of Emmis Communications. Others have called him "a man of great integrity" and a "thinker." In sum, Henabery has been a man of great influence in broadcasting during a tumultuous time; the years, in fact, that took us from 78 rpm records to mp3 files, the modern day equivalent of horse buggies to space ships.

Here's his story.

•

"Henabery's father, Joseph Henabery, a pioneer in silent films, was D.W. Griffith's assistant and, believe it or not, played the part of Abraham Lincoln in Griffith's classic 1915 film, "Birth of a Nation." In his later years, Henabery, the father, directed many of the big stars of the time, including Douglas Fairbanks, Rudolf Valentino and Fatty Arbuckle.

Henabery, the son, was educated by the Jesuits at Fordham College in New York - one of his classmates was Vin Scully — and he started his radio career at WBEC, a station licensed to Pittsfield, Massachusetts that served Berkshire County. After WBEC, Henabery spent ten years as Program Director of WWJ/Detroit.

Looking back, he claims the decade wasn't particularly productive. "I was lousy (at the job) and left because I knew I'd never go anywhere unless I had a success under my belt." He set his sights on New York City and within a short time was hired to produce the morning show at WCBS-AM. When that station's ratings rose, Henabery — his card newly punched — headed north to Boston to become Director of Programs for RKO Radio at WNAC.

WNAC-AM was originally part of The Yankee Network, a chain of regional stations that operated in Massachusetts, Maine and Rhode Island. Founded in 1930, the network's primary competition was RCA, a company headed by David Sarnoff, that took particular exception to the fledgling network's use of FM relays to link their stations together and also opposed Yankee's launching of the nation's first FM network, a move that had been made in conjunction with Edwin H. Armstrong, the inventor of FM. By the time Henabery arrived in Boston, RKO had owned WNAC for over ten years.

As Director of Programs, one of Henabery's first moves was to flip WNAC from middle-of-the-road to talk. Next, in anticipation of an FCC ruling mandating FM stations broadcast unique programming (instead of simulcasting their AM signals), Henabery automated WRKO-FM with Top 40 music, broadcast in mono. He called the station ARKO.

According to staffer, Bill Hahn, WNAC-AM's days doing talk were always numbered, and after-the-fact, Henabery says he'd guessed things were going on in the company that were above his pay grade. "I always suspected that (by dropping the talk format and killing the network) the owners got a huge tax write-off and were planning to go into the Drake format."

In 1966, Henabery had no Top 40 experience and wasn't much interested. In fact, he'd been toying with the idea of heading back to New York to program WOR. But, WRKO General Manager Perry Ury was nothing if not a great salesman.

"Stay with me," he told Henabery, "and we'll do this thing."

•

Behind the scenes there *was* a lot going on at RKO General and little doubt that WNAC would go Top 40, following the lead of other RKO stations. As early as the spring of 1966 Ury says he realized that Bill Drake, the company's programming consultant, hated Boston winters and would refuse to come east from California until the weather warmed up. He also knew the format change couldn't wait. So, Ury told Henabery to pack his bags and head to the west coast.

Boss Radio – KHJ/Los Angeles — had been in format for about a year when Henabery arrived in LA. He parked himself in a hotel room and began monitoring the station. "I listened to KHJ for a few days and returned with my report," he says.

(The report, dated June 21, 1966, can be found online in its entirety. What follows are high-lights.)

To: Jerry Bess

From: Bob Henabery

Subject: KHJ – Boss Radio

"Boss Radio," is a tightly formatted, well-produced, skillfully-staffed and promoted, modern music station.

All categories of programming rate high. The personalities, their material, the music and service features, the station's distinctive sound. KHJ news and on-air promotion blend together in a fast-moving, non-stop continuous flow.

Personalities and Material

The KHJ program day is divided into three-hour segments hosted by various "Boss Jocks."

All deejays have young voices and "dig" what they are doing on the air. Unlike some modern music stations staffed by older performers, the "Boss Jocks" are enthusiastically responsive to the goals of the station and react positively to everything happening there.

The two most distinctive on-air presentations are those of the drive-time personalities, Robert W. Morgan (AM) and The Real Don Steele (PM). Morgan and Steele seem to be the only men who have gimmicks of their own which are introduced into the overall format and which are exclusive to themselves. Morgan uses an up-dated dedication device in which the names of individuals are submitted to him without their knowledge and then read on the air.

EXAMPLE: "Mr. Cusato, science teacher at Encino High — are you listening on your birthday? ZAP! You're Morganized!"

The Real Don Steele is the most articulate of the "Boss Jocks" in respect to the argot of the youth. He delivers this language flawlessly at a furious and witty pace. Steele is the most intelligent and talented of the "Boss Jocks."

Music

The "Boss 30" is a tight music playlist which contains no untested or speculative records. Everything played is a proven hit or a "Goldie." The format is highly repetitious as far as frequency of play is concerned. The music is selected on the basis of popularity. Listener requests taken on the "Boss Line" are tabulated throughout the broadcast day by special operators on duty at the station. This list is then compared to record sales in Southern California for validation purposes.

16 records are played each hour of the day. We estimate that 7 of the records are derived from the top ten (and) 6 of the records from numbers 11-20.

3 of the records are "Goldies" valuable to balance tempo. The merit of such repetition consists in the audience anticipating that a hit tune will soon be played. Thus a listener will stay tuned to hear his favorite and will be rewarded in a few minutes when it is, indeed, played.

The high quality of the music is obvious. Records such as "Paperback Writer" by the Beatles, "Along Comes Mary" by The Association, [and] "Band of Gold" by Mel Carter, out-distance so-called adult standard music not only by the enthusiasm and vitality of the performances but by obviously superior musicianship.

Service Features

Outside of news KHJ restricts service features to mention of the time after <u>every record</u> ("KHJ Big Kahuna Time 11:20, etc.") and weather twice an hour.

No effort is made to present extended traffic features.

Distinctive Sound

KHJ's distinctive sound is tied together by jingles and catchphrases.

Short, fast jingles express the following phrases:

"KHJ Los Angeles"

"93 KHJ"

"93 KHJ plays more music"

"93 KHJ Golden"

"KHJ Weather"

"93 KHJ Sports"

"KHJ Boss Hit-bound"

"The Big Kahuna 93 KHJ"

In connection with the basic one-hour format it is important to point out that lee ways are provided that the jingles do not appear in exactly the same sequence every hour. Except for this variable, required in the selection of the various musical elements, there is little variation from hour to hour.

Catchphrases express the overall "Boss Radio" concept <u>or</u> the current KHJ promotion.

On-Air Promotion

KHJ's current promotion is The Big Kahuna. The Big Kahuna is an actual person — an Hawaiian dressed in the costume of a Polynesian king. The Big Kahuna — speaking only Hawaiian, is escorted to various high schools and recreational areas by a KHJ personality. Tapes are then made for play-back on the air.

"This is Gary Mack at Encino Junior High. We're here today to introduce the Big Kahuna. (BIG KAHUNA SPEAKS IN HAWAIIAN.) The Big Kahuna says to listen to the sound of the conch shell on KHJ to win your coconut for the big KHJ Luau June 22. (BIG KAHUNA SPEAKS MORE HAWAIIAN.)

The Big Kahuna also says to always stay tuned to the much-more-music station in Los Angeles. KIDS THEN SING. 93 KHJ. THE BIG KAHUNA."

One of this type of spot is used every two hours during the KHJ program day. Every other hour a special record called The Big Kahuna is played.

All intros and outros on the station refer to The Big Kahuna.

News

KHJ presents "20-20 News."

Five-minute reports are scheduled 20-25 and 40-45 from 6:00 — 9:00 AM. All other times of day the news is heard 40-45.

KHJ makes great use of mobile units to cover breaking local stories in Los Angeles. Three or four reporters are assigned to different stories in various parts of Los Angeles and spend their entire day with the story until it is wrapped up.

Although the entire KHJ operation is marked by a high level of professionalism, we think the station's success can be attributed to the following:

1) The imaginative promotional schemes developed at the station.

2) The general excellence of the "Boss Jocks."

3) The tight list of established hits and avoidance of "picks."

4) An enlightened commercial policy of 12:20 commercial minutes per hour compared to NAB's 18 providing for "much more music."

Ury and Bess liked what they read and gave Henabery his marching orders. Looking back, Ury speculates Drake's reaction was probably, " 'They'll do it, they'll fail, and they'll need me even more.' "

Henabery and his team didn't fail. On March 13, 1967, WNAC-AM went Top 40 as WRKO. "I take no credit for the originality of the ideas," Henabery told me, "but, the interpretation at WRKO was mine."

From the distance of years, Henabery's view is that the Drake format was terrific. "Bill Drake was the #1 radio guy – period," he says. "But, I never got along with him. I always thought we could never work together because our styles were so totally different."

How did their styles differ? Henabery says his management philosophy was collaborative, while Drake's was autocratic. So, when Drake and his Canoga Park troops arrived in Boston the next spring, Henabery decided it was time to move on.

It was 1968 and, for Bob Henabery, the decision to leave Boston wasn't a hard one because, just as he'd used his success at WCBS to get to Boston, he planned to use his WRKO success to leverage his reputation in the industry. "So, somebody would hire me for a good job," he says.

That somebody turned out to be ABC, and here's why: Rick Sklar programmed WABC/New York at the same time that John Rook was the PD at WLS/Chicago. Both men were ambitious and aspired to be named ABC's National Program Director. But, despite their talents and reputations, ABC turned to Henabery instead. "I was the compromise candidate," he says. "My title was Program Development Manager." NOT National PD.

In fairness to Henabery, his experience in talk radio (at The Yankee Network) and with music radio (at WRKO) uniquely qualified him for the job. But, that didn't mean that the job was going to be a walk in the park. Henabery says his job was to mind the store. "The ABC program directors were not my subordinates," he says, today.

"We all agreed that the radio stations had to be done locally." His job, he says, was to advise and strategize.

By the fall of 1969, the ABC AM group had the highest cumulative radio audience in the nation. But, the ABC FM group was in trouble.

•

In the spirit of the times they called it "The Love Format."

It was ABC's sanitized and automated version of Album Rock and, from start to finish, it was only on the air for one year. Dispirited, in late 1970, ABC tried again with what would best be described as local versions of the free form progressive format Tom Donahue had created at KSAN/San Francisco. Henabery laughs and, sarcastically, describes this approach as... "Here's your morning dope report. The good grass is on the corner of..."

Still, his gut told him that this "no-format-format" had legs. So, he convened a meeting of the ABC programmers in Chicago. "We were told the free-form was dead, explains RCS's Dwight Douglas, "and that many of the disc jockeys would have to be reigned in, or turned out to pasture. Bob's first job was to teach the freaks to format."

The new idea was called "Rock 'N Stereo" and that's the slogan ABC used to promote it on the air. "We had a certain style, and all the stations used that phrase," says Douglas, pointing to KLOS/Los Angeles as the station that used the slogan and approach the longest. "The format succeeded because you could maintain a hip image and still play hit music," Henabery says. "It was just a different kind of hit music."

By 1974 Henabery had tired of corporate life. The last straw was when ABC turned him down for the General Manager's job at WLS/Chicago. Shortly after getting the WLS news, he resigned from ABC and announced the formation of his new business, Bob Henabery Associates, describing himself as "specialist in new radio format development."

On June 20, 1974 the company opened its doors. At the time, Henabery wrote, "Radio has been changing more significantly in the last few years than even in the early '50s when television arrived. Yet, these newer changes evolve so subtly they go virtually unnoticed by broadcasters in their day-to-day work." He suggested there was an accelerating need to step back and take a fresh look at what was going on — in radio and in communications in general. He said he thought it was important for broadcasters to learn the nature and the extent of the changes that were occurring.

Among other things, he was referring to how FM was going to change the playing field. He also assumed, especially in the late summer of '74, that the country was fed up with Vietnam and Watergate and would begin to look for a new musical and lifestyle release.

He was right and discovered it on the streets of New York.

It was called Disco.

•

SJR (San Juan Racing) owned foreign language WHOM/New York. When the company asked Henabery to do a format search, one of the suggestions he returned with was Disco. "I had a couple of tapes I'd prepared of disco mixes and the one that scored highest, with everyone, was the Top 40 mix with no oldies, all currents," he says. But, SJR said no. (Ironically, they embraced the format later, as WKTU v 1.0).

"So, I brought a cassette of the format to Washington and played it for Harold Green, the General Manager of WKYS and WRC," Henabery says. "We were sitting in a car outside Guards restaurant in Georgetown and Harold said — these are his exact words — 'So, that's disco. I like it. Let's do disco.' "

WKYS debuted with a seven point two share. "That made them #3 12+, and #1 with 18-34s," says Henabery.

While Henabery got press for discovering the format, the financial rewards went to Kent Burkhart, largely because Burkhart took WKTU/New York to #1 in only thirty days and, with his staff of programmers at Burkhart/Abrams, he was able to parlay the 'KTU success quickly. "Bob didn't cash in on it as much," says Douglas, "but he certainly had a major role in creating the format and in making rhythmic music a non-race issue for broadcasters."

The disco format and movement became so successful, so quickly, that Bob's friends, jokingly, called him The King of Disco. Like many American trends; however, the music, the lifestyle and, then, the format became so pervasive and so much of a cliché, that, by the end of its run, it was a non-entity. (Think of the Bee Gees' career.)

Henabery seems uneasy taking credit for his role in creating the format. One gets the impression that it doesn't really matter to him. (My view is that to diminish Henabery's place in the evolution of the Disco format does the man a disservice. That said, to suggest that Disco is the centerpiece of his career would be like saying Chuck Berry's claim to fame is *My Ding A Ling*, instead of *Johnny B. Goode*.)

•

Henabery's next discovery was the antithesis of Disco. He called it "The Magic Format" and says the genesis of the idea came when he began to think about an office populated by young women. "Let's think of them in terms of their musical needs," he suggested.

The format debuted on WMJC/Detroit, but had its greatest success at WMGK/Philadelphia. "Bob Craig did a masterful job of combining the music with great imaging. I think he got a 9.0 share," Henabery remembers. "After that, a lot of folks copied it."

Bob Henabery Associates consulted actively during the '80s (We Let The Music Do The Talking at WENS!) and '90s (SETS FM™, a new format Bob debuted on KXST-FM/San Diego.) With each idea, came the Henabery touch and philosophy. "The first response to a new programming idea is denial by the enemy — even as they're going down the tubes," he explains. "Generally, reasons for the denial flow from the top down in the company, not from the bottom up."

Today, when asked about his career and his contributions, Henabary isn't quite as definite. "I'm too aware of my own limitations," he says, modestly.

But, think about this: As a programmer, Henabery put his finger-prints on Talk, Top 40 and Album Radio. As one of the nation's first successful consultants, he identified the formatic holes for Disco and Lite Rock and, beyond that, advised many of the nation's major broadcasting companies on matters that transcend basic programming issues.

In 1976, on behalf of ABC, his former employer, Henabery submitted a report to the FCC dealing with the question of whether the Government should have any say in format changes.

> "Assuming a good ownership situation, the quality of local management is the single most important function in the radio station equation. Logic would also seem to dictate that in an egalitarian society, which perceives no one type of format superior to another, that a good classical station is superior to a bad rock station, and that a good rock station is better than a bad classical station.
>
> In other words, it is the local management that determines success, not the choice of formats."

"No one can touch him, intellectually or creatively," says Joe Capobianco, a Vice President at Sirius Satellite Radio.

Still, Henabery remains humble. "If I'm proud of anything, it's that I tried to be a good example to a younger generation of programmers in the quality of my work product – letting them see that you could win without smelling up the joint."

That sound you hear is applause.

CHAPTER 24

DAN INGRAM: THE BEST TOP 40 DJ OF ALL TIME

It was summertime and the living was easy.

The President and his Attorney General were on vacation, and so were lots of other Americans. In New York City, baseball fans, 74,246 of them, gathered at Yankee Stadium to cheer on Mantle and Maris as they batted at the Babe's record. It was Thursday, June 30, 1961, and the #1 song in the country was *Quarter To Three*, by an artist named Gary U.S. Bonds, which seemed ironic, or at least coincidental, since the country's birthday was only four days away.

That night, at WABC, a disc jockey went on the air. He didn't say his name; he'd been asked not to. Instead, he identified himself by simply saying, "This is the Chuck Dunaway Show, without Chuck." He admits he was nervous, but he focused on the task at hand. Meanwhile, downstairs, the American Broadcasting Company switchboards were lighting up. Apparently, things got so crazy and so hectic that the frazzled operator called up to the studio to ask, "What the hell is going on? What are you doing up there?"

"Just doing a radio show is all," replied the DJ.

He wasn't new to radio, but he'd been out of the game for five months, working at MARS Productions, a company in Connecticut that created contests for radio stations, including WABC. Prior to that, he'd worked all around the New York area, spent a year or so at KBOX/Dallas, and had become a Program Director at WIL/St. Louis, where he also did the morning show.

But, by 1960, he'd gotten tired of getting up in the middle of the night — he'd been a morning man for most of his short radio career — and that was one of the reasons he'd grabbed the MARS job.

(Another might have been that at MARS he got a piece of the action, which is to say that he was making enough money to not worry about whether he could afford roast beef or hamburger).

Earlier in the year he'd been offered a job at WMCA, WABC's Top 40 competitor. But, when the station brought up a salary, $25,000, he'd responded by suggesting it wasn't enough money to do afternoon drive in New York City. Today he says it was a negotiating ploy the station's manager, Steve Lubunski, didn't bite on.

He remembers leaving the meeting, wondering if he'd made a big mistake, and thinking how much he wanted to be on the radio again.

He was twenty-six, a native New Yorker, and his name was Dan Ingram.

•

Born in Oceanside, New York, Ingram grew up in Queens and on Long Island. His parents were professional musicians; his father was a sax player, his mother a cellist. With deep affection, he talked about them. "Dad was a handsome, swashbuckling, rogue tenor sax player in the big band era. And my mother was a concert cellist, who was getting marvelous reviews." Growing up surrounded by music had an impact on him, says Ingram. "Their interest in music interested *me* in music, especially classics and jazz. When I started playing records on the radio I could feel the structure of it (the songs), and that made it easier to do talk-ups."

In the mid '40s, when big bands were still booked for live network radio shows, his father would sometimes take his son to work with him. "Nobody'd bother me," Ingram remembers. "They'd say, 'He's Johnny Ingram's kid, he's OK,' and I'd go sit in a corner somewhere and watch the rehearsals. It was exciting." One of the programs his dad played on was "The Fred Allen Show" (Allen, who never successfully made the transition from radio to television, once famously said, "I'd rather have a full bottle in front of me than a full frontal lobotomy.") and Ingram has vivid, pre-adolescent memories. "There were five girls on the show called the DeMarco

Sisters and, when I was eleven, I fell in love with the youngest one. I thought she was really great, except she was an older woman; she was fourteen."

By Ingram's mid-teens, around 1950-51, the first golden age of radio was on its last legs. Panicked local stations were forced to fill the void left by the network radio shows that were being phased out or becoming television programs. It was a strange and changing time, when a maverick disc jockey could play what he wanted on the radio – there were no playlists – and create a following. In New York, on 1010/WINS, there was Alan Freed. "I remember hearing him beat a phone on the table in time with a Bill Haley record," says Ingram. "Yeah, I heard him, and had heard OF him. Lots of energy."

But, at the time, Ingram was more interested in jazz, and says he listened to WOV, a big New York City station with a jock named Freddie Robbins. Some nights, he says, when New York radio wasn't enough, he'd spin the dial on his Emerson until it landed in Chicago, where he listened to a rhythm 'n' blues jock named Daddio Daylie. "He was on a clear channel fifty-gallon station and the remarkable thing about him was that he rhymed every intro and made it work. I mean, this guy was sharp, had a great sense of the English language, knew how to use it AND how to be hip. All at the same time."

•

Ingram's first radio job was at WHCH, the college station at Hofstra University, his alma mater on Long Island. (Other Hofstra graduates include: Alan Colmes of "Hannity and Colmes," Philadelphia radio legend John DeBella, Director Francis Ford Coppola, Songwriter Ellie Greenwich and a 1997 Noble Prize Winner, Robert Muller). After college, in quick succession, he worked for a number of small northeast stations, with market climbing on his mind. At one point, he worked for two stations at the same time — on WNHC he used his real name and on WICC, about an hour away, he called himself Ray Taylor.

Then, sometime in 1959, he got a call from a man named John Box. "I wanna blast you out of New Haven," said Box. "What's it going to take?"

Ingram had a one word answer. "Money."

And, so it was that Dan Ingram headed south to Dallas for twice his New Haven salary.

The Top 40 battle in Big D was between Gordon McLendon's KLIF and KBOX (one of three stations owned by Balaban Broadcasting). On the day Ingram arrived in town, KLIF was claiming that more people listened to KLIF than to all other Dallas stations combined. By the time Ingram left for St. Louis, in 1960, KBOX – yes, it was named after John Box – had taken a big bite out of KLIF, but as well as the station did and as good as it sounded, it was never quite enough to win.

One Dallas morning, just as his show ended, he got a phone call. On the other end of the line was a woman he knew by name only. "My name is Ruth Meyer," she said. "You may not know me, but I'm the Program Director of WMCA in New York, and I just wanted to tell you that I like your work. I'm not offering you a job, but I wanted you to know that, someday, when you feel like you want to get to New York, give me a call."

I could hear Ingram smile as he remembered a telephone call from almost half a century ago. "It was very nice of her," he says. "It made my day, probably my week and my month, too."

•

Hal Neal, the General Manager of WABC/New York, was a former network announcer who'd traded his sound booth for an executive suite.

In 1960, WABC, according to its long-time programmer, the late Rick Sklar, was "the last bulwark of radio soap-operadom" and trying hard to become a rock 'n' roll radio station.

ABC wasn't a company flush with cash. So, when Neal arrived from

Detroit, his pleas for money to hire a full-time program director
fell on deaf ears. Get a DJ to do the job part-time, the corporation
suggested. While there's no public record of the words Neal used
when he heard this, his actions spoke loudly, and when he moved
quickly to hire an in-house consultant, a move that didn't require
approval from personnel, there was little or no outcry.

The consultant's name was Mike Joseph. Joseph's plan called for a
long playlist based on the station's frequency, 77. This meant seventy
currents, seven album cuts, seven soaring singles — you see where
I'm going with this. Meanwhile, down the hall, it was really Neal
who was calling the hiring shots and, in short order, Herb Oscar
Anderson and Scott Muni were plucked from WMCA, Charlie
Greer came in from WAKR/Akron, Chuck Dunaway was drafted
from WKY/Oklahoma City and Jack Carney arrived from WIL/
St. Louis. Add to them Farrell Smith and staff announcer, Bill
Owen, and you had version 1.0 of a team that would eventually
be called "The All-Americans."

•

Dan Ingram wasn't surprised when Jack Carney was fired from
WABC. "He was very talented, but also very egocentric," Ingram
says. "Whenever anyone criticized his work, Jack had a bad habit
of responding, 'Well, why don't you get yourself a new boy?'"

Carney, apparently, pulled the line out too many times and one day
Hal Neal took him up on it. "Alright, haul your ass out of here.
Right now." Carney's afternoon-drive replacement was a TV host
from Miami named Fred Hall. "Fred had been doing a kiddies
show and had tremendous ratings," says Ingram, explaining that
Neal hired people based on their ratings. But television for tykes
wasn't the same as big-city Top 40 for teens, and if nobody else
knew it, Ingram did. "Fred was on the air at ABC saying things
like, 'Hey gang, here's your rock 'n' roll record!'"

Never shy, Ingram decided to tell Hall what he thought.

"Jeez, man!" Ingram said, "You gotta start thinking that these kids are pretty hip and pretty well grownup." Then, as if to let Hall in on the secret of the century, he added, "You know, you may be surprised to learn that they're all screwing."

Hall was incredulous. "What?!? Are you kidding?"

"No, I'm not," deadpanned Ingram.

He listened for a few more days and knew exactly what Hall's problem was. "He was, as they say, in the wrong ballpark. So, the next time I was at the station to see Hal Neal and drop off tapes, I said to him, 'Hal, you know the guy you have on afternoons isn't helping your station. His focus is towards little children, not towards adolescents, who we know are pretty hip these days.' "

Neal just stared. Then, in a flash of anger, said. "YOU. Shut UP! You're a peddler. You're here to peddle your stuff. Give it to me, and then get out."

Ingram says he replied with two words: "Yes, sir."

He says he wasn't offended and that he understood Neal simply didn't want an outsider telling him how to run his business. "I gotta tell you, I agreed with him totally. He was absolutely right."

So, the moment passed and the two men began to listen to the Mars tapes Ingram had with him. After listening to all ten contests — Neal loved them all, remembers Ingram — the manager turned to him and asked, "By the way, who do you think would be better on my station?"

"Me," Ingram replied.

"I thought so."

Ingram had an aircheck with him, but was reluctant to hand off a master, so he promised to send a dub. Several days later, Neal called. "I like your work. It sounds good. I just don't know how you'd sound on my station."

Ingram said, "No problem. I'll have a tape on your desk in the morning, before you get in."

Neal laughed. "You got to be kidding. I get in at seven 'cause I can get two hours of work done before the bullshit starts. So, don't worry about it. Today's Thursday, anyway, and tomorrow's Friday ... so, bring me a tape on Monday."

Ingram said, "Nope. I always keep my word. I'll have a tape on your desk in the morning, before you come to work."

•

He was determined to land the afternoon show at WABC, but wasn't sure how he could create a tape that would allow Hal Neal to hear what he'd sound like on the station. "That night I went into the Mars studio and found an aircheck of Jack Carney that I'd taped off of WABC-FM, which was simulcasting their AM signal. The tape was clean — no passing cars, none of the sparkplug noise you got on AM — like it was recorded right in studio. So, I had the records, all of their jingles, everything, and I even transcribed the commercials so I could put them in my own words."

He had the dummy tape done by three in the morning. Knowing he had less than three hours before he had to head for the city, he decided to sack out in the ladies' room, the only place in the building he could find a sofa. (Ingram told me all ladies' rooms in Connecticut had to have sofas back then. I didn't ask why.)

With a start, he awoke at six-fifteen. Neal was due at his desk by seven. "I made one hell of a drive down into New York, parked in front of the ABC Building on 66th Street, went inside and asked the guard if I could take the tape up to Mr. Neal's Office."

The guard looked him over. "What, are you kidding?"

"No, I'm not," replied Ingram, "I really mean it. And I want you to come with me so, uh, nothing wrong happens."

The guard was still hesitant.

"So," Ingram says, "I reached in my pocket and took out a ten dollar bill, which was a lot of money in those days."

Up they went, with Ingram always in the guard's sight. "You're not going to disturb anything, are you?" the guard asked.

Ingram promised he wouldn't. "So, I put the tape on Hal's desk, took his pen and wrote him a note."

> Dear Hal,
>
> I always keep my word.
>
> (signed) Dan

"Then I took the note, stuck it on his pen, thanked the guard, left the building, drove back and sacked out again in the ladies' room — until a lady came in and asked what I was doing there.

That night, Hal Neal and Dan Ingram made the deal of Ingram's lifetime. Just like the deal that blasted him out of New Haven, it was for twice the money he was making.

He had no idea it would last for over a quarter of a century.

•

"So, tell me," I said. "What was surprising about your first day at WABC?"

Ingram answered by saying something not many know about. "When I got to WABC," he says, "I was the 'unofficial programmer.' "

"Excuse me?"

"The first day I was there Hal Neal told me to go down the hall and make Mike Joseph think he hired me. So, I did and I guess to this day, Mike thinks *he* did."

Ingram stops to weigh his words. "Joseph's a nice man and we had a good relationship, but he was on the way out and knew it."

One of the first things Ingram did was cut WABC's playlist to forty records. "The bottom five or so were new records, and that was it," he explains. (This, of course, happened well before June 11, 1962, the day Rick Sklar joined the station.) "Rick Sklar was the best promotion man in the world," says Ingram. "He could take an idea and turn it into a huge contest."

Case in point: "The Principal of The Year," a high school targeted promotion, created by Bob Whitney, which had originated at KALL/Salt Lake City. "At KALL entries were submitted on an 8" x 10" piece of paper," recalls Ingram. "But, when Sklar ran with the contest in New York, he decided that a smaller file card would work, a 3" x 4", I think. Because of that, there was a shortage of file cards along the entire east coast. People actually had friends send them boxes of cards from California." (In his book, "Rocking America," Sklar revealed that students could vote more than once, and that over one hundred seventy-six million votes were cast.)

"How do you stay humble at a radio station as big as WABC?" I asked.

Ingram told me that, for years, he kept two letters from listeners on his den wall that helped him understand his parameters. One suggested he "shut the f**k up" because the listener, who wrote his message in crayon, was recording the music. The other, single-spaced typing on onion skin stationary, thanked him for his contributions and made mention of a Scandinavian girl who was bettering her English by listening to him. These were what he called his "two poles of audience reaction."

•

Twenty-five years is a long time. Enough time to take us from Hank Williams to Jimi Hendrix, and a long time to miss John Lennon.

It's also slightly less than the number of years Dan Ingram spent at WABC, where he once posted a twenty-eight point share, making his show the most listened to radio program in the history of New York radio.

In the spring of 1988, as WABC was flipping to its new talk format, Ingram's voice was one of the last to be heard. "This is WABC, New York," he said, sadly. Then, he just walked away, showing no interest in the new format, although some discussion had gone on about him staying.

What were his plans for the next day? "Well," he says, "there was a satellite idea Rick Sklar had come up with called "Super Radio." But, when the ABC Board heard it would lose half a million dollars in its first year, the concept was stopped in its tracks."

Ingram, always in demand for voice-over work, didn't find himself at odds and, eventually, he ended up at WKTU before beginning a thirteen year run at WCBS-FM.

"So, what do you think of the business today?" I asked.

"I think it's been pretty well ruined by the sharp pencils," he replies. "Many stations are automated, which is a good way to save money and lose audience. It's one of the worst eras in radio and there's no place for someone to learn their trade anymore."

"Would you go back on the air today?"

"I'd consider anything that was offered," he answers. "It all depends. I tend to think of myself as being somewhat expensive. I made good money (at ABC, when he was voted the #1 disc jockey in North America); of course, it was nothing like what's going on today."

One thing you probably don't know about Dan Ingram is that for most of his life he's been involved with the labor movement. "My home was always a labor home," he explains. "My parents were some of the first members of Local 50 of the Musicians Union in Pittsburgh and they felt that people should have the right to band together to bargain collectively." Ingram says he believes it's a fundamental right. Today, after over forty years of active union involvement, Ingram is First Vice President of AFTRA in New York, a non-salaried position. He says the financial part doesn't bother him a bit. "When I'm walking home from a meeting at night and I've done some work that I know is going to help ten thousand people, there's no amount of money that can buy that good feeling. It's so rewarding, wonderful."

When told by media types that he's the reason they got into radio, he laughs. "You'll get over it in a few days," says Dan Ingram. "Just drink a lot of water."

In 2007 Dan Ingram was inducted into the NAB Radio Hall of Fame.

CHAPTER 25

RON JACOBS: THE BOSS OF BOSS RADIO

"The first thing that gave me a rush," says Ron Jacobs, "was sitting in that balcony with that one little knob. I'd been given the responsibility of adjusting the levels on a mono PA system during chapel service."

School was a drag, but running sound gunned his engines, he says. "It was a control thing, and if I didn't like what some teacher was saying, I could just cut her off. I had no problem making an ass out of myself, but this was a way to make an amplified ass out of myself."

The future that was coming hadn't been imagined yet.

Like most who gravitate to radio or show business, at first it was all about attention and getting girls. But for Jacobs there was more. He didn't want to be a merchant like his father and knew he wasn't the doctor or lawyer type. What he wanted was to get off the island of Hawaii, and he thought radio might be the ticket.

Lord knows he couldn't hop a bus.

•

"There were probably no more than two hundred TV sets in Hawaii," says Jacobs. "So, when people talked about Soupy Sales, I had no point of reference." With television coming to the islands late, Jacobs's attention stayed focused on radio and the power of sound. "I got to do my first shows on 'The Voice of Junior Hawaii.' We had scripts, a guy from the agency supervising, and did it very precisely, just like they did it in the 1930s." It was like the Golden Age of Radio — big auditoriums, studio organists and announcers who'd stroll through the lobby, with hands cupped behind their ears. "I got a taste of the back cusp of what radio used to be in the golden years, which I think were much more creative," says Jacobs. "I know it's not hip to talk about Amos and Andy, but creatively doing old style radio live on the network with a full audience and studio orchestra, and creating characters — I mean, that was real theater of the mind. Anybody could start a record and sit back and smoke for three minutes."

In 1955, the all night man at KHON/Honolulu was fired. Jacobs dropped out of school and conned his way into the job by claiming he was experienced. "I was in the slot, to get to the gate, to make it down the ramp that could get me, someday, to Los Angeles," he says. "Where, maybe, the chicks were nicer and, more importantly, where radio offered a lot more opportunity."

The big NBC outlet in the Pacific was KGU and when Jacobs heard there was an opening ("It was like hearing there was a position open on the Yankees!"), he used the "I work cheaply" ploy and got the job. Five nights a week he called play-by-play bowling — really — and, when he wasn't lugging a three hundred pound Ampex to the lanes, he wandered the late night halls of the station reading memos and getting into files. "That's how I learned about management," he says, sheepishly.

The control room of KGU had other lessons. "The big thing about KGU is I was sitting in the chair where Dave Garroway once sat."

Jacobs says he spent much of his time at KGU listening to everything he could get his ears on. "The show 'Biographies In Sound' just blew me away."

Thirteen years later, at KHJ, he would re-create the show's format, with rock 'n' rollers instead of historical figures, and call it "The History of Rock 'n' Roll."

•

In 1957 Elvis Presley was bigger than Jesus.

By the fall of that year most of the staff of KGU, including Jacobs and his best friend, Tom Moffatt, had been lured to a new station, KHVH. Owned by industrialist Henry J. Kaiser, KHVH's studio was perched high above Waikiki, on the fourteenth floor of the

Hawaiian Village Hotel, a structure Kaiser had built. "It had the best view anyone had ever seen," says Jacobs.

In November, news spread about Presley coming to Hawaii. The two young men went crazy. When they discovered Presley would be staying on the thirteenth floor of their hotel — one floor below them – it was like, well, the second coming.

Jacobs still remembers Presley's arrival. "He comes into the building, thousands of chicks are down by the pool, and he comes out on the balcony a few times and they go berserk."

You won't believe what happened next.

Right after Presley arrived at the hotel, Jacobs and another jock, Donn Tyler, left the building. Tyler, pretty much the same build as Presley, wore a wig and was made up to look like Elvis, from a distance. The two jocks raced to the car, jumped in, and proceeded to tour the island. Meanwhile, upstairs, on the air, Moffatt told his listeners that Jacobs was out cruising with Presley.

"We went to the U of Hawaii," Jacobs says, "and chicks come pouring out of their dorms, like fish being dumped out of an aquarium."

Jacob's hadn't even begun yet. Next, he and his Presley impersonator drove to a nearby stadium where a high school football game, scheduled for broadcast on KGU, was about to start. "The big goal in those days was to get your call letters on another station," reveals Jacobs.

He says he knew the stadium layout like the back of his hand; for two years he'd mixed the audio for the games every weekend. So, with *his* Elvis by his side, Jacobs drove right in. "The school band and players went nuts and the play-by-play guys from KGU got hysterical. 'Elvis is here! Elvis is here!!!!' "

Jacobs decided he had to get out of there without being stopped or lynched. He jammed his foot on the accelerator and raced back to the station.

When he and Tyler got to the studio they, excitedly, told Moffatt what had just happened. They were out of breath and still couldn't believe what they'd just pulled off.

All of the sudden the phone rang.

"Are you the boys that did that Elvis thing?"

"Yeah..."

"Well, we're right below and Colonel Parker (Presley's manager) wants to see you."

Jacobs was convinced they'd be skinned alive. "So, we put Tyler on the air and Moffatt and I went down."

They passed the Samoan bodyguards and walked out on the lanai. "And, Colonel's out there smoking a cigar, and he doesn't even get up," says Jacobs. "He tells us to sit down and then he says, 'Are you the guys that did this thing?' "

The boys — Jacobs was twenty, Moffatt a little older — were frozen with fear. Then Colonel Parker looked at them and said, "Let me tell you. That was one of the funniest things I've ever heard."

Whew! Jacobs started breathing again. Then, unexpectedly, he felt the hair on his neck rise. "And, I turned around and it's fricking Elvis. I mean, this is the guy whose records we've been playing."

Colonel Parker introduced them. "This is Mr. Jacobs," he said to Presley.

Elvis nodded. "How do you do, sir?" (Jacobs remembers thinking Presley was the best looking guy he'd ever seen. "You could tell why most guys hated him.")

Parker continued. "Elvis, these guys were playing our records before anyone else and they did a great stunt this afternoon. I think they should MC tomorrow's concert."

Elvis agreed. "Sounds good to me," he said.

Jacobs almost fell off the balcony. Then, he says, Presley turned to him and said, "See you tomorrow, sir."

Meeting Elvis was a big deal, of course. But, more importantly the stunt brought Jacobs face to face with Colonel Parker. It was the beginning of a forty year friendship, which influenced every promotional activity Jacobs did from that day on. "The Colonel became one of the idols of my life. Whenever I've produced anything since, I ask myself, 'How would Colonel do this?' "

"Honest to God."

•

It was a cocky move.

When Moffatt, the most popular jock in Hawaii, was offered a deal at KPOA, he and Jacobs announced, "We go together or we don't go at all." KPOA agreed, but there wasn't a shift open for Jacobs, so the station appointed him PD.

KPOA was a chop suey of divergent elements — Filipino opera, Japanese-language programs, re-created baseball games — but it gave Jacobs a chance to learn and work long distance with Bill Gavin, the Music Director of "Lucky Lager Dance Time," a pre-Top 40 countdown show. "Gavin taught me discipline and the overall concept of a show; how to get from here to there. He said, 'We're not here to sell records, we're here to play the hits.' " Jacobs admits that at this stage of his career ideas like this simply hadn't occurred to him.

KPOA also gave him a chance to meet consultant, Mike Joseph. "Before Joseph, there were no pie charts, no clocks," he explains. "Joseph was into formatics: 'You wanna get this in the first half hour.' For the first time I could picture a wheel and shrink things down to an hour."

In 1958, KPOA sent Jacobs to meet Joseph in Flint, Michigan. "It was one hundred degrees colder!" he remembers. What he heard on the air knocked him out. He found disc jockeys cloaked in echo,

talking fast and hitting vocals. When Jacobs returned to Hawaii he
was a convert.

•

KPOI — say it, K-*poy* — was a monster radio station.

Named after the Hawaiian food staple, the station went on the
air in May of 1959, Honolulu's first full time rocker. Initially,
Jacobs programmed and did both morning and afternoon drive
while Moffat did nine to noon and six to nine at night. "It was
like on-going street theater," remembers Tom Rounds. He's
referring to KPOI promotions that included cars hanging from
cranes, donkey basketball games and countless marathons. One
marathon, designed to get Rounds and the station on the front
page of the Honolulu Advertiser, the local paper, was called a
"Wake-A-Thon." By the time it was over and Rounds was rushed
to the hospital, he'd been awake and broadcasting for over two
hundred hours. "After staying up over forty-eight hours," says
Rounds, "you start to lose it. I don't remember anything about
getting to the hospital." What he does remember is his picture on
the front page of the paper. "There I was, zonked out."

KPOI's staff was young and committed. "We lived at the station
and the energy – funny, creative and alive with great promotions
– never, ever stopped. K-Poi was #1 in every demo," says Rounds,
proudly.

This success made Jacobs a hero and, when the owners bought
a station in Southern California, they sent Jacobs to program it.
San Bernardino and Los Angeles had little in common, but Jacobs
didn't know it yet.

He was bulletproof, in his middle twenties and, to him, Southern
California meant Hollywood.

Jacobs checked in the Hollywood Plaza, soaked in some starlets,
and the next day made tracks for San Bernardino and KITO.
"By the time we passed our first gravel pit in Colton," he says, "I
realized it wasn't going to be glamorous."

Still, he had a job to do.

He changed the call letters to K-M-E-N, and visited the PD of KFXM, San Bernardino's Top 40 leader, to give him fair (and foul) warning. "We're going to kick the shit out of you," he told him.

"We started doing the circus things we'd done at KPOI," he says. Out in the community Jacobs had the jocks pick a charity, dress in goofy costumes and walk till they dropped. On the air, he had them hitting hard. KFXM, used to taking it easy, began to feel the punches, but Jacobs didn't stick around to celebrate because, just as KMEN began to zoom up in the Hoopers ratings, his bosses called. "Get to Fresno," they told him. "We're buying KMAK."

What happened next, historically, has been labeled "The Battle Of Fresno."

•

Jacobs marshaled his forces.

He hired a jock named Frank Terry and another named Bob Morgan. He wanted to trash the call letters but, when a search for new calls found nothing better, he got radical, at least by 1962 standards. He placed a lower case *e* after KMAK, forcing people to see and say the word K-MAKe. "We'll K-Make the hits and be the K-Makers," he decided.

He put himself on the air and did what he does best – rabble rouse. "The first day I said, 'Fresno State sucks.' I jive-assed and put callers on the air, like I'd done in Honolulu." It was circus time again. Frank Terry played drums, so he invented a "Drum-A-Thon," and Terry attempted to set the world record for continuous drumming. "He went for days," says Jacobs. "Musicians were sitting in and by the time it was over, there was a mob." ("The worst thing in the world is to have a drummer for a roommate," Jacobs notes.)

K-MAKe was on the map, but KYNO, the big dog in Fresno, was only twenty kilocycles away on the dial. "So, the kids started to switch back and forth to hear who was playing the best record,"

Jacobs says. "KYNO's owner, Gene Chenault, took notice, too, and hired a new Program Director, Bill Drake.

Around the same time Jacobs realized his mid-day man, Bob Morgan, had great chops. "He had the bits and he had great timing." Taking one for the team, Jacobs decided to take himself off the air and to move Morgan to morning drive. Meanwhile, across town, Drake took over KYNO's defense and the battle heated up. "Drake's first instinct was to give away money," says Jacobs. "My first instinct was to have fun *while* you gave away money."

The checkbooks came out. Jacobs set KMAKe's jackpot at $1,500 and left the station. Before he made it home, KYNO upped the ante to $2,000.

It was Top 40 beautiful, but it required capital and, when Jacobs called his bosses in New York for emergency cash, they suggested he write it all up in a memo.

"We can't compete like that!" he screamed.

"Memo," they insisted.

"Aloha," he replied.

It wasn't fun anymore and, within days, Ron Jacobs was back home in Hawaii.

•

Drake and Jacobs never actually met in Fresno. Their meeting came later, in Hollywood.

But, it was in Fresno that Jacob's lifelong relationship with Robert W. Morgan began. Jacobs still remembers their late night talks, the ones about one day working together in Hollywood. "Yeah," Morgan would say. "You could be the PD and I could be the morning man."

In the "93-KHJ Silver Anniversary Souvenir Scrapbook," Jacobs recounts what happened next. "I wasted a year in Hong Kong working on a pirate station that never signed on. This was followed by a month in the Halawa Jail for possession of three milligrams (3/1000) of marihuana." (Yes, spelled with an *h*. And, yes, it still throws his nose out of joint.) Within twenty-four hours of splitting the slammer, Jacobs was in LA connecting with Morgan, who'd just been hired by Bill Drake to do mornings at KHJ. Morgan told Jacobs that the station didn't have a Program Director yet.

What happened next deserves a book-sized narrative, but here's a condensed version: Willet Brown, the owner of KGB/San Diego, intervened on Jacob's behalf with Tom O'Neil, RKO's Chairman. The pot thing — remember it was 1965 — was getting in the way. Brown and O'Neil were friends and when he was asked for his advice, Brown said, "The guy can program your radio station. That's all that really matters. 'I say, give him a shot.' "

O'Neil did. The decision made, Jacobs signed on. One of the first things out of his mouth (again) was a comment about the call letters. KHJ carried too much baggage, he thought, and he wasn't even a *little bit* impressed that the letters stood for Kindness, Happiness and Joy.

During one of the many meetings before the new format launched, Jacobs told Drake and Chenault what he thought. He was animated that night, going a million miles an hour and Drake and Chenault were trying to keep up with him. "We've gotta get rid of these call letters," Jacobs told them.

Silence.

Drake and Chenault glanced at each other.

Then, very quietly, Drake said, "Ron, you can do almost anything you want. But, trust me, you'll never get RKO to change them. Ever."

That's close to how it happened.

On May 3, 1965, from studios at 5515 Melrose Avenue, KHJ/ Los Angeles debuted. Five months later, it was #1. "It was an awesome entertainment machine," says consultant Guy Zapolean.

"Everything was excellent: jocks, contesting, promotion and, especially, the seamless production."

Ron Jacobs' KHJ years were 1965 to 1969, and effectively ended with the release of "The History of Rock 'n 'Roll."

•

After leaving KHJ, Jacobs and Tom Rounds launched Watermark Productions, a Hollywood based company that produced short and long form programming for radio. Its biggest success, in 1970, was "American Top 40," which was quickly followed by "The Cruisin" Album Series (an industry insider favorite) and numerous other programs that were to become integral parts of American radio over the next ten years.

But, Jacobs was itchy, and in 1972 he joined KGB/San Diego.

KGB's format was a San Diego version of Boss Radio, a pale imitation of what he'd created at KHJ. It was the last thing he wanted to do. The whole trip, he thought, was so passé for the '70s. To explain his thinking and to present KGB's new format, he wrote and produced "The KGB Recycle," a half-hour plus journey through the evolution of rock 'n' roll that played on the station, repeatedly, for two days. (Listen at www.reelradio.com).

Once the new KGB was established, Jacobs introduced the "Homegrown" albums for charity, a concept he described as "amateurs performing their own songs." Another idea he hatched was the KGB (later known as the San Diego) Chicken.

In 1973, "Billboard" magazine named Jacobs Program Director of the Year and, a year later, the magazine named KGB Station of the Year.

•

After KGB, Ron Jacobs returned to Hawaii. At home again, he joined KKUA and went back on the air by launching "Whodaguy Ron Jacobs," a high-profile morning show that went out of its way to highlight Hawaiian music and artists.

In 1980, Jacobs tried his hand at country. He took over KDEO and called it "the western most country station in the nation."

During the rest of the decade Ron Jacobs followed his muse, writing for magazines (he was a contributing editor to both "Honolulu" and "Hawaii"), creating radio promotions ("The Hawaiian Chief," sponsored by American Airlines and Sheraton Hotels, which aired in forty-eight U.S. markets) and writing his first book, "Backdoor Waikiki," which was published in 1986.

In 1994, Jacobs returned to Los Angeles to work with Tom Rounds. Their goal this time was to create a countdown show for the entire planet — think "American Top 40" for the world. The result was "The World Chart Show."

By Christmas day, 1995, the program was heard on three hundred and sixty stations in fifty-four countries, with co-productions in twenty-seven different languages.

•

On July 7, 2007, from his jungle headquarters in Kaneohe, Oahu, Hawaii, Jacobs launched an internet radio station, www.WhodaguyHawaii.com. "It's not a gig or an ego trip," he told "The Star-Bulletin." "It's a labor of love, a mission, my final one."

In the mid '50s, when he was a teenager, Ron Jacobs couldn't wait to get off the island. Today, if what I hear is a true reflection of his feelings — and I think it is — it sounds like he'll never leave. (Fortunately, given technology's gifts, he doesn't have to.)

Robert W. Morgan once said, "Ron Jacobs is the best radio program director who ever lived." If you have a chance, listen to Ron's new work. I think you'll understand what Mr. Morgan meant.

(Ron Jacob's latest book is "Obamaland: Who Is Barack Obama?" The cover price is $19.59, which, if you don't know, is the year Hawaii became a state. Jacobs doesn't miss much.)

CHAPTER 26
TOM JOYNER: FLY JOCK

Most of us never get this call.

"Hello."

"Mr. Joyner? Stand by, please."

Thirty or forty seconds pass.

"Tom Joyner, is that you?"

He recognizes the drawl.

"Yes, sir."

A laugh rings down the line. "Well, you know, I may not be President anymore," says Bill Clinton, "but, I'm not dead. How ya doin?"

Put Clinton and Tom Joyner on the air together and they're magic. This wasn't lost on Clinton's handlers during the '90s, nor was it lost on the man himself — which is why he still calls. Clinton, in all fairness, might be interested in reaching Joyner's five million listeners. "The show is a match that lights the flame," says Joyner. "It's a responsibility I take seriously."

This man means what he says. His morning show is all about fun and entertainment, but Joyner knows what's important to his audience and from time to time, he's been compelled to raise his voice.

"I choose the battles I think we can win," he says.

•

He wasn't alone in his anger.

New York politician, Al Sharpton, brought the Katz memo to the press. (Katz was a national radio rep firm.) When Joyner read it, he saw red. There'd always been rumors about a non-urban dictate, but it was just talk, right?

Nope. "The memo proved it was real," say Joyner.

So, he took it to his listeners and they took it to the wall. Letters, faxes, calls. In fact, so many people called the Katz office in New York the phone system blew out. Katz was embarrassed. The memo recommended that advertisers and buyers not spend money on urban stations, because the format's listeners were suspects, not prospects. Joyner's advocacy campaign was on the air for less than a week when Katz finally called.

"I told them we expected an apology," says Joyner, "but that it wouldn't be enough." He said he wanted to know which advertisers had refused to buy black media, and he wanted Katz to pitch them again. Katz agreed. One of the companies, they said, was Dallas based CompUSA.

Joyner turned up the flame. Instead of phone calls, he asked listeners to send him their CompUSA receipts. "We boxed up about $700,000 worth, took them over and said, 'Look. This is what you're getting from African-American consumers.' " Then, Joyner looked into their corporate baby blues and said, "If you want to continue to get this money, you'll have to advertise with Black Media."

"It's not about black and white," he told them. "It's about green."

CompUSA got it, did what he suggested, and even gave a ten percent discount (on their next purchase) to everyone who'd sent a receipt.

Radio does work.

•

This hurts.

"I'd climb up on the amplifiers and jump," says Joyner.

He'd leap off the stage, land on his knees, and sliiiiiidddddde. "What I lacked in talent, I made up for in showmanship."

He was in a working band called The Commodores. Yes, *those* Commodores, as in *Brickhouse* and *Easy*. But, when he got his first radio job at WABT/Tuskegee, he left the group.

So, picture this: he slides on home and tells his folks he's going on the radio. "And my folks say, 'Right?!? Well, ok, that crazy group wasn't going anywhere, anyway.' "

Joyner's first full-time job was at WRMA/Montgomery. "I was a newsman, but when anybody got sick, I'd fill in and dee jay."

He says WRMA's afternoon jock had a fondness for the bottle. "I hate that I did this, but I used to get him whiskey just so I could go on the air." Joyner pauses, "He's fine now, went to AA. He 12-stepped."

From Montgomery, Joyner stepped up to WLOK/Memphis and from there it was north to KWK/St. Louis. That's where KKDA/ Dallas Station Manager Chuck Smith found him. "He flew me to Dallas to listen to the station," says Joyner. "The dee jays didn't sound like any I'd ever heard."

Smith offered him morning drive, but said he'd have to change his style. "All that rhyming and trash talking has to go."

"He wanted me just to talk to people, to one person," Joyner explains. "He coached me and changed my style."

So, everything was coming up roses, right? Well, no.

"It didn't work at first and I was about to be fired," says Joyner. "The Arbitron ratings were horrible, but when the Pulse rating results came out I'd done pretty well."

For the weeks in between, however, it had been touch and go. Joyner says the station had even hired his replacement, but he never started and Joyner kept his job at KKDA for the next five years.

"If you don't have stories like that," laughs Joyner, "you're really nothing in this business."

Mohammad Ali was another phone buddy.

"He didn't know me from nobody," says Joyner, "but he liked to talk, and I had him on the air all the time."

Bart McLendon, Gordon's son, thought an interview show with Ali might work in syndication. "You have this relationship with Ali," he told Joyner, "and if you work with him, we'll do these five minute vignettes." Joyner liked the idea, so he resigned from KKDA to pursue it. He says it might have been the greatest, except after only a few weeks, Ali decided it was too much work.

"But, I quit my job," Joyner protested.

"Come work with me," Ali replied. "You can be my personal PR man."

Joyner says the job was a joke. "How are you going to do PR for the world's greatest PR man?"

So, he crawled back to KKDA. "I think I stayed for a year and a half and then I went to Chicago," he says.

He worked for WVON, WBMX, WJPC, and WGCI – all in Chicago. "I did a lot of radio," he agrees. He says he even tried doing a TV show, but it didn't pan out.

So, in 1983, Joyner returned to KKDA. Again. "It was a two year deal," he says. "Then, in 1985, I started fly jockin.' "

•

It's still hard to believe. For eight years Joyner did the morning show at KKDA/Dallas and then flew to Chicago, to do afternoons at WGCI. Even harder to believe is that he was #1 in both cities at the same time.

"The plan was to work myself to death, then retire and do a weekend show."

He wanted to be like Casey Kasem. Instead, in 1994, he went nationwide in the morning for the ABC Radio Networks. Four years later, in 1998, Joyner created the Tom Joyner Foundation. In the years since, it's raised over fifty-five million dollars to provide financial assistance to students at historically black colleges and universities.

In 2005, a late night television spin-off, "The Tom Joyner Show," got great ratings among African-Americans but, when it proved difficult to push into prime time, Joyner pulled the plug. The same year he published a book, "I'm Just a DJ but ... It Makes Sense to Me."

Tom Joyner is a man of influence. The names of the awards he's won are too many to list, as would be a list of the people he's influenced. But, think about this: he reaches ten million ears every day. "First, we get people laughing. Then we get them to listen," he says. "If you can get people to listen, then they begin to think and that's when they start making a difference."

Whether you call him "Fly Jock" or "The Hardest Working Man in Radio," Tom Joyner is committed to making a difference.

CHAPTER 27
CASEY KASEM: AMERICA'S TOP COUNTDOWN HOST

He was working at KEWB/Oakland-San Francisco. It was 1962 and he was the night jock. His name was Casey Kasem and he was a "wild-tracker."

The show was scripted. It had to be for the engineer to keep up. He used audio drops — funny stuff, clips from movies, TV, records – anything he could get his hands on, and bounce off of. He was as fast as a brakeless cable car; so frenetic he drove one of his engineers to drink; yes, it's true. Some nights Kasem would get to work, look at old red-eyes and know he was in trouble. He'd been doing the show for about a year and a half when the General Manager asked to see him.

"Casey," said John McRae, "I'm changing things and I want you to stop wild-tracking."

Kasem stared. "What do you want me to do, John?"

"Be a regular disc jockey."

Kasem didn't need to be told that the other wild-trackers at the station had been fired. He needed some direction, though. "Talk about the artists, the music," said McRae. "And, by the way, start doing it tonight."

"I figured I'd do time, temperature and weather," he says, "and be out of a job the next morning."

He was thirty years old and thought his career was over.

•

Kamal "Casey" Kasem wanted to be a radio actor.

George Shapiro, the Radio Club's sponsor at Detroit's Northwestern High, was skeptical. "Do you have any idea what the average radio actor made last year?" he asked.

Kasem answered, "No."

"Fifty dollars," replied Shapiro.

Kasem was between high school and college. He'd done a sports show over the high school PA system — he still has the scripts, he says – but he wanted to do more radio. Even if it didn't pay.

"Shapiro recommended me to WDTR," says Kasem. "I became the chief sound effects man and did some drama, too."

In the early '50s, radio drama was still alive. "Detroit was the home of a few network shows," Kasem says. " 'The Lone Ranger' was on ABC and 'Challenge of the Yukon' was on Mutual. And they both had the same cast."

In 1950, because of a part he played on WJR/Detroit's "Scoop Ryan, Cub Reporter," a fifteen minute show presented by the Wayne State Radio Guild, Kasem was invited to audition for "The Lone Ranger." "I had the voice range to play anyone from twelve to twenty," he says.

When he got the part — his national debut — were his parents impressed?

"No," says Kasem, "They just expected me to be successful. But, I do remember my Grandmother saying, 'Maybe one day you'll be like Arthur Godfrey.' "

•

In 1952, Kasem was drafted and sent to Korea. Believe it or not, the Army actually gave him a broadcasting assignment. "There were nine radio stations," he says, "and I created a production team at headquarters to do comedy and drama."

Then destiny reared its head.

"There was a Saturday night Top 10 countdown show and they asked me to fill in," he explains. All was going well until he hit the #1 song, Les Paul and Mary Ford's *Vaya Con Dios*. "I said, 'here's the song that's #1 in America from coast to coast: 'Go Buy a Dose.' " (Casey assures me it was funnier than it reads.)

Out of the Army and back in Detroit, Kasem re-joined "The Lone Ranger" cast, went back to college, started acting — he did summer stock with George C. Scott — and dabbled on the air at WJLB and WJBK/Detroit. He says he really didn't want to be a disc jockey. "I just fell into it."

But, when he filled in on a popular night-time show and the ratings sky-rocketed, he stayed. Within three months, he was the #1 disc jockey in Detroit. What happened next may surprise you.

"I quit," says Kasem "I left at my peak and went to help my parents in their grocery business." The family needed help and so, he worked seventeen hours a day, seven days a week — stocking, packing, and mopping. "I did it for a year, but it paid off. We quadrupled business and I was able to go to New York to become the serious actor I was hoping to be."

It was June of 1958.

•

Today, Eugene Victor Walsk is a successful New York Producer, but back then he was just another Wayne State graduate starting his career. When Kasem arrived in New York some Army buddies threw him a welcoming party. Walsk was there.

"I've got to be able to audition," Kasem told him. "Do you know of anything?"

Walsk sent him to audition for the part of a "drunk, gay Russian" in the #1 off-Broadway play that season, "Ivan of."

"I did really well," Kasem remembers. "The guy I auditioned for was so impressed that he called others in to see me, and I did it again. I knew I was going to get that part."

But, he didn't. Thirty years later he discovered he lost out to Ed Asner. "I didn't get it, but I feel better now that I know I lost it to a guy who's won six Emmys," says Kasem.

Kasem took stock of his situation; he had no money, not even enough for a cup of coffee. "So, after six months, I put my tail between my legs and went home." When he says "home," he means Detroit. He could just as well have meant radio. He began looking for work. "I put feelers out and sent off some tapes," he says. "Milwaukee wanted me, but then the people at WJBK heard I was back in town."

WJBK was owned by Storer Broadcasting and its sister station in Cleveland, WJW, had just flipped to a pop format and wanted Kasem, too. "So, I went there because they also offered me the Cleveland Bandstand show."

It was in Cleveland that Kasem started wild-tracking and calling himself "Casey At the Mike." "I was looking for something to keep me on the edge of my seat," he says. "Wild-tracks were the answer." WJW was a pop station that played artists like Perry Como and The McGuire Sisters, but at night Kasem leaned heavily on rhythm and blues (just as Alan Freed had done on the same station less than a decade before).

Within three months he was #2 in Cleveland, right behind WHK, and this success took him to WBNY/Buffalo, but the job didn't last very long. "I was fired because I was insubordinate."

Then Chuck Blore entered his life.

Blore programmed KFWB/Los Angeles but he also had a corporate programming role with Crowell-Collier Broadcasting, the company preparing to buy WMGM/New York, where Blore intended to send Kasem. When the FCC killed the deal, Blore sent him to KEWB/Oakland-San Francisco instead.

It was there, in a trash can by the control room door, that Kasem found something that changed his life.

•

Farley McLuth was the janitor at KEWB and he was running late that night. Kasem, still shaken from the edict delivered by John McRae, was beside himself with worry. "There was a big trash barrel wedged in the door piled high with reams of news copy," recalls Kasem. "And, on top of it all was a magazine called 'Who's Who in Pop Music in 1962.' "

The magazine was full of thumbnail sketches — birthdays, first hits, favorite foods, etc. Kasem says that at that moment he knew he'd been saved. "I'd always teased upcoming records, but this was different, this was people, lives, feelings – storytelling."

That night he went on the air without his wild tracks. "Coming up," said Casey Kasem, "is the man who's had more #1 records than anyone else since the beginning of the rock 'n' roll era." Sound familiar?

"Ten seconds later and Farley might have moved that trash can," says Casey Kasem. "It was supposed to be there for me to see."

•

In May of 1963 Kasem went to work for KRLA/Pasadena-Los Angeles. Bill Drake's and Ron Jacobs' version of KHJ was two years away, so KRLA's only direct competition was KFWB. "Within three months, I was #1," says Kasem.

He did mid-days at KRLA, but his real goal was to use the station as a launching pad for voice-overs, TV, even movies. In late '63 KRLA had collaborated with LA's Channel 13 to do a local music show. "My job was to introduce two people who'd died – Johnny Horton and Sam Cooke," remembers Kasem. The script was rough, he says, so he asked if he could ad lib his part. "I did them both in one take," he says.

Several weeks later Kasem ran into Bob Lee, the producer of a new and still un-named Dick Clark Production (that would become "Shebang"). Lee told him he thought the work he'd done on Channel 13 was terrific. "We'd like you to come down and talk to us about hosting a new show we're putting into syndication."

The show never was syndicated nationally, although it did become a hit in Hollywood. "I did "Shebang" for two years. It went off, and then, by popular demand, it came back on," says Kasem. Six hundred and fifty episodes later, he was established on Los Angeles TV.

Did I mention his movies? Kasem chuckles as he recalls his first flick — Dennis Hopper's "The Glory Stompers."

"I played a bad guy, a motorcycle bandit," he says.

•

In 1967, at the insistence of his friend, record mogul Mike Curb, Kasem tried his hand at voice-overs. His first hit was as the voice of Robin in the "Batman and Robin" cartoon. "That was the beginning. Eventually I did several other features, including "Josey and The Pussycats" and letters and numbers (a segment) on "Sesame Street."

I don't have to tell you about "Scooby-Do," do I? In 1968 Kasem became the voice of Shaggy in the cartoon series. The role lasted for twenty-three years and Kasem says there's always talk it may come back.

In 1976 he was hired by NBC television, and over a period of five years, he recorded over twenty-five thousand promos for the network.

But still, and always, there's "American Top 40," a national institution. According to Ron Jacobs, AT 40 is the most listened-to program in the history of radio. "I can't imagine it having done so without Casey's energy and creative contributions," he says.

On January 4, 2004 Kasem turned hosting duties for "American Top 40" over to Ryan Seacrest, the host of "American Idol." As of this writing he continues to produce "American Top 20" and "American Top 10" for Premier Radio Networks.

•

In 1981, Casey Kasem was given his star on the Hollywood Walk of Fame. Eleven years later, in 1992, he became the youngest broadcaster in history to be inducted into the Radio Hall of Fame. Then, in 1997, "Billboard" magazine presented him with its first-ever Lifetime Achievement Award. Kasem is humble. Yes, he says, the awards do mean a lot but what's most important is the connection he's forged with his audience. "We've flown together," says Marty Raab, a Premier Radio VP, "and people stop him and say, 'Casey, I've listened to you all of my life.' Or, 'I remember a long distance dedication you did and the song you played.' "

The music, of course, is American Top 40's calling card, but — after four decades that have taken us from singer-songwriters to hip-hop divas — the show's only real constant has been Kasem and the stories he tells.

This weekend check out your local oldies station; that is, if you still have one. If you do and the stars are aligned, you'll hear AT 40 in a re-run from years gone by. Casey will be there counting down the hits. He'll have a story or two and, perhaps, a dedication. And, then, at the end of the show, you'll hear him say, "Keep your feet on the ground and keep reaching for the stars."

By the way, he was getting tired of wild-tracking.

(Over the Fourth of July weekend in 2009, thirty-nine years after rolling out his first "American Top 40" hit, Casey Kasem left the show he'd created. He said he had a "myriad of projects' to attend to.

To say goodbye to his long-time audience, he played *Thank You for Being My Friend*.)

CHAPTER 28

MURRAY "THE K" KAUFMAN: THE FIFTH BEATLE

New Yorkers, particularly those old enough to remember radio in the late '50s and early '60s, know all about Murray the K and his antics.

But, I'm not a New Yorker. If I were, I'd tell you there's a late night vibe to the city that can be scary if you don't get it, perfect when you do, and that Murray the K got it, and gave the night a vibe of his own.

Murray, despite what you may have heard, really wasn't a Top 40 disc jockey. The truth is he never would have put up with the formatics and restrictions. Murray had his own game and he played by his own rules. This means he played the records he wanted to play when *he* wanted to play them, and this was true whether he was on WINS/New York during the '50s or WOR-FM, one of the first FM rock stations, in the middle '60s. And, of course, you've heard he was called "The Fifth Beatle." Right?

•

Murray Kaufman was born in Manhattan, in 1922, to show biz parents. Vaudeville was the family's main source of income, but in the '30s, they ventured out to Hollywood and Murray, still a young boy, appeared in a few movies. When the war started after Pearl Harbor, Kaufman joined up, but instead of fighting for his country, he provided entertainment for the troops, a skill that came in handy when he returned home and began to book talent in the Catskills.

Booking turned into public relations, which led to song plugging. In 1953, it was Murray who brought Bob Merrill's song, *How Much Is That Doggie in the Window?* to Patti Page. It became Page's fourth #1 hit.

Kaufman's next step took him to radio.

He became the producer and co-host of WMCA's late night program, "Day With Night," which starred Laraine Day, the wife of New York Giant's Manager, Leo Durocher. Eventually Kaufman got his own show. While it was successful, it paled in comparison to what happened next.

In 1958, Kaufman moved to 10-10/WINS. His first assignment was the all-night show but, before long, he was moved to the seven to eleven shift, where he stayed for the next seven years. (If you talk to Cousin Brucie Morrow, who Kaufman replaced at WINS, you'll get a sense there was a little behind-the-scene's character assassination going on against Morrow. Kaufman's not here to defend himself but, it *was* New York and careers were at stake.)

It was from his night-time perch at WINS that Murray the K came to own New York City radio.

"This meeting of the Swingin' Soiree is now in session!"

•

His act was infectious. He was loud, fun and always playing to his teen audience. He'd say, "It's what's happening, baby!" and they'd believe him. He created his own on-air version of pig Latin — he called it Me-a-surray — and they understood it. Most of all, he let them know how much he loved the music and, for that, his audience loved him back and made his show #1 in New York.

The Beatles knocked on his door when they came to America in February, 1964, and on their first night in America Murray did his show from their Plaza Hotel suite. (Brian Epstein had been told that if they wanted to conquer New York, they needed Murray in their corner.) According to the story, the moniker, "The Fifth Beatle" came from a comment by either George Harrison or Ringo Starr. Someone was sucking up.

In 1964, a few months after returning from England, where he'd been visiting The Beatles on the set of their first movie, "A Hard

Day's Night," Murray discovered that Westinghouse Broadcasting, the owner of WINS, had decided to change the station's format. While the change wasn't scheduled to occur until April 1965, Murray went on the air in December of '64 and resigned publicly — letting the cat out of the bag and embarrassing the company. Only the extent of his popularity can explain why WINS management allowed him to stay on the air for two more months.

On February 27, 1965 Murray the K did his last show on WINS/New York. An era was over, but another was about to begin.

•

What Kaufman liked about FM was he didn't have to hype records to his listeners anymore. He said the music spoke for itself. In 1966, he became the Program Director of WOR-FM/New York, an RKO station, and the format he created was loose, varied and expressed a hip, counter-culture attitude. For a year, Murray's vision of WOR-FM is what the audience heard. Then, as sure as the sun was going to rise the next morning, the station's management tried to impose a playlist on him. Murray refused, resigned and promptly had a heart attack. (Shortly thereafter, Bill Drake, RKO's programming consultant, showed up and installed an oldies format on WOR-FM.)

Murray survived, but not in New York. First, he went to CHUM/Toronto, then it was down to WHFS/Washington and finally, in 1970, he returned to New York to take up duties on "Monitor" — NBC Radio's (network) weekend show.

From there, Murray had a short stint at WNBC/New York, where he did early evenings, preceding Wolfman Jack, but the show — both his and the Wolfman's — didn't really catch on, and Murray's last New York radio appearances were on WLIR/Long Island, in 1975, and on WKTU later the same year.

Murray the K did it all. Radio, Television, concerts and consulting. During the last years of his life he was a special advisor to the stage show "Beatlemania" and, from Hollywood, he hosted the syndicated radio show "Soundtrack of the '60s."

But, his health was failing.

Murray Kaufman died on February 21, 1982.

Fifteen years later he was inducted into the Radio Hall of Fame.

CHAPTER 29
ART LABOE: THE ORIGINAL

I typed my question. "Tell me about Art Laboe," and hit "send." The next day I had mail.

"The man virtually invented Oldies radio. He's a successful DJ-cum-entrepreneur, perhaps only second to Dick Clark." The reply was from Ron Jacobs, a broadcast legend and a man who fingers a devastatingly accurate keyboard. "Laboe did those pioneering remotes, started a record label, built one of the first Hollywood rock 'n' roll recording studios and was buying Los Angeles real estate when most jocks could barely afford rent."

Can you say "appreciation?" Jacobs, who's been around the block a few times, took delight in claiming that Laboe, his friend of forty-five years, started in radio about the same time as Marconi.

I think Jacobs just likes to stir things up.

•

Art Laboe didn't have his ham radio operator's license the night the FCC came pounding. "They had one of those cars with a loop," he remembers, "and I was bootlegging and got caught." The government slapped his hand, but that didn't discourage him and, by the time he was thirteen, he had the licenses he needed to be legal. Then came the war.

Laboe wasn't old enough to enlist but that didn't stop an Army recruiter from enrolling him in a radar engineering program. "You turn eighteen, kid, and we'll make it official."

He got a First Class Radio Telegraph license and it took him from Los Angeles Community College to Stanford, on the Army Signal Corps' dime. "I started on the engineer side," Laboe explains. He thought it was the best way to kick open a radio station's door and, once inside, he figured he'd go for his goal — getting on the air.

In 1943 Laboe marched into the offices of KSAN/San Francisco.

"I don't have a job," the manager told him. "Besides, you don't have the voice for it, you're too young and you need a license."

Laboe pulled his First Ticket out. "You mean this?"

The manager fell all over himself. "You're hired," he said.

"But, I thought...."

"Look, I need that license. I'm operating illegally."

It was a part-time job, but it was radio, even though he still had Army obligations. But, since signing up, Laboe had discovered that Signal Corps graduates had an eighty-five percent casualty rate. "I don't like this gig," he thought.

So, when he turned eighteen, he joined the Navy instead, and spent the rest of WWII flying cargo planes over the South Pacific.

•

The war was over and Laboe was back in Los Angeles. "The competition for radio jobs was tough," he says. "Big time network announcers came back looking for work and I couldn't get much going." Finally, for sixty dollars a week, he landed at KPMO/Pomona. Again, it was his license, not his on-air work that got him the job.

By 1949, Laboe was working in Los Angeles doing the all night show at KRKD. The pay wasn't much, so, to supplement his disc jockey salary he sold advertising time, which put him on the streets. "I bumped into this guy at an all-night drive-in called Scrivner's," Laboe says. "And he said, 'Why don't you do a show out here?' "

That got Laboe thinking. He knew doing a remote was technically possible and also knew LA was home to the aeronautics industry, with its swing swifts, which meant there was a market for shakes and burgers all hours of the day. Including the dead of night.

He came up with an ingenious idea for a show, one that didn't include having to beg a Program Director for a job. Instead, he bought the air time himself. He figured with the radio station's 10,000 watts he could draw a live audience to all three Scrivner drive-ins, and he was right. "At one point," Laboe says, "we were getting two hundred cars at a time."

He called himself "Art Laboe, Scrivner's Roving Disc Jockey," and he actually did rove in his car. "I'm passing Florence and Western," he'd say on the air. "And, while I'm traveling, here's Big Joe Turner!"

He began to get noticed.

In late 1954, Laboe left the drive-in show and moved to KFWB to do an interview program. "Lana Turner, Gary Cooper, folks like that," he says.

The next summer he headed back to the drive-in, ready to pull daytime duty and to introduce a new concept that would get his audience actively involved with his show. "I'd come up with an idea," he says. 'Come to the drive-in, pick a record and dedicate it.' " Dedications had never been done in LA and the show exploded! By the end of 1955 Laboe had a 33.0 Hooper ratings share in Los Angeles.

His playlist always included twenty or thirty current records, but he began to get requests for older tunes, which he began to refer as "oldies but goodies." Laboe doesn't claim he was the one who invented the phrase, but he does say, "Until then nobody'd done anything with it." Before long, it caught on and he owned it. "That drive-in is where the whole concept of oldies started," he says today.

In 1959, Laboe founded Original Sound Recording and released "Oldies But Goodies in Hi Fi." He only expected Los Angeles sales but, to his surprise, the record became a national best-seller. "Pretty soon, I had a big company on my hands." (The company is still going strong and still doing business from it's location at 7120 Sunset Blvd., Hollywood, CA.)

•

During the '60s Laboe focused his energy on Original Sound. (In 1966, Original's *Talk Talk* by the Music Machine went to #15 on the Billboard chart.) Then, in the early '70s, he joined

Wolfman Jack on XERB/Tijuana, a station which covered both Los Angeles and San Diego.

As his radio audience grew, so did his other businesses, including a nightclub he owned that specialized in playing oldies. One night, in 1972, Hal Rosenberg, the newly named GM of KRTH/Los Angeles, made a sales call on the club. "How'd you get all these people in here?" Rosenberg asked.

"They've come to see oldies but goodies," Laboe told him.

Rosenberg, says Laboe, was amazed and immediately changed his formatic plans for K-Earth. (The original plan for K-Earth had been progressive underground — earth, ground — get it?) But, according to Laboe, Rosenberg was so impressed by the club's draw and the demographic it represented, that he convinced RKO to go oldies.

Stranger things have happened.

•

Between 1975 and 1981, in a myriad of roles, Laboe guided the programming of KRLA/Los Angeles and still managed to grow his flourishing business — something he's still doing. In the middle '90s, he bought a group of radio stations in Tucson and, in the new century, sold them for seventeen million dollars, earning a significant profit.

There's a lesson here.

For more than sixty years Art Laboe has refused to let the vagaries of the radio business stop him. He used engineering to get in the door, and showmanship and salesmanship to get on the air. Most importantly, he never lost sight of the fact that *he* was the brand.

"Do just what I did," he says. "Get a sponsor."

Said another way: CONTROL YOUR DESTINY. It's good advice. Particularly now.

"At this point," Laboe says, "I just feel blessed."

Now you know why.

CHAPTER 30
LARRY LUJACK: THE JOCK OF CHICAGO

Larry Lujack is not a big city guy.

For the past twenty years, he's lived outside of Sante Fe in relative obscurity. Yes, occasionally he's gone back on the radio in Chicago – by remote control – but, mainly he likes the quiet of the desert. "I've never liked big cities," he says. "Lots of people, too many cars and those damn expressways."

Still, for the twenty years beginning in 1967, Lujack dominated rock 'n' roll radio in Chicago on WLS and at WCFL. No small potatoes for a guy who grew up in Idaho. "I've always loved wide-open spaces," he says. "But, with the career direction I took, I ended up spending most of my adult life living in places I hated."

Ah, c'mon Uncle Lar! Was it really that bad?

John Records Landecker, who was at WLS with Lujack, says he thinks Lujack was having a great time, but won't fess up to it. "I think he loved what he did for a living," Landecker says. "Nobody held a gun to his head to make him stay."

But, in 1987, Larry Lujack hung up his spurs. "On my last day at WLS, I walked out of the station and felt like a great weight had been lifted from my shoulders," he recalls. "I was thinking, 'This is great. I don't have to do this anymore.' "

Then he punched the car radio and heard Landecker putting callers on the air. "Honest to God, people were in tears about me retiring. By the time I got home, I felt guilty that I had somehow let these people down."

So, does this mean he had second thoughts?

"Not *that* guilty," says Lujack.

•

The Larry Lujack story could be a book. In fact, it is, although "Superjock" is long out of print. Aside from mentioning that he camped out in an Arizona motel room to force himself to write it, Lujack says, "Don't ask."

But, before there was someone to write about, there was an eighteen-year-old kid who did mornings at KCIL/Caldwell, Idaho — that is, when he made it to work on time. "You can't get drunk the night before and expect to get up at four the next morning," explains Lujack.

KCIL's General Manager, for whatever reason, didn't fire young Mr. Lujack. But, the writing was on the wall and Lujack quickly relocated to KRPL/Moscow (where there actually *was* writing on the wall). "Back then," explains Lujack, "lots of stations had big signs up in the control room that said SMILE, and everything that came out of your mouth had to sound friendly, upbeat and bright."

The thing is, Lujack didn't do upbeat and bright. "I'm sarcastic and cynical, and that got me in trouble in the early days," he says. Besides, he really wasn't *himself* yet. "There was a guy in Seattle, at KJR, named Dick Curtis and I thought he was just the coolest damn thing I'd ever heard on radio," Lujack says. He copied Curtis, but that still didn't stop KRPL from canning him for not sounding friendly enough.

Job? No. Plan? Yes.

"I went to Ogden's Radio School in Burbank to get a First Class Radio Operator's license and then, after a stint in the Air Force National Guard, I got a job at KGEM/Boise, Idaho. It was the capitol of the state, it was 10,000 watts and I thought 'Hot damn, I'm in the big city now.' "

Lujack stayed in Boise for eighteen months and then things started heating up when he was hired by KNEW (later KJRB), the Kaye-Smith station in Spokane, WA – the farm station for KJR/Seattle.

•

One night in Spokane Lujack got carried away on the air. "There was this Volkswagen dealer and I forget...uh...exactly what I did," he kinda confesses. "But, it was stupid."

Pat O'Day, who was Kaye-Smith's National PD, has more details. "Larry played a spot for a local VW dealer and followed it by saying, 'We love those German cars, don't we?' The response, from a recording made in Berlin during the war, was 'Seig Heil, Seig Heil.' " This, says O'Day, touched a nerve. "It turned out the VW dealer had been involved with the Gestapo and (while he) deeply regretted his involvement, he was very, very paranoid and thought it was a personal message from Larry to him."

Ouch! Not friendly enough. Pink slip. Again.

Lujack quickly turned up across town at KPEG playing "cowboy music." But, when KFXM/San Bernardino called he headed to California, living to regret it. "They fired all of us within four months. No kidding. It was one of those deals that used to happen — that still happens."

It was 1963. Lujack was twenty-three and out of a work again. "I said to myself, 'You're married, have one kid and another on the way, and you can't do this with the rest of your life.' "

•

He decided to go back to college, get a degree in forestry, and "to live happily ever after in the woods."

Just picture it: Larry Lujack – FOREST RANGER. "My parents thought radio was stupid," says Lujack, and they encouraged his college plans. "I was all set to do it," he says. "Then I heard about an opening at KJR/Seattle." Lujack insists he really *was* committed to a life in the great outdoors, but KJR, after all, "was as big time as you could possibly get."

So, he placed the call to Pat O'Day. "I told him my whole sad story," Lujack says, "about the U-haul trailers and getting fired and how I had decided, 'Screw it, I'm out of radio.' And O'Day said (and this just floored me), 'You wanna get back in?' "

In 1964, Larry Lujack went to KJR, a move O'Day says "seemed to leave the impression that the way to get to Seattle on a fast track in our company was to piss off an advertiser."

He stayed at KJR for two and a half years. Once there, he had to re-work his on air approach because Dick Curtis, who Lujack had worshipped *and* copied, worked at KJR, too. "I came to the realization that it was far easier to just be myself on the air." To this day, Lujack believes KJR was the best sounding Top 40 station in the country. But, KJR couldn't pay him what WMEX in Boston could, and KJR wasn't offering him afternoon drive, so he resigned and prepared for a long haul to the east coast. But, he hated Boston, hated WMEX; in fact, he hated everything about it.

Fortunately, after only four months Ken Draper, PD of WCFL, called him about coming to Chicago. Then, after only four more months, ABC called him with an offer to join them to do afternoon drive. Yes, the offer often included more money. "So, when I was twenty-seven I went to WLS," Lujack says.

"It was the age of the super-boss jock," says Scotty Brink, who was at WLS with Lujack. "We were fast paced and tightly produced. But, Larry – well, Larry pretty much abandoned all that stuff. He was sloppy in a lot of ways and, as a result, really stood out."

Lujack says Brink's observation is very "perceptive." He also confirms that kicking trash cans on the air wasn't out of the question.

•

It's a jock meeting at WLS, where the important stuff was "getting said" for Chicago. Gene Taylor's the manager and he's conducting the meeting. Young Mr. Lujack is sitting in a room full of rock radio legends, including Art Roberts, Clark Weber and Ron Riley.

Taylor calls the meeting to order. "Larry's doing it the way I'd like the radio station to sound," he says. He pauses. "I'd like the rest of you to listen and get closer to that sound."

It was at WLS that Lujack started "The Crank Letter of the Day," which evolved into "The Clunk Letter of the Day." "I changed the name because a lot of the letters were really stupid," says Lujack.

Stupid? Perhaps. Funny? You betcha. David Letterman, a student at Ball University, used to get up early to listen. So did a kid from Kansas City named Rush Limbaugh.

•

In 1971, Larry Lujack called John Rook the greatest program director of his generation.

The feeling, says Rook, was mutual and when Rook returned to Chicago the next year to consult WCFL, Lujack got a call and an offer. "I had it so good at WLS that I was a little leery about leaving, so I threw them what I thought, at the time, was an outrageous proposal. It was basically a five-year no-cut deal for $100,000 a year" (about $400,000 a year in today's dollars.) Lujack acknowledges that radio salaries have grown since then. "Some of the contracts I read about today amaze me," he says. "But, for that time, I don't think anything like that existed."

In 1972, Lujack returned to WCFL and stayed for four years. "Initially it worked out great," he explains. "We beat WLS, and that had never been done." But, it's hard to fight the fight and three years into his deal – for reasons not entirely clear — WCFL gave up and changed formats. One day the station was Top 40, the next it was beautiful music. Lujack, however, had a no-cut deal and a stroke of luck, because Marty Greenberg, the General Manager of WLS, came to his aid.

"WCFL had changed formats and Larry was required to announce beautiful music," says Greenberg, adding he sensed there might be an opportunity to get Lujack back to WLS. What happened next was unprecedented. "I called Lew Witz to ask for permission to talk to Larry, and Lew said to me, 'Marty, not only will I let you talk to him, but I'll pay for part of it.' "

As unlikely as it sounds, a deal was structured that brought Lujack back to WLS with half his salary, covering the remaining term of his contract, paid by WCFL.

Greenberg remembers ABC's legal department couldn't believe that two competing stations had negotiated that kind of deal.

•

Lujack would arrive at work between three and four in the morning.

He'd smoke one hundred cigarettes, down a gallon of coffee, do his four hours, take a walk and then come back and listen to an aircheck of the show. "This is a guy who worked very hard at what he did," says Greenberg.

"He came in early because he was cheap and wanted to park on Lower Wacker," jokes John Gehron. Gehron, at Oprah Winfrey's Harpo Productions until late 2008, was the Program Director of WLS when Lujack returned. "WLS was a very unique radio station," he adds. "I always tried to make sure the format didn't get in the way of what the talent did best."

Gehron says this hands-off approach allowed Lujack to be who he was – "cynical, creative, and loose. Larry's punch lines," Gehron observes, "came out of left field and were generally something that hadn't occurred to you."

That brings us to "Animal Stories" and the notorious anteater tale. "Anteater tongues are incredibly fast," says Lujack. "So, one day, off the top of my head, I made this comment: 'I'll bet a lot of housewives would like to have an anteater around.' "

Tommy Edwards, Lujack's sidekick, cracked up. When he started laughing Lujack says he realized that what Edwards was thinking wasn't what he'd intended. "Then it suddenly occurred to me what he was laughing about, and I just burst into hysterical laughter and started falling on the floor."

Larry Lujack, Superjock, has appeared on Chicago radio sporadically over the past ten years. First, at WUBT and, most recently, with Tommy Edwards on WRRL-Real Oldies 1690. Wherever and whenever he shows, his fans find him. It's because he's part of the fabric of their lives.

Listeners recall Lujack opening the mic and saying, "We'll be doing a show in Fargo, North Dakota Saturday night and, if Larry Lujack can fly across the frozen tundra to go there, you clowns in Fargo better turn out to see me."

"I was on the air what I was off the air," says Lujack, "and I think listeners can sense that."

"He can take people right down to what they *really* think and feel and *not* offend them," says Pat O'Day. "He's a magician!"

A member of the Illinois Broadcast Hall of Fame, since 2002, Larry Lujack was inducted into the NAB's Hall of Fame on April 15, 2008. In preparation for the ceremony, Lujack had this to say to his old friend, John Rook: "Gheez, had I known it was this big of a deal, I would have put a little more effort into my show."

CHAPTER 31
BILL MACK: THE SATELLITE COWBOY

The truck was weaving in and out of its lane.

The driver wasn't drunk, he'd had a heart attack. "When they finally got to him he was already dead," says Bill Mack. Even after thirty years at WBAP/Ft. Worth, and even after talking to millions of late-night listeners, this isn't an easy subject for Mack. "When they opened his cab, they said my radio show was going full blast. I've often wondered what I said that night. You know, in the middle of the night there's so much loneliness."

It was the summer of 2001 and Mack had just been hired by XM Satellite Radio. "We'll be doing my show from our studio in Ft. Worth. I'll feed it to Washington and they'll shoot it to the moon."

It's a long way from Shamrock, Texas to the moon.

•

The manager of KEVA/Shamrock, Texas was the owner's son-in-law, and Mack should have known that would be a problem. But, it was his first job. He did a few livestock reports; mostly he vacuumed the control room, where a picture of the owner's mother stared down at him. He did this for eight months and then the son-of-a …the *son-in-law* fired him. He auditioned for a job at KLYN/Amarillo and was hired, but says, "I wasn't very good, so I worked news until they finally let me do a DJ show."

Compared to Shamrock, Amarillo felt as big as New York City and he says it took some getting used to. The same was true about the music. "I didn't really care for country music," he says. "I was a big fan of Perry Como and The Mills Brothers. But, then I heard Hank Williams sing *Mansion On The Hill*."

That's when things changed. Or, maybe it was that phone call in the night. "Hank called me," Mack says. "He said he'd been in his car for over thirty minutes and hadn't heard a Hank Williams song yet."

He swears Hank wasn't joking. "He was serious."

Mack stayed in Amarillo until the end of 1952. "Then I was offered a job at KWFT/Wichita Falls and it was really my big springboard, my university," he says. KWFT was 5,000 watts of country at 620, and it was there, with total freedom, that Mack began to spread his wings. "They let me play whatever I wanted," he says. "And, they allowed me to book shows, and didn't ask for a dime. It was there that I met Elvis for the first time.

On August 22, 1956, Mack booked Elvis Presley and Johnny Horton (*North to Alaska, Battle of New Orleans*) into Spudder Park. "Elvis was third billing, so he opened the show," explains Mack. "When we brought Horton on, they were still screaming for Elvis." Presley was scared, he says. "I'll never forget the way he looked that night." He also remembers that, after the show, Presley went directly to the hospital to meet Mack's new baby, a daughter who'd been born the day before.

Sweet memories.

•

In 1959, after six years in Wichita Falls, Mack went to work for KDAV/Lubbock and, as part of the deal the station threw in a rental house. On the day he was moving in, Mack remembers a tall man appeared at the door. "He said, 'I live one door down and I heard on KDAV that you were coming, so I wanted to welcome you.' "

Mack says he nodded and said thank you. "Excuse me, sir, what's your name again?"

"Holley," the man responded. "L. O. Holley."

A few weeks later a bulletin sounded on the teletype machine. It was February 3, 1959. "Wes Youngblood ripped the copy off the wire, turned off the alarm, ran into the room and handed it to me," says Mack. Without thinking or even looking at the words, Mack opened his microphone and began. "Richie Valens, The Big

Bopper and Buddy Holly were killed today in a plane crash out in the midwest."

He remembers that he began to shake and that it got worse quickly, when Youngblood ran back into the studio and told him that Mrs. Holley, Buddy's mother, was on the phone. "She was ironing," said Youngblood, "and heard you on the radio."

Mack says he froze and couldn't pick up the phone. "You can imagine how I felt," he says. Instead, he ran out of the station, jumped in his car and drove straight to the Holley's home, where the press was already circling.

"I walked in and Mr. Holley came up, put his arm around my shoulder, and said, 'Bill, I know this had to be tough on you.' "

They weren't angry," remembers Mack. But, they were hurt.

"I'll never forget it," he says.

Ya think?

•

It was late 1962, maybe early '63 and Bill Mack was working for a radio station in San Antonio. On that particular evening he was backstage with Patsy Cline, and she was in a mood.

"Let me hear it," she said, "I don't have much time."

"I borrowed Roger Miller's guitar," says Mack, "and I sang *Blue* to her." He knew, even as he was singing, that it wasn't a CMA-quality performance, but, at least, she was listening. When he finished, all Patsy said was, "Send the damn thing to me."

And that was that — except that it wasn't.

On March 5, 1963 Patsy Cline died in a plane crash. She never recorded *Blue*, and Bill Mack, who was spooked by the whole thing, put the song away and didn't think about it again for almost thirty years.

WBAP stands for We Bring a Program. Named in the '20s by President Herbert Hoover, the station's been around almost as long as country music, but it had little truck with country until Mack arrived.

It was Saturday night, March 2, 1969, three days short of the anniversary of Patsy's death. Mack played his first tune just after midnight. "I got this phone call, one of the first," he remembers, "and this guy says, 'I'm listening to you here in Minnesota and it sounds like we got us a Midnight Cowboy.' "

Mack says he hadn't planned to do a trucker's show, "but they kinda adopted me."

Almost overnight, the show earned a national audience. But, in the 'ear'-conditioned halls of WBAP, Mack says he went over "like a pregnant pole-vaulter. The old heads of state at 'BAP didn't like this hillbilly coming in and messing up their Sinatra music," he says. Regardless, WBAP was his home for a dozen years, until 1981. "We had a Program Director who didn't like me. When I disagreed with him, they axed me."

But, PDs come and go and, after a three-year separation, WBAP asked for reconciliation. In 1984, Mack returned, opened his mic, and casually said, "Well, as I was saying…"

•

He almost blew the meeting off, but his wife insisted he go. He brought two songs on cassette. One was *Blue*.

"Wilbur Rimes, LeAnn's dad, thought *Blue* was too old for her," Mack says. "But, when LeAnn heard it, she begged him to let her do it."

You know what happened, don't you? LeAnn Rimes recorded *Blue* in August of 1994.

"If Patsy Cline had recorded that record," says country legend George Jones, "I'm sure it'd been good. But, it's hard to tell if she would have outsold LeAnn."

And how does George Jones feel about Bill Mack?

"I've always loved Bill like a brother," Jones laughs. "And if he'd been a girl, I'd have probably married him."

Bill Mack was inducted into the Country Radio Hall of Fame in 1982 and the Texas Country Music Hall of Fame in 1999. Now that his show is on Sirius/XM Satellite, he's called "The Satellite Cowboy."

CHAPTER 32
GORDON MCLENDON: THE PROMOTION MAN

There is a romantic notion that Top 40 radio was born because local radio owners, particularly young men, loved rock 'n' roll. Don't kid yourself. The format was born because these owners wanted – no — *needed* to make money. That rock 'n' roll was inventing itself at the same time was a serendipitous coincidence.

According to legend, the idea of Top 40 was born in an Omaha bar when Todd Storz and Bill Stewart, the owner and the programmer of KOWH Radio, noticed a waitress playing the same song over and over on the jukebox. It may have been cocktail think, but after several hours the men concluded that the same thing – that is, repetition of records — might work on the radio. (While probably anecdotal, those who knew the two men insist the story is true.)

Regardless, the concept came and conquered, and before the old-line media moguls even noticed, Top 40 was pervasive and on the air everywhere. One of the men most responsible for this turn of events was a Texan named Gordon McLendon.

•

McLendon's flagship was KLIF in Dallas, a station he'd bought in 1947. It was there, on the strength of his sports know-how and imagination, that he launched The Liberty Broadcasting System.

In the late '40s broadcast rights for team sports weren't any cheaper than they are today, but this didn't concern or stymie McLendon because, frankly, he had no intention of broadcasting the games live, or paying for the privilege. His plan was to re-create the games using wire copy and sound effects. For some reason, team owners let him get away with it.

Sure, some of his play-by-play was made up, but it worked in his favor because, if the real games got boring, he could call a foul that never happened or talk about a pretty girl that had never walked by.

"What harm is there in making a hundred thousand people happy on a hot summer afternoon?" he asked.

McLendon launched his network in the spring of 1948. From the beginning, he understood that the key to attracting an audience was to be different — to attract attention. So, among other things, he trained a parrot to chirp the call letters and instructed his music director, a young man named Tom Merriman, to produce jingles for KLIF; singers sang the call letters, at a time when Dallas, the city that would become the radio jingle capital of the world, didn't know from jingles.

But, by 1952, baseball's owners had had enough of his audio hi-jinx and, despite all the sponsors he had, or the number of fans he'd attracted to the game, pro baseball pulled the plug.

On May 15, 1952, The Liberty Broadcasting System — the second largest radio network in the nation – went under, and Gordon McLendon, who'd become one of the most respected play-by-play men in the country, never pursued sportscasting again.

But, that didn't mean he didn't want to play.

•

In 1953, two years after Ike Turner recorded *Rocket 88* for Sam Phillips at Sun Records (the record was credited to Jackie Brenston and his Delta Cats), and a year before Elvis entered the same building, McLendon heard about the formatic experiments being conducted by Storz in Omaha and decided Top 40 might be a home run.

At the time, KLIF still had some block programming on the air — shows like "Lullaby in Rhythm" and "Hillbilly Roundup" — but McLendon was ready to rock. One of the first things he did was hire Bill Stewart away from the Storz organization. Stewart arrived in early 1954, took it all in, and promptly cut the playlist. "We're only going to play forty records," he said.

Within ninety days, KLIF was the #1 radio station in Dallas. At first, the gains were attributed to the music. After all, Alan Freed had already demonstrated that rock 'n' roll was a drawing card. But, closer inspection proved that McLendon and Stewart's genius was about what went *between* the records. "Storz may have been responsible for figuring out the music component, but it was Gordon who came up with the promotions and marketing that made the Top 40 format fly," says Ken Dowe, McLendon Broadcasting's first Executive VP.

By today's standards, some of the promotions appear a bit careless. For example, KLIF disc jockeys threw hundred-dollar bills from buildings and caused riots. Another promotion, "The School Spirit Campaign" (the school with the most signatures got a record hop hosted by one of the KLIF DJs), paralyzed the entire Dallas school system because the kids did nothing but collect names. The Superintendent of Schools begged KLIF to stop.

Then, to top himself, McLendon wrote a check for $50,000. The check was placed inside a bottle and hidden, as the on-air promos stated, "somewhere" in Dallas. McLendon called the contest "The Great Treasure Hunt." Teenagers went wild. Lawns and gardens were torn up, laid to waste. Good citizens – probably not KLIF listeners – didn't see the humor in it, and complained to the FCC. But, McLendon laughed it off, explaining that legal problems were why he had lawyers. Besides, he said, the contest created great publicity for the station. And, yes, someone found the bottle and cashed the check.

In 1957, as McLendon bought more stations, he sent Don Keyes, the chain's first National Program Director, to Houston to launch KILT. To draw attention to the station the two men decided to run "The Great Treasure Hunt" contest again. Promotional announcements hit the air and, as in Dallas, teenagers hit the streets. Then it all went wrong. "In the excitement of the contest," said Keyes, "one of the treasure hunters fell off an eyebeam at a construction site and was killed."

The next day the story was plastered all over the Houston papers. Representatives from the Blair Advertising Rep firm, in town to acquaint themselves with KILT, and wise to McLendon's shenanigans, thought it was just another one of his gimmicks. Sadly, it wasn't. According to Ken Dowe, McLendon's contesting led to the FCC writing more specific rules about radio promotions.

•

Gordon McLendon loved to do things that had never been done. In San Francisco, he invented Easy Listening for KABL; in Los Angeles, he created the first All News Station on XETRA. And, once, he put a station on the air that only ran commercials.

In 1971, McLendon sold KLIF to the Fairchild Corporation for ten million dollars. At the time, it was the largest amount of money ever paid for an AM radio station. At the last minute, over coffee, McLendon offered to throw in KNUS-FM for an additional $150,000, but Fairchild executives declined, saying they'd stick with the AM cash cow. Left with a stand-alone Dallas FM, which had not been mentioned in the no-compete clauses, McLendon slyly decided to take on KLIF. Fifteen months later KNUS-FM was the #1 radio station in Dallas.

McLendon was never a hands-off owner. On November 22, 1963, while the city and nation waited to hear John F. Kennedy's fate, it was McLendon himself who reported from outside Parkland Hospital. In a faltering voice, full of disbelief, he spoke simply. "The President…" he began. "President Kennedy … is dead."

•

My guess is that McLendon would be torn about the state of broadcasting today. Always a maverick, he probably would have applauded the deregulation and consolidation of the industry. After all, this was a man who offered to buy Armed Forces Radio from the government.

But, on the other hand, I suspect he'd be troubled by the relaxing of standards (think obscenity and lack of commitment to community) and the exodus (read as *firings*) of on-air talent in the name of cost cutting. "Keep your eyes on the programming," he used to say. "And, the sales will follow."

On September 14, 1986, Gordon McLendon died at his ranch outside of Dallas. Eight years later he was inducted into the Radio Hall of Fame. Today, his influence can still be heard on every contemporary radio station in the world.

CHAPTER 33

JOHN MCRAE: MAKING WAVES
WITH FORMULA 63

(This story was written a few weeks before Christmas, 2001. It was a fortnight after Beatle George Harrison died, shortly after I'd done a piece on Casey Kasem, and is about a man I never met.)

It's been a tough few days.

A week ago I received an e-mail from John McRae, a seventy-five year old man I didn't know or know anything about. Mr. McRae wrote that he'd been the General Manager of KEWB/Oakland-San Francisco in the early '60s and thought my characterization of his relationship with Casey Kasem was misleading. "I haven't seen the item in your publication," he wrote, "but, while it's nice to have someone remember my name, it apparently tends to report me as a hard-nosed individual who told Casey Kasem, about forty years ago, to knock off the wild tracks and do as I recommended."

The long and short of it is this: Mr. McRae said he'd never had the conversation with Kasem, that it wasn't the way things were handled at Crowell-Collier Broadcasting, and that I had the story wrong. So, I called him.

It was Thursday, November 29, 2001.

McRae and I talked for over ninety minutes, and he regaled me with tales of keeping disc jockeys out of jail and radio promotions we wouldn't dare try to do today. I found what he had to say interesting, funny and, yes, even insightful, and so I decided to write about him.

I had planned to write these words: "No, John McRae isn't a legend in the way that, say, Casey Kasem is, or Robert W. Morgan and The Real Don Steele were. But, he was there, rubbed elbows with the best of them, greased the way for some, and remembers when radio was like a hormone-raging adolescent – aching to grow up, squawking for attention, and trying to keep it fun."

Now I have to write in the past tense. You see, John McRae died in a plane crash last Sunday night. Just about the time I'd stopped thinking about George Harrison.

•

"I was seventeen and a half and went straight out of high school into the Canadian Air Force," McRae began.

In 1943 the Southeast Asian Command operated out of India and Burma, east of Afghanistan, in the same geographical region as Bangladesh. By the time he was eighteen, McRae was a Squadron Gunnery Leader, a commissioned officer who flew in B-24 Liberators, the four engine plane that was the bomber of choice during World War II.

McRae's interest in radio had begun before the war. "I don't know whether I should tell you this," he laughed. "One day my next door neighbor — an engineer at the local radio station – asked me if I knew anything about Shakespeare." It seems the station had a big jackpot but was having trouble giving it away. "You going to be home tonight at seven?" the engineer asked. "Who knows, we might call you."

"They called and asked me the question, and damned if I didn't know the answer," McRae recalled. The jackpot was $31 – worth about $300 today. "It was more money than I'd ever seen in one place at one time," said McRae.

Flush with his winnings, he went to the station to hang out and, before long, he was working sixty-hour weeks playing sixteen inch ETs — electrical transcriptions — and some 78s. But, he wasn't a disc jockey, he insisted. "There was no such thing back then. The term *disc jockey* didn't come around until the time of Martin Block."

Then the war came. When it ended, the twenty-year old McRae returned to Winnipeg, where he admits his target was mostly nightclubs and women, at least until he ran out of money.

•

McRae was ambitious, seasoned by combat, and eager to get on with his life. In 1946 he found work as a producer at CKRC/ Winnipeg and by the end of the '40s he'd moved onto The Canadian Broadcasting Corporation as a staff announcer. "Lorne Greene (Ben Cartwright on Bonanza) was doing news out of Toronto when I was doing it out of Winnipeg," McRae told me.

From Winnipeg, he headed south to KFTM/Fort Morgan, Colorado, gave up announcing, took up sales, and eventually became Station Manager. Next, he went to Denver, then it was off to KOBY/San Francisco to run the West Coast's first rock 'n' roll station.

Then, in 1959, McRae got a call from the President of Crowell-Collier Radio, Bud Purcell. "Come to Minneapolis," invited Purcell.

"They had KFWB, without question the number one rock station in the United States," McRae explained.

In other words, he couldn't say no.

•

The promotion was a Chuck Blore idea.

The commercials started before sunrise. Morning men all over the Twin Cities joked about the copy and offered unsolicited testimonials. "I've tried Formula 63 and it really works."

"But, nobody knew what Formula 63 was," recalled McRae. Not yet. Blore hired Cajun politician and entrepreneur, Dudley J. "Couzin Dud" LeBlanc, the inventor and sometimes spokesperson for a product called Hadacol, to voice the spots. "Hadacol was ninety percent booze," says McRae. "Anybody who took a couple swallows of it was feeling good."

Crowell-Collier bought time on every radio station in Minneapolis. "This is Dudley LeBlanc," the spot began. "And I'm here to tell you about Formula 63. It'll wake you up, put a smile on your face and make you feel good. If you'd like a free sample, go to your local drug store."

"We had Formula 63 on the outside of this little box," said McRae. "And inside was an invitation to a free rock and roll concert that night in Minneapolis."

As the sun rose, radio station managers driving into work started to catch on. Not only were their morning men talking about it, but virtually every available billboard in town was advertising it. Formula 63, to their surprise, was a new radio station, KDWB.

Some of the managers went ballistic, and lawsuits flew; remember, in 1959, some radio stations still refused to even take advertising from television. Others saw the humor in it, liked the money, and kept running the spots. As for KDWB; well, its ratings went through the roof.

But, don't try this today. The government would frown.

•

In 1961, McRae returned to San Francisco to manage KEWB. At various times during his tenure the staff included Casey Kasem, Robert W. Morgan, Bobby Dale and the Real Don Steele.

"In '63 or '64, Don was up for DJ of the year," McRae told me.

It was ten in the morning. Steele and his lady friend, Gracie, were getting seated on a plane bound for Vegas. "Don had had a few toddies," McRae explained, "and they were discussing a new record Gracie thought was going to be a hit. Steele thought it was a stiff.

"It's a bomb," Steele said loudly. "It's a bomb!"

A little old lady across the aisle heard the word, bomb, and freaked.

The plane pulled back to the gate. Security and the FBI arrived.

"Don provided a wealth of opportunities for me to keep him out of jail," said McRae. "I forget what time they called me that night to confirm that, yeah, The Real Don Steele was a disc jockey."

•

In 1965 McRae left KEWB and headed to Sacramento to manage KRAK and eventually move into ownership. Twenty years later, he cashed in his chips and applied his wealth of knowledge towards bass fishing. "I never really *re*-tired," he laughed, "because I was never tired."

That's all I know about John McRae.

I never met him, didn't know what he looked like until I got his picture two days after he died, and I never even shook his hand. But three days before he died I heard his laugh, and I'd like to think that counts for something.

Rest in peace, new friend. Be sure to say hello to Robert W. and Don.

And if you see George…well, you know.

Chapter 34
Ruth Meyer: The First Lady

In the Middle East, a woman can get arrested for being in a car with a man who's not her husband. In the United States, during the '50s, a woman who wanted to program a radio station couldn't get arrested at all. There was, however, an exception. Her name is Ruth Meyer.

Ruth Meyer was raised in Kansas City where she dreamed of growing up and writing for newspapers. After graduating from Kansas City Junior College, she hit the pavement and started knocking on newspaper doors, but was told there were no jobs for those without experience. Her mother had given her sixty days to find a job or to enroll in secretarial school, so, in desperation, she started calling local radio stations looking for a job writing commercials.

Lady Luck intervened. KCKN, a 250 watt AM station, gave her a job as a continuity writer, but the station was so under-staffed that she was also allowed to pick the music.

Todd Storz was still in his twenties, but was already well known in the radio business for his role in inventing Top 40. When he arrived in Kansas City to run WHB, a station he'd just bought, he heard about Meyer and offered her a job. "There weren't any women in radio back then," she says, "but that didn't seem to bother Todd."

Storz taught Meyer the basics of Top 40, a tutelage that in many ways was like being given the keys to the kingdom. "He made radio so exciting to me that I never wanted to do anything else," she says.

•

In 1958, at the urging of disc jockey, Peter Tripp, Meyer arrived in New York City to take the programming reigns of WMGM. At the time, the station was playing rock 'n' roll, but its heavy commitment to sports – WMGM was the radio home of the Yankees – left it vulnerable to stations that played more music.

Meyer tried to make changes, but was met with opposition and, after three months at WMGM, she quit. "The station's management wasn't able to grasp the fundamentals of Top 40," she says. Since Meyer was one of a handful of broadcasters in the country who actually understood Top 40 and the environment it needed to succeed, the statement speaks volumes.

Across town, WMCA had a new General Manager, Steve Labunski. Labunski was not only a former Storz employee, but he'd also worked with Ruth in Kansas City, so he was aware of what she could do. But, when Labunski hired Meyer to program WMCA he didn't name her Program Director. "In *those* days a woman didn't get the title," Meyer says. Instead, she was named Production Director, but she did everything a Program Director does.

Today, she laughs about it and insists that she isn't bitter. But, she admits that had she been a man, she would have gotten a lot further. "Everyone used to ask, 'Who's really programming the station?' They just didn't believe a woman could be doing it.

I just wanted to do the stuff that I heard in my imagination," says Meyer. "I didn't think of myself as a woman Program Director, just a Programmer."

•

Meyer was at her desk when the phone rang.

On the line was Bob Sharon, a friend from Kansas City. Sharon told her that Chuck Blore, the Program Director of KFWB/Los Angeles, was using a promotional line on the air she should know about. "He's calling the KFWB air staff 'The Good Guys,' but, he's really not doing much with it."

"I got excited and wanted to use the phrase on WMCA, but my boss thought it was a dumb idea," says Meyer.

Then, WABC started calling *their* DJs 'The Good Guys.' Like Blore, ABC was only playing with the idea and didn't seem committed; for Meyer, it was the straw that broke the camel's back. Despite

Labunski's objections, she began to build a team around the name.

At first, the men at WMCA didn't take Miss Meyer seriously. "The talent thought of me as a 'Dotty Dippy' and humored me by doing what I told them to do," she says. One of the things she told them was that they didn't have to like each other, they just had to behave as if they did. Despite their skepticism, the WMCA Good Guys — among them Joe O'Brien, Harry Harrison, Jack Spector, Dan Daniel, B. Mitchell Reed, Johnny Dark and Gary Stevens — played along and found out that being a team worked. (In 1965, Gary Stevens replaced B. Mitchell Reed.)

Stevens, now a successful broker, says Meyer was ahead of her time. "In retrospect, I believe her appointment to PD was a function of management's disdain for the programming function and its desire to assert control over what it figured would be a weak leader. They were to be disappointed on both counts."

As strange as it may sound today, 'The Good Guys' styled their hair alike, dressed alike (in their Good Guy sweatshirts) and even showed up together, at record hops, personal appearances, wherever the station sent them. Ruth even wrote a song about them called *We're The Good Guys*.

•

WABC had a signal that could be heard as far as Philadelphia, but in New York, it was WMCA that was the real deal, and it showed in the ratings for years. Meyer, however, never sought the limelight. "I wanted the jocks to be the stars," she says.

How about recognition from her peers, or from the radio press of the day? "None, whatsoever," she answers. "But, I didn't need a lot of adulation. I got my kicks from watching it all happen."

•

After ten years at WMCA, Meyer decided to leave. It was 1968 and time for something new. For the next five years, from her base in New York, she consulted. Her clients included Radio Luxembourg and Radio Caroline; each defined radio for England and Western

Europe during the late '60s and early '70s.

Then, in 1973, she took on a new challenge working for WMGM/ New York. WMGM had dropped Top 40 in 1962 and started playing a middle-of-the-road format: Sinatra, Ella and, by the early '70s, most likely, The Carpenters. In 1973, station management decided to change the format to country, a decision Meyer didn't agree with. "I didn't like country," she explains. "In fact, when I found out, I quit."

But, as she was working out her notice, she heard someone in the sales department say, "Country will never work in New York," and that raised her competitive hackles. She changed her mind about leaving and took on the challenge of creating New York's first full time country station.

The call letters were changed to WHN. "You started to hear it in cabs," says Steve Warren, the station's Music Director. "Then, when we started to bring artists in to do concerts, the advertising community became aware of us."

As she'd done at WMCA, Meyer stayed behind the scenes to build her team. "Ruth was never an attention grabber," Warren says. "She worked with people who knew how to grab attention and believed that anything that pulled the focus from them was counter-productive. Ruth's radio stations are always built on personality and one of her great talents is that she's able to marshal groups of extremely talented and diverse people and aim them in the same direction, like a ball team."

•

Meyer was devoted to New York. Once she felt WHN was on its way, she left to spend time at Metromedia's WNEW, where she worked with a sales guy named Karmizan.

Then, interested in trying something new, she returned to WMCA to lead the launch of the station's talk format. It was there that she discovered Sally Jessy Raphael.

In 1978 Meyer was named Vice President of Programming at the NBC Radio Network, where she was part of the team that created The Source. "We did concerts and news, and even created a program called "Sex, Drugs and Rock 'n' Roll" that drove NBC management bananas," she laughs.

After NBC, Meyer went to work for the ABC Radio Network, but it wasn't a good fit. "At ABC women were almost invisible and had no impact on decision making," Meyer told me.

Frustrated, she returned to WHN.

•

Ruth Meyer wasn't the first female radio programmer; that distinction goes to Bernice Judis, General Manager of WNEW in the '30s and '40s. But, Meyer was the first woman to lead, compete, and win major market radio battles during the second half of the twentieth century. While she's quick to reject the notion, that makes Meyer a pioneer and a legend.

When she retired, she returned home to Kansas City. Today, she says she has trouble listening to music radio because she always wants to fix the problems she hears.

"So, what do you do in your spare time?" I asked.

"I listen to sports radio, because I don't know anything about it."

"Are you sure?" I asked. "After all, you know radio and you know how to build a team."

I heard a polite laugh. Just what you'd expect from a lady like Ruth Meyer.

CHAPTER 35

ROBERT W. MORGAN: "ZAP! YOU'RE MORGAN-IZED!"

The sun wasn't even up in L.A.

The April riots, five months before, had sapped the city of its energy for a while. But, if you'd been listening to K-Earth 101 on that hot August morning, you'd never have guessed there was anything wrong with the world.

The song playing was The McCoy's *Hang on Sloopy*. As it started to fade, the morning man excitedly exclaimed, "God almighty, it's fun playing these records!"

Then Robert W. Morgan slowed down. "Don't get me wrong," he said. "There's nothing wrong with Perry Como, but enough's enough."

Those in the know knew that until the month before, Robert W. had been across town at KMPC, playing Sinatra and Streisand songs. And, while he'd always sounded at home on KMPC, playing the music he'd played long ago on KHJ seemed to be getting his blood rushing.

It was a Thursday or Friday morning — uh, I mean, morgan — a few days before he was scheduled to officially start at K-Earth, but Robert W. couldn't wait to get on the air and, by five-forty, he'd been discovered and K-Earth's phones were jammed.

"It's been an awful month without you on the air!" said a guy named Greg.

Another caller said, "You're the only voice that can wake me up. Welcome back."

"We went from station to station looking for you. Now, we have a home again. Robert W, we love you."

After nearly thirty years on the radio in the Southland the affection might have been expected. But, why the practice run? Why did Morgan jump in early, when he could still be out fishing? Robert W., former KHJ Boss Jock, got right to it. "I'm actually here before I should have been," he explained. "I wanna make all the mistakes and get them out of the way by Monday."

Then, slyly, he delivered the punch line. "This," he said, "is kinda like a premature e-jock-ulation."

•

In 1955, when he was eighteen, Bob Morgan left his home in Galion, Ohio, and headed east to nearby Wooster, where he played at being a student at the town's college and studied radio at WWST, the local station. In the spirit of the times, he went on the air as "The Rooster from Wooster." It was, as you'd expect, a name he didn't take with him when he headed west.

Morgan's California journey began with the all-night show on KACY/Oxnard — a station Shotgun Tom Kelly would work at a dozen or so years later — which originated live from The Wagon Wheel Bowl and was called "Kegler's Spare Time with Bob Morgan." Then, in 1959, he got a call from Uncle Sam, who sent him to Fort Ord, near Carmel, CA. (Not bad duty if you can get it.)

After the service, Morgan spent six months playing classical music on KTEE/Felton. If this seems bizarre — a rock "n" roll disc jockey announcing classical music — consider this: he co-hosted the program with Bob Elliot, a former Marine heavyweight boxing champ, who would later morph into Top 40 jock K.O. Bailey. Shortly thereafter, Morgan joined KMBY/Monterey to do mornings.

That's when things started to get interesting.

•

Ron Jacobs was a hot-shot programmer, wrapping up a ninety-day winning streak at KMEN/San Bernardino, when he got word from his corporate office to get up to Fresno. Responding quickly,

Jacobs and DJ, Frank Terry — their worldly possessions bouncing in a U-Haul — headed north in Terry's Corvair.

Within hours of arriving in Fresno, Jacobs did two things. First, he hired a man named Sunny Jim Price to program the station, KMAK, and second, he took Price's advice concerning a kid named Bob Morgan, who he was told was working at KMBY in Monterey. "Sunny Jim did me, maybe, the biggest favor of all," Jacobs told me.

The next day found Jacobs and Morgan staring at each other through KMBY's double-glass studio windows. "This wasn't just a first impression," Jacobs recalls. "It may well have been, for both of us, a look in the mirror."

They didn't say much to each other.

"Sumo check, very Zen," explained Jacobs. "But, our monosyllabic grunts and nods signaled the start of a relationship as intense as I have ever had with anyone, in or out of radio."

•

Morgan joined KMAK to do mid-days, while Jacobs did the morning show himself until he realized how good Morgan was and handed the shift over to him.

Next, Jacobs came up with the "Good Morgan" concept, as in morgen — the German word for mornings. Still not completely satisfied, Jacobs decided the name *Robert* sounded cooler than *Bob*. He, also, had another idea. "Do you have a middle initial?" he asked Morgan.

"Sure," Robert replied. "W."

And so it was that Bob Morgan became Robert W. Morgan.

•

At night, Jacobs and Robert W. would sit around talking and dreaming about the big time. They knew they had something special. All they needed, they believed, was "the shot."

But, radio being radio, KMAK cratered when Jacobs's bosses wouldn't ante up with promotion money to combat Bill Drake at KYNO. In a rage, Jacobs quit and, not a big fan of the mainland, he headed home to Hawaii.

As for Morgan, well, Morgan did what all jocks did — he moved on. He spent eight months at KROY/Sacramento, biding time before he got a call to join KEWB/San Francisco. No, it wasn't a morning show, it was nights following a man he'd never met before, The Real Don Steele.

Then, in 1965, the future began to unfold. Morgan and Steele were hired by Bill Drake and were headed for Los Angeles to work for RKO General's perennial loser, KHJ. The goal was to take on KRLA and KFWB.

For some reason lost to history, Drake had hurriedly signed up the talent, but even as he was planning the launch, he'd yet to name a Program Director. Morgan immediately thought of Jacobs, got in touch with him and begged him to call Drake. Jacobs hesitated. Morgan pushed, probably screaming and yelling at Jacobs; such was the nature of their relationship.

Finally, a nervous Jacobs placed the call.

The first meeting between Drake and Jacobs went well and another was scheduled for later the same evening. With time on their hands and a tank full of gas, Morgan and Jacobs drove all over L.A. "It was raining," remembers Jacobs, "and we were running on pure adrenalin."

Later that night, Jacobs met with Drake again and walked out with a new job. He was now the Program Director of KHJ/Los Angeles, the station that would call itself Boss Radio.

•

During his prime at KHJ, Morgan scored a twenty share, a number that indicated that twenty percent of the people listening to the radio in LA were listening to him. It's a feat that's never been duplicated. Claude Hall, an Editor at "Billboard" at the time, suggests it may have something to do with how much fun Morgan seemed to be having on the air. Scotty Brink, who worked with Morgan at KHJ, is more specific. "I think Robert W. was the best disc jockey I ever heard."

"One of my most vivid memories is what happened one morning when Robert was coming out of his house carrying a hair dryer," recalls Charlie Tuna, a Boss Radio legend himself. "The police were going by and they thought the hair dryer was a gun. So, they stopped him and did a whole pat-down. Robert was just incensed and got on the air and went on for three hours about the L.A.P.D."

•

Lancaster/Palmdale, California had none of the glitter of Hollywood, but Don Imus could have cared less; he figured if something worked on the radio, it would work anywhere. Besides, imitation is the sincerest form of flattery, right? "I went to disc jockey school in Hollywood," says The I-Man. "Then I got a job at KUTY/Palmdale, about sixty miles up from LA, and every morning I'd listen to Robert W. Morgan's show while I was on the air."

Actually, Imus did more than just listen, he copied Morgan exactly. Morgan would play a record on KHJ and do a bit and a few minutes later, Imus would play the same record on KUTY and repeat the same bit.

Of course, Imus wasn't the only DJ in America to emulate Morgan. "There were airchecks of Robert W. floating all over the country," says consultant Lee Bayley.

"A friend from LA sent me a tape and I was stupefied," says WPLJ's Scott Shannon. "His intelligence and one-on-one manner were an inspiration and, when I was designing my early Scott Shannon 'personality,' I tried to borrow Robert W.'s speech patterns and intelligence and combine it with some of Don Steele's energy – as weird as that seems."

Morgan's influence on the entire radio industry was so pervasive that morning jocks in town after town across the country began "Morganizing" their audiences. And, if they didn't know why they were doing it, it didn't matter, because if it was good enough for Morgan and Boss Radio, it was good enough for them.

"Good Morgan, Cheboygan!!"

•

Imus and Morgan become fast friends and talked on the phone once or twice a week. As they were getting to know each other in the early '70s, Morgan, except for a quick trip to WIND/Chicago, stayed in LA, while Imus began his market climb: Palmdale to Stockton, Stockton to Sacramento. "Then," Imus told me, "I went to WGAR in Cleveland."

In 1971 or '72, along with WJR/Detroit's J.P. McCarthy, both Morgan and Imus were up for "Billboard Disc Jockey of the Year." The convention was going to take place in New Orleans.

"I'm not going unless I win," Morgan told Imus, "And you shouldn't either. Unless you win."

A day or so later Morgan called Imus again. "I just found out that you've won."

"So, Jack Thayer gave me the money and I went to New Orleans and checked into the hotel," says Imus.

That night at the banquet came the announcement. "And the winner is (drum roll, please) — J.P. McCarthy."

"They announced McCarthy's name," recalls Imus, "but, I still thought they'd said mine. I mean, I'd been told that *I* won." (And, with more than a little buzz on, Imus began walking towards the stage.) Later that night, he returned to his room to find a telegram from Morgan. On the piece of paper was one word. "Gotcha!"

"I never could get even with him," complains Imus.

Well, maybe once. Several years after the incident Morgan was coming to New York and insisted that a limo be waiting for him at JFK. Imus promised to take care of it. When Morgan arrived, he was met by a driver in a garbage truck.

Perhaps you saw the picture in the trades.

•

To aspiring Boss Jocks KHJ/Los Angeles must have looked like heaven. But, to Morgan, LA's "promise land" was KMPC and, specifically, Dick Whittinghill's morning slot. "Robert and I were in awe of KMPC in those days," says Charlie Tuna. "We were on a hot station, KHJ, but KMPC, owned by Gene Autry, had a traffic watch, news people all over, and was the station of the stars."

Freedom from Drake's formatics may have appealed to Morgan, but equally important was the money — the $100,000 a year that KMPC's morning man, Dick Whittinghill, supposedly made. (In fact, during the late '60s Morgan and Steele, both making about $35,000 a year, had staged a walk out at KHJ. Boss Radio PD, Ron Jacobs, responded by putting Tuna on in both shifts.)

By 1970; however, Jacobs was gone from KHJ and Morgan was good to go. That's when he got the call from WIND/Chicago.

"He really liked the idea (of WIND and Chicago)," says Tuna. "He was a music connoisseur – the great bands, great vocalists, not just the Top 40 – so it was an opportunity to play music he loved and have fun."

WIND was also a chance to earn the kind of money Morgan thought he was worth. But, things didn't work out, perhaps because Morgan only stayed in Chicago a year. He'd wanted to take on WLS's Larry Lujack, but WIND didn't play Top 40, WLS's format, so the two men never competed directly. A station closer in format to WIND was WGN, but their morning man, Wally Phillips, was an insurmountable hurdle. "As Robert explained it," Tuna told me, "Wally owned Chicago and he just couldn't do it."

Morgan returned to Los Angeles where he was to spend the

remainder of his career. One morning, back at KHJ, he played *The First Time Ever I Saw Your Face* by Roberta Flack — apparently not one of his favorite records. Referring to it, but perhaps speaking to a larger subject, he opened his mic and said, "Radio, like life itself, is a series of peaks and valleys. This is one of the later...."

•

By 1974, the year his daughter, Susanna, was born, Morgan and Steele were re-united on K-100/Los Angeles. Listeners (particularly insiders) were and weren't surprised when the ex-Boss Jocks began throwing verbal bombs at their former employer, KHJ.

K-100 turned out to be a valley for Morgan. Perhaps it had to do with the signal, suggests the station's Program Director, Lee Bayley. "It was a low power station with a tower in the hills and a signal that barely got across town."

But, off the air things were moving for Morgan. He took on side projects, including "The Robert W. Morgan Special of the Week," "Record Report," television announcing on "Solid Gold," and he even hosted "Morgan Manor for TWA." Then he got his shot at KMPC.

At first, it was the swing shift: weekends and fill-in. "It was strange to hear Robert doing the Saturday over-night show," says Arbitron's Ron Rodrigues, who was KMPC's Music Director. "But, he seemed to suck it up."

The real deal, of course (and most everyone knew it) was that Morgan was parked and in place for when Dick Whittinghill retired. When it finally happened, it seemed to be pre-destined. "One of Robert's greatest strengths, and why KMPC coveted him, was he was an advertiser-friendly guy," Rodrigues says.

Remotes and meet-and-greets; Morgan was good with all of it. And, while his ratings at KMPC never approached what he'd achieved at KHJ, monster ratings weren't really an expectation because KMPC's sales department consistently outperformed its numbers.

For fun, on the day he took over the reigns of the morning show, August 6, 1979, Morgan started by playing his boss's signature song, *Back In The Saddle Again*.

•

Three years later, Morgan left KMPC to join Magic 106/KMGG, but after four years and no great success, KMGG changed formats (to become Power 106), and Morgan returned to KMPC, where he stayed until 1992.

Then, as if it were déjà vu all over again, he and The Real Don Steele were reunited at KRTH. It was their fourth radio station together. (KEWB, KHJ, KIQQ-FM, KRTH). On his first day on the air, on that August morning, Morgan mentioned that he'd signed a ten-year deal.

•

Robert W. Morgan died right after six in the morning on May 22, 1998 — roughly a month before his sixty-first birthday. He'd vowed to prolong his fight with cancer long enough to see his daughter graduate from college and it was a promise he kept.

When notified of his death, K-Earth stopped everything for five seconds. There was dead air, total silence.

The day after he died, a twelve-year old girl named Holly Amos posted these words on a memorial website:

> "I've been listening to Robert W. since I was eight years old. Last night I heard about his death, and I was so sad that I started crying."

Something tells me Holly wasn't alone.

CHAPTER 36

BRUCE MORROW — WE'RE ALL COUSINS

A letter was posted on Bruce Morrow's website on August 4, 2008.

> Dear Cousin Brucie,
>
> I've been listening to you since the '60s! I'm so happy that you're on SIRIUS and look forward every week to hearing your show. I'm an artist and like to listen while I paint. I especially like it when you play songs that aren't played often, as I know the music of that era thoroghly [sic] and miss hearing more arcane tunes. Keep up the great shows!
>
> Signed,
> (Name Withheld)
> Crownsville, Maryland

•

Joe McCoy, Vice President of Programming at WCBS-FM/New York, was on the train heading home, but his mind was still at work. He had a Saturday-night slot open and hadn't figured out what to do with it yet. "Oh well," he thought. "I'll deal with it later."

It was an early evening at the end of a day, on a night in 1982. McCoy fished into his briefcase for a copy of "Billboard" and began thumbing through it. He glanced at the charts. He was curious but since CBS-FM was an oldies station, knowing what the #1 record was really didn't matter. Then, he saw an article mentioning Bruce Morrow and his radio stations in New Jersey and upstate New York. "And the light just came on," says McCoy. "That's it! Cousin Brucie."

Morrow had been off the air in New York City for five years, but to those who remembered him from WABC, time had never passed. Several phone calls and meetings later, McCoy and Morrow had a deal and Cousin Brucie, already a New York legend, joined WCBS-FM where he appeared weekly for the next twenty-three years.

"When people first arrived at WCBS-FM, they were greeted by a massive photo of Bruce interviewing The Beatles," says Dave Logan, the last PD of WCBS, before the parent corporation turned the station into Jack FM, in 2005. (July 12, 2007, WCBS-FM was revived.) "The picture, taken at WABC in 1964," says Logan, "is impressive by itself, but even more so when you consider that Brucie was already a legendary performer when it was taken."

When CBS corporate blew WCBS-FM up in favor of the newer Jack FM, Morrow, responding to the move, told "The New York Daily News" that it was like "replacing Yankee Stadium with a fruit stand." Michael Bloomberg, the Mayor of New York, was a bit more colorful. "I'll never listen to that f***ing CBS radio again," his honor said.

After the demise of WCBS-FM, Morrow signed a long-term agreement with Sirius Satellite Radio, where he still broadcasts twice a week and still has fans who've been listening to him forever.

But, unless you live in New York or listen to Sirius, I'll bet you still think of Cousin Brucie standing with the Beatles, at WABC, like I do.

That, cousins, ain't the half of it.

•

Bruce Meyerowitz's girlfriend's mother told him that if he was going to go on the radio, he needed a stage name. "Ok," he told her, "but the name has to begin with the letter "M."

She opened the Manhattan phone book, closed her eyes and pointed. "Morrow," she said. "That's it." Today Morrow laughs about the whole thing. "I could have been named Brucie McNulty," he says.

His first radio job was at ZBM/Bermuda, where he was given the name, "The Hammer." It described his pace on the air. He was very young and the first disc jockey to play rock 'n roll on the island. Morrow says Bermuda was fun, but not always. He remembers the day a black church burned to the ground and its Pastor asking for help. Morrow went on the air and announced a big dance to raise money. On the day of the event, thousands of people, of all races, showed up. But, some citizens weren't happy. He says angry calls and threats on his life were made. He started carrying a lead pipe for protection. Finally it got to be too much for him.

On the day Morrow left Bermuda, it was his new church friends who drove him to the airport. There were lots of tears. He flew home a little wiser, a little sadder, too.

•

His father knew someone at WINS/New York and the connection helped Morrow get an entry level job as a staff producer. Then, AFTRA went on strike and everyone at the station was drafted to go on the air, including young Bruce Morrow.

One night, security let an old woman in to see him. "Mr. Morrow, do you believe we're all related?" the old woman asked him.

Here we go, he thought. "Yes, ma'am, I do."

"Mr. Morrow, I'm broke and can't get home," she continued, softly. "Cousin, can you lend me fifty cents?"

Morrow remembers giving her the money and thinking she had beautiful eyes. Driving home that night, through the Brooklyn Battery Tunnel, a thought hit him like a northbound train. "I knew I had something very special," he says. "I knew I had my handle."

Mel Leeds, the Program Director of WINS, was a tough, no nonsense kind of guy. Morrow wasn't even close to being tough, but he was sold on his idea. The next morning he took a deep breath and walked into Leeds' office.

"Mr. Leeds," asked Morrow, "can I call myself Cousin Brucie on the air?"

Leeds frowned. "That's the stupidest thing I've ever heard, kid. This is New York City, not Cheesequake. That is so corny, it'll never work here."

Morrow stood up to him. "I'm a Brooklyn boy and nobody's cornier than New York kids," he said.

Leeds was surprised Morrow stood up to him. "Alright, kid, try it. But if you're wrong, you're fired."

That night, Morrow became Cousin Brucie. Early the next morning, Leeds called him at home. "Get in here," the older man barked. "We've got problems."

When Morrow arrived at the office, Leeds glared at him and said, "What'd I tell you?"

"Well, I guess I over did it," said Morrow.

"You more than over did it!" exploded Leeds. "I'm letting you go."

For a moment, you could hear a heart break. Then Leeds broke the silence. "I'm putting you under contract right now," he announced. "From now on, you're a radio personality. You're Cousin Brucie."

It turns out that WINS had been flooded with telegrams and phone calls wanting more Cousin Brucie. Morrow was on top of the world and would have stayed there, if it weren't for one Murray Kaufman, "Murray the K."

Morrow doesn't divulge much except to say that Kaufman convinced WINS management Cousin Brucie talked way too fast and was costing the station advertisers. "They bought the argument," says Morrow. "I was off the air and out of work."

There's probably more to the story, but Kaufman's gone and Morrow's a gentleman.

•

Cousin Brucie wound up at WINZ/Miami. Today, remembering, he says it always felt like out of town tryouts. Sure, there was the Top 40 battle between WINZ, WQAM and WMBM, but it sure didn't feel like New York. He says the last straw was when he noticed Christmas lights strung up on palm trees.

Morrow was halfway through a two-year deal at WINZ when Hal Neal, the General Manager of WABC, came to his rescue. Still embarrassed about it all these years later, Morrow says he told a white lie to get out of his contract. "I told WINZ management I had to get back to New York because my wife was cracking up." The station was sympathetic and released him. It was 1961.

•

In pre-Beatle America, Vietnam was barely a blip on the radar screen, and we were still dancing in the streets, not marching. But, rock 'n' roll scared some, and WABC, with its 50,000 watts covering New York and a total of twenty-two states, was cast as the devil's messenger — if you took that sort of thing seriously.

One New York newspaper columnist, who didn't understand the music or those who played it, wrote: "They must chain Cousin Brucie up in the ABC basement, feed him six times a day and let him out every night at seven." Morrow has a different take on it. "We were a friend on the radio," he says. "The kids listened to us more than they did to their own parents." "It's true," says former TM Studios President, David Graupner. "I requested a song and not only did he play it, but he mentioned Westfield, N.J. and my name. I was a star in my school for a week."

WABC was an exciting radio station and, at times, it seems as if everyone in the New York area was listening. But behind the curtain, says Morrow, it wasn't quite so much fun. In 1974, WABC management offered their disc jockeys a new deal: IF the ratings went up, they'd get an incremental raise. BUT, if they went down, salaries would go down, too.

Morrow was livid. "I put my life into that station and they were going to throw us to the wolves. How dare they do that?"

He says it forced him to make one of the toughest decisions of his life. "I made a deal with WNBC (to replace Wolfman Jack), and then I called Rick Sklar back and told him I'd accept the WABC terms, if they'd tear up my contract and start fresh."

WABC agreed and, no longer contractually obligated to the station, Bruce Morrow walked out, after thirteen years. It was August 7, 1974, two days before Nixon resigned the Presidency.

•

The ad campaign proclaimed:

GOOD MOVE, COUSIN BRUCIE!

The hype was huge, but WNBC never lived up to it and how Morrow feels about his experience at the station is probably colored by what the new Program Director, Bob Pittman, said to him as his three-year contract with the station drew to a close. "You ought to move over and allow some younger guys a chance."

Bruce Morrow was forty years old and found himself at a crossroads. That's when he met Bob Sillerman, who's one of the four hundred richest people in America today. (Among other things, he owns Elvis Presley Enterprises). In 1978, Sillerman and Morrow formed a partnership called SFX Broadcasting to acquire two radio stations in upstate New York. Eventually the group included seven radio properties and a television station. "Bob was the businessman, and I did everything else, from installing transmitters to hanging curtains," says Morrow.

When SFX was sold, Morrow says, "It made your Cousin Brucie a very happy man."

•

"Very few personalities in New York are as beloved as he is," says Dave Logan. "The affection is universal, from the Mayor and our Senators, to a guy who runs a sandwich shop in Brooklyn. The people of New York love him." Logan says the affection is for more than what Cousin Brucie does on the air. "He's served as President of The Variety Clubs for years, helping raise enormous sums of money and goodwill for children. He's always offered his time and his personal devotion to those who needed it most, and he's never asked for anything in return."

On Tuesday, April 24, 2001, Cousin Brucie Morrow was inducted into the NAB Radio Hall of Fame. I wasn't there to hear him accept his award, but I suspect when the applause died down he reminded the audience that there is no better theater in the world than the one that lives in our minds and imaginations.

Then, I'll bet he winked, paused and softly with purpose, said, "Remember, nothing captures your imagination better than radio."

CHAPTER 37

PAT O'DAY:
"WHAT A DIFFERENCE O'DAY MADE"

Pat O'Day's father was a radio evangelist in Tacoma, and from the time he was seven or eight, O'Day knew he wanted to follow in his footsteps. "Not as a minister," he says, "but as an announcer, a newsman or play-by-play man."

Bremerton, WA, is a Navy town west of Seattle, across the Puget Sound, in Kitsap County. By the time he was in high school O'Day was doing PA announcing for the Bremerton High football team and, before and after school, he was sweeping floors at a local radio station, where Linc Perry was the General Manager. Perry didn't think O'Day had a prayer. "You're wasting your time getting your hopes up for something that will never happen for you. I'd suggest you just not hang around here anymore."

O'Day's heart was broken, but he didn't give up. In 1956, Neil Sargent, the Program Director of KVAS/Astoria, gave O'Day his first full time job. "He had everything," says Sargent. "Personality, humor, competitiveness, intelligence, creativity and a great work ethic."

The next year O'Day moved on to KLOG/Kelso, Washington, and it was there that he was discovered by his hero, Washington radio legend Wally Nelskog. "Wally, in typical Wally fashion, walked in the back door of the station and said, 'I've been listening to your program and find what you do quite attractive.' " Nelskog offered O'Day his first programming job at KUTI/Yakima, and O'Day jumped at the chance. A year and a half later KAYO/Seattle called his name and he jumped at that, too. Then, after he'd been in the Emerald City for less than a year, the phone rang again. This time, it was Seattle's big dog, KJR.

It was January of 1960.

•

Les Smith bought KJR/Seattle in 1953 and, in 1958, sold the station to Essex Productions, a company owned by Frank Sinatra and Danny Kaye. KJR had had a brief fling with rock 'n' roll in the mid '50s, but in 1958 the payola scandals were brewing, the music itself was struggling and Smith, who'd stayed on after the sale, was somehow convinced by his manager that rock 'n' roll had no future. So, KJR flipped to a safer middle-of-the road format. But, it failed to gain an audience. The following year the station re-entered the rock 'n' roll arena, hired Programmer Chris Lane — who stayed for about a minute — and as the new decade was beginning, the station hired O'Day to do afternoon drive. Things started to get exciting.

"Rock 'n' roll was still in its infancy, and we were deciding, on an hourly basis, what a great radio station should sound like," O'Day says.

He studied Chuck Blore's KFWB/Los Angeles and the Bartell Brothers' San Francisco powerhouse, KYA. But, mostly, O'Day kept his eyes on Seattle. "The Northwest is unique," he thought to himself.

Sure. Heard that before. But, even his programming peers agreed with him. On national music calls, where programmers compared notes on new record releases, O'Day would proclaim, "You gotta play this record!" What he'd get in response was, "*That* isn't going to happen *here*, Pat. That's just *your* thing; your area's so different."

Perhaps it was, he thought. At any rate that's how he decided to play it. "I believed local artists could be as important as national acts," he says. "Why not? Our station's local, why not play local music?

KJR broke The Wailers' version of *Louie, Louie* and it was a Seattle hit twice, almost three times. But, as much as O'Day championed the record, it didn't become a hit until a Portland group, The Kingsmen, copied the Wailer's version, and their label, Wand Records, slyly implied that the group was from the east coast. With no Pacific Northwest stigma, The Kingsmen's version stormed into history.

Meanwhile, back in Seattle, KJR — with O'Day and a long list of big-personality jocks, including Dick Curtis, Jerry Kay, Larry Lujack, Tom Murphy, Mike Phillips, Charlie Brown, Norm Gregory, Scotty Brink and 18-year old Kevin O'Brien — set the town on its ear. "O'Day's intense passion for entertaining programming is second to none," says O'Brien (Kevin Metheny). "He's a remarkable human being."

•

James Marshall Hendrix was a Seattle boy O'Day had known for years.

O'Day was always fishing for new ideas. "So, I got to thinking the concert business was changing," he says. "Sound and lighting requirements, security problems with drugs and artists falling victim to how good or bad a local promoter might be. So, I said to Jimi, 'Why don't we handle your performance everywhere you go? We'll bankroll the tour, arrange the advertising — do it all. At the end of the tour we'll sit down, pay the expenses and then split the rest.' "

They called the company *Concerts West* and it changed the way live performances were done.

O'Day was involved with KJR until the middle '70s. "He didn't just talk the talk," says Metheny. "He could go on the air and shame us young Turks, leaving us to eat his creative dust."

In 1976, O'Day bought KORL/Honolulu and commuted between the islands and the mainland. Then, in 1977, he took over KYYX/Seattle. "That was the FM that finally beat my alma mater," he says, proudly.

•

"**That was then** and this is now," says Edie Hilliard, former CEO of Jones Radio Network/Seattle. "But, back then, Pat was indisputably the king of Seattle radio."

Today, KJR-AM is a sports station, and O'Day runs a real estate brokerage in the San Juan Islands and is no longer actively involved in radio. But, he still listens and still talks like the great programmer he was.

"Here's a great line I heard on the radio the other day," he told me. " 'Hey, we're having another fun weekend with good-time oldies!' "

"What kind of horseshit is that?" O'Day asks. "I mean, c'mon. Those aren't even real words."

Indeed.

CHAPTER 38
GARY OWENS: THE MAN FROM BEAUTIFUL, DOWNTOWN BURBANK

Gary Owens collects South Dakotans. They're stashed in a little box in his desk drawer, a box he pulls out whenever he has to prove he comes from some place earthly, as opposed to, say, out of this world. ("Look, here's a tiny Tom Brokaw. This is my miniature Mary Hart. Oops, where's Cheryl Ladd? Be careful, now. Watch where you step.") As he shakes their little hands and puts them back in the corn-lined box — Owens is nothing, if not friendly — I sneak in the hard question.

"Are you really as twisted as you seem?"

Owens laughs. "I have an offbeat sense of humor," he answers. "Don Imus told George Carlin he thinks I'm awfully squirrelly and George said, 'Well, of course he is.' "

•

"A woman came up to the house," says Jonathan Winters. "We'd left the iron gate to my property open and she said, 'Oh, Mr. Winters, I see there's a man pushing you in a wheelchair, and I've obviously come at a bad time.' "

It was a photo shoot for a new Winters-Owens comedy CD, *Out Patients*, and easy to explain. Owens took control. "I'm Dr. Nedlinger and please don't bother Mr. Winters now. Even though we've got him taped to this chair and under heavy medication, he could spring out and hurt you."

The woman genuflected, turned and ran.

"Gary's quick and has a very imaginative mind," says Winters. "We're always doing crazy things."

Then Mr. Winters turned introspective. "Friends are hard to come by. Period. I've found him to be a great friend in many ways."

Plankenton, SD, Owens's home town, is twenty-five miles west of Mitchell, SD, which is seventy-five miles west of Sioux Falls — a hop, skip and a jump north of the Iowa state line.

"We told my folks we were going to Iowa for the weekend," says Owens. Instead, he and his best friend, Lee Harris, both about fifteen years old, crossed the Rockies and drove to California. "I'd never seen a palm tree or the ocean before," says Owens, "And I said to myself, 'This is where I've got to be.'"

But, he was still a kid, the '50s had barely dawned and his dreams were still on the drawing board. "I didn't know whether I was going to be a cartoonist or go into radio and TV," Owens told me. So, he drew ten different characters and sent them to Minneapolis in response to an invitation he'd found on the back of a matchbook cover (Draw me and win a scholarship!!!) Owens struck gold and won the scholarship. The kicker is the judge was Charles Schultz — yes, *that* Charles Schultz — as in Snoopy, Lucy and Charlie Brown. Then the radio bug bit. He didn't give up cartooning, though; it'd become a big part of his life, but not in the way he'd imagined.

At sixteen, with a voice that had changed from a pre-puberty squeak to one with an announcer's mellifluous tones, Owens joined KORN/Mitchell and became, as he put it, "a hyphenated teenager-newsman-dance band remote-announcer." He stayed at the station for a while and still remembers it well. "The only way you could hear yourself on those remotes was to put your hand up to your ear."

•

Don Burden, the owner of KOIL/Omaha, was colorful.

Owens arrived at the station in 1957, hired as a newsman, not a jock. He was teamed with a morning man with a head full of steam. One morning, the jock exploded, shot a deleted expletive at Burden and walked off the air.

The phone rang. It was Burden. "Gary, you've got to take over."

Owens couldn't run a board, so he spent half the show apologizing for his technical mistakes. But, he got better. Very quickly. In fact, it turned out he was a natural, which explains why Todd Storz and Bill Stewart, across town at KOWH, conspired to get him out of town.

He moved to KIMN/Denver. There, he did radio in the morning, a kid's TV show in the afternoon and followed that with a local newscast. "So, I was dressed in a very bad chicken suit," Owens recalls.

He only had a few minutes to shuck the outfit. On the way to change, he ran into a friend in the hall and lost track of time. The stage manager panicked. "My God, Gary, you've only got two minutes."

Now normally that would have been time enough for a quick turnaround, but the zipper broke. "So, I ended up doing the newscast with a beak over my head. 'Good Afternoon. Federal Mediators on Capitol Hill...' "

The station manager's feathers were ruffled, and Owens kissed news anchoring goodbye. But, he kept the kid's show and fell in love with television. Shortly thereafter, the McLendon boys called.

•

Don Keyes was Gordon McLendon's National PD. "Don was a wonderful radio man who should be in the Hall of Fame," says Owens. Keyes called Owens about joining KILT/Houston, but Owens didn't stay in south Texas very long. "I became a troubleshooter for McLendon," he says. "We'd get the ratings up, and I'd go somewhere else." From KILT, he went to KLIF/Dallas, WNOE/New Orleans, then on to KTSA/San Antonio. "I learned so much about Top 40," Owens says. "McLendon had it down to a science. We'd prepare three hours off the air for every three hours on."

In 1958, Owens left the McLendon Chain to join WIL/St. Louis. "I think we were the last music station in St. Louis to be #1," he says.

Then, in 1959, Chuck Blore called him with an offer to go to KEWB/San Francisco. "I'm embarrassed," Blore told him. "You're probably making more in St. Louis."

Owens was tempted because he still dreamed of California. "Can I think about it overnight?" he asked.

That night a tornado hit St. Louis. The next day a rattled Owens accepted the job and headed west and, in short order, he blew KSFO's Don Sherwood out of the water.

From there, it was a short trip to Los Angeles and KFWB.

•

Someone should make a movie.

Owens hit his stride at KFWB. It was Top 40 heaven, top of the heap. But, he wanted more. In 1962, despite the risk, he left his #1 morning show at KFWB to join KMPC. "I was taking a tremendous chance," he says.

KMPC was a different world. It had nothing to do with rock 'n' roll and everything to do with reaching the ears of Hollywood's movers and shakers, and Owens hoped the move would lead to voice work, cartoons, television and movies.

It did.

Step back and look at Gary Owens career: Top 40 pioneer, the voice of the television networks and thousands of commercials, tons of cartoon work ("Garfield," "Roger Ramjet," "Ren and Stimpy"), plus movies and comedy. And, anyone who ever watched "Laugh In" will always remember Owens' cupped-ear introduction from "beautiful downtown Burbank."

Over a career that's lasted more than half a century, Owens has won virtually every award broadcasting can bestow. Walk down Hollywood Boulevard today and you'll find his star right next to Walt Disney's.

GARY OWENS

More than that, the man is loved. Why? Because the way he's gone about the business of doing business stands as a shining example of how to do it: with character, heart and a sense of humor.

"I'm a great fan," says Jonathan Winters.

Mr. Winters has a lot of company.

Chapter 39
Elvis Presley: Me, Sam, and Dewey

(This story was written in August of 2002 just before the 25th anniversary of Elvis Presley's death. It's about KZEW-FM/Dallas, a legendary radio station created by Ira Lipson, and about Elvis and Sam, and Dewey Phillips, an incredible radio man.)

KZEW-FM/Dallas never played Elvis Presley songs. It didn't matter that he was the King of Rock 'n' Roll or that half the musicians we *did* play owed their very existence to him. ("Before Elvis," said John Lennon, "There was nothing.") Elvis had ceased being hip long before FM was, and frankly, we never gave him much thought.

It was Tuesday afternoon, about 3:25, August 16, 1977. We'd just wrapped the news — light, fluffy, lifestyle stuff — and the radio station was blasting a six-minute song by Argent called *God Gave Rock and Roll To You*. The studio door was closed, the monitors were blaring. Then, news ace Carol Hotlett ran into the room.

"You're not going to believe this!" she screamed.

"Believe what?" I asked.

In the background I could hear the Associated Press teletype alarm bells going for broke.

"Elvis is dead," she said.

"Jesus," I said.

For a moment I froze. *It's Only Rock and Roll* by the Rolling Stones was cued up and ready to go, but for some reason it didn't seem right to go there.

"Whadda we do?" I said, aloud.

"Play one of his songs," said Hotlett. Smart lady.

"I don't think we have any."

Panic set in. I started rifling through a stack of never played oldies LPs in the corner and, to my surprise, I found 1959's "50,000 Elvis Fans Can't be Wrong."e But, nothing on it seemed to fit the moment, so I kept searching. With less than a minute to spare, I unearthed *Heartbreak Hotel*. I cued it up and turned on the mic. "This is, uh, very strange," I said. "And very unexpected."

I stopped to clear my throat. "I've got some awful news. We've just been told that Elvis Presley died in Memphis today…"

I started the record.

Next I went to the phones. "Hi, it's the Zoo."

At first I thought no one was there, but just as I was about to punch another line, I heard a sound. It was soft and pained. Suddenly I realized someone was crying.

•

The heat was oppressive, over one hundred degrees.

It was Memphis, in July of 1954, so hot and muggy that clammy clothes stuck to a body's skin like peanut butter to the top of your mouth. It was early in the week — some accounts say Monday, 7/5, some say Tuesday, 7/6 — and nineteen-year old Elvis Presley was recording professionally for the first time. Yes, that's when he cut *That's Alright, Mama* and *Blue Moon of Kentucky*. Within a few days his whole world would turn upside down.

WHBQ/Memphis disc jockey, Dewey Phillips, was damn near certifiable. In his book, "Elvis," author Albert Goldman describes Phillips as a natural-born freak. "No tricks of typography," wrote Goldman, "no Tom Wolfe razzamatazz on the top buttons of the typewriter — #*%&*!!! — will ever simulate the sound that this nut made over the late-night, deep-South radio circa 1954."

Goldman's a character himself, but he's closer to the truth than he's not. Dewey's show, "Red, Hot and Blue," was like Mecca to R and B lovers and, in fact, he was so committed to his vision of what was worth playing and what wasn't, that he refused to play anything by white artists. Considering the pop charts at the time, it wasn't such a bad policy.

But to his friend, Sam Phillips, it was a bugaboo. Why? Because in the first week of July 1954, Sam wanted Dewey to hear something he'd just recorded by a kid from Tupelo, MS. "He was asking Dewey to consider something that had never previously existed on this earth," wrote Peter Guralnick, author of "Last Train To Memphis."

"There was an element of Dewey that was conservative," Sam Phillips told Guralnick, long after the fact. "When he picked a record he didn't want to be wrong."

•

It was Wednesday night, July 7th. That's the night Sam played Elvis's songs for Dewey. Sipping on a beer, the Memphis DJ listened. He just sat there, never said a word. Sam was quiet, too. In later years both talked about knowing that what Elvis had done wasn't white, pop or country, and about wondering what the next step was or should be.

But, when Dewey woke up the next morning he knew.

On July 8, 1954, somewhere between nine-thirty and ten p.m., Dewey Phillips told his WHBQ audience that he had a new record he wanted them to hear. "It's not even a record yet," he confided. "It's a dub of a new record Sam is putting out next week, and it's going to be a hit!"

That night, for the first time in the world and for the first time anywhere, Dewey Phillips played Elvis Presley's first recordings like there was no tomorrow. To hear it told, the phones exploded and before the show was over Elvis himself — pulled out of a movie theater and brought to the radio station, where he was nervous, but polite, and, obviously, way over his head — was on the air with Dewey, live on WHBQ.

His mama heard him that night.

Don't you wish you had, too?

CHAPTER 40

DICK PURTAN: SIX DEGREES OF SEPARATION

Six degrees of Kevin Bacon or six degrees of separation. Whatever it's called, the game supposes that no matter who you are you're only six people away from anyone else in the world.

Wanna play? Here goes.

John Lennon (1) toured with Roy Orbison (2) who was at Sun Records with Elvis Presley (3) who met Richard Nixon (4) at the White House, where his Vice President, Spiro Agnew (5) seldom went because he was busy attacking the media. Agnew was Governor of Maryland before he became Vice President. In the spring of 1968, he called Al Burke (6) the GM of WBAL/Baltimore, to complain about Dick Purtan, WBAL's new morning man.

"Fire that son of a bitch!" demanded Agnew. "He made fun of me."

Purtan had always done parodies of social and political types; in Detroit, his targets got the joke, but Baltimore wasn't Detroit and Agnew didn't see the humor. When Burke fired Purtan, he'd only been at WBAL for five weeks.

Of course, that's not how the story ends. Purtan returned to Detroit and became a legend, while Agnew went to Washington and became an embarrassment. Looking back, one can't help but wonder if Dick wishes he'd never heard Agnew's name.

Purtan, not Nixon.

Ok. Both.

•

He went to Syracuse for school and to work.

At the time, not that it's really changed, radio was a transient business and disc jockeys were always coming and going. So, trying to mitigate the problem of always having someone new on the air, some stations had house names, names that stayed with the station. No one will notice, they thought. And, so it was at WOLF, where Purtan joined a long line of jocks who'd been *The Buckaroo Sandman*. "Dick Clark was the Buckaroo Sandman, too," Purtan says.

After Syracuse, Purtan returned to Buffalo, where he became Guy King, on WWOL. Other "Guys" included Tom Clay, Bruce Bradley, and Purtan's hero, Frank Ward. In 1958, Purtan became the new King for fifty dollars a week.

For the most part, his parents were supportive of his radio ambitions. But, when he married his college sweetheart, his new in-laws were skeptical. Purtan didn't give an inch. "I want to be a disc jockey," he told them. When it was pointed out that he had a brand new Masters Degree in Telecommunications, and that television might be a smart move, Purtan said he didn't care; he only had eyes for radio.

And, when a visiting lecturer named David Susskind asked Purtan what he wanted to do now that he had his degree, Purtan stuck to his guns. "Radio," he answered.

Susskind offered to help.

Ben Strauss owned WWDC/Washington and Susskind suggested Purtan send him a tape. When Strauss responded, he told young Purtan, "I've got nothing in Washington, but I've got a station in Richmond and one in Jacksonville. Jacksonville might be better for you."

In 1960, Purtan and his bride, Gail, headed south to sunny Jacksonville, where God's own humidity co-existed with Spanish moss and sulfur water, and he went to work for a radio station so pathetic that he forgot to tell me the call letters. "We were Top 40," Purtan says. "A CBS affiliate with news at the top of the hour and a five minute show at the bottom." To make matters worse, the competition was The Big Ape, WAPE/Jacksonville. Purtan says it was barely a fight and, within a year, he was on the air at

WSAI/Cincinnati. "A fabulous radio station," he says. "We had a forty-two share in the Pulse (ratings)."

Then Detroit called.

•

In 1965, the year Purtan joined WKNR/Detroit to do the morning show, Motown Records had four #1 hits, and the radio battleground in the Motor City was Top 40.

Two years later, when the Drake format came to CKLW/Windsor — Paul Drew was the Program Director — Purtan's morning numbers held, but the rest of the day went up in flames. The fireman called to the rescue was consultant, Mike Joseph. "Joseph told everyone, including me, to shut up and play the music and do ten second intros."

Purtan refused. "You can't just play music in the morning," he said.

Joseph threatened action, but Purtan refused to give in and after a "come to Jesus" meeting with the General Manager, Purtan got his way. But, the rest of the day went to Joseph.

The next year ABC offered Purtan $40,000 to jump ship and join WXYZ/Detroit. But, the job was afternoon drive and Purtan said he was a morning man. Instead, he went to WBAL/Baltimore and although morning shares increased by ten points in the short time he was there, by the time the ratings were released he'd already been *Spiro-ed,* and was back in Detroit during — guess what — afternoons for WXYZ. For $25,000.

But, behind the scenes, things were happening.

"Purtan had just arrived when Martin and Howard, the old-style MOR morning guys, went on vacation," recalls Bob Henabery, ABC's Program Development Manager, at the time. "So, Chuck Fritz, the General Manager, moved Purtan to mornings to do an audition, and asked me to listen in from New York. "I laughed and laughed and laughed," Henabery says.

Later that day, Henabery told Fritz to keep Purtan on in mornings. "If you don't, you're out of your mind."

"Poor Martin and Howard," Henabery says. "They went on vacation and never came back."

Purtan, however, stayed for the next ten years.

•

WJR's morning man, J.P. McCarthy, had owned Detroit for almost thirty years. When he died on August 16, 1995, those in the know were convinced Purtan would replace him. Purtan, however, wasn't convinced it was a good idea. "I didn't want to be Deborah Norville," he says, referring to the "Today Show" co-host who replaced Jane Pauley and only lasted two years. "I wanted to be Katie Couric."

Finally, feeling pressured, he accepted the job, but got an 11th hour reprieve when ABC put WJR on the block. While the sale never happened, WJR still let Purtan off the hook. "I admire them for being so forthright about it," Purtan says.

Six months later, on Valentine's Day, 1996, Mel Karmizan, then the President of CBS/Infinity, flew to Detroit to offer Dick Purtan mornings on WOMC-FM. Purtan said yes.

Today, over thirteen years later, Purtan is still with WOMC, and has a Marconi Award from the NAB to put on his mantel. "I've been at five different (Detroit) radio stations in thirty-six years," Purtan told me, in 2001: "WKNR, WCYZ, CKLW, WKQI and, now, WOMC. Fortunately, I take my audience with me."

By the way, if you're wondering how to connect Purtan back to John Lennon, there's a simple answer. In 1964, it was Dick Purtan who brought the Beatles to Cincinnati.

Chapter 41

Bobby Rich: Bobby, You're A Rich Man

At the time, he says, it seemed like a good idea.

It was 1981 and Bobby Rich was in Los Angeles, working as a programming consultant for Drake-Chenault Enterprises. Under Rich's purview was KYNO/Fresno, one of Gene Chenault's original stations (and, historically important because it was where the Bill Drake-Gene Chenault relationship began). "So, the competition, KFRE, was doing a bank vault contest," says Rich. "My brilliant suggestion was that we guarantee KYNO would give away more. You know, if they give away a car, we'd give away two."

Rich says he convinced Chenault that the most KFRE could possibly give away was $12,000. But, then, go figure, KFRE loaded their treasure vault with too many large denomination bills — who knew? — and their winner scarfed up $54,000. This was thirty grand more than Rich had projected and since KYNO had promised *double* the winnings, the number turned out to be astronomical. "We were stuck with having to come up with $108,000," Rich says, sheepishly. He was surprised he didn't lose his job.

I told this story to Rich's friend, Bob Henabery, and he just laughed. He points to Rich's incredible success at KFMB/San Diego and tells me how WABC PD, Rick Sklar, reacted when Bobby took over WXLO/New York. "Bobby scared Rick to death." (I told Henabery I didn't think Rich had any idea.) Then Henabery gave the ultimate compliment. "Bobby's stations are fun to listen to," he said.

Tucson must agree. For years, Rich's station, Journal's KMXZ-FM, has been the most popular radio station in southern Arizona.

I wonder if they have a big cash giveaway.

•

KSTT/Davenport, Iowa, at 1170 AM, had an eye-to-the-world-window that allowed listeners to look in and see their favorite disc jockeys, one of whom was Bobby Rich, the station's Program Director.

The station had signed on in 1946, gone rock 'n' roll during the mid '50s and by the time Rich arrived, in 1968, it was the Quad Cities' favorite Top 40 station. When he left three years later, in 1971, KSTT had a 31.0 share in the ratings, which means Rich had a shot at his ultimate dream — working for KJR/Seattle. The program director of KJR, Gary Taylor, was aware of Rich. "I thought Bobby was a great talent and showed tremendous promise," recalls Taylor.

So far, so good. But, by the time Taylor called to see if Rich might be interested in coming to Seattle, Bobby's on-air act had changed a little, and Taylor didn't know it, until he listened to Rich's aircheck.

"What happened to you?" he asked.

"Whadda you mean?" replied Rich. "I got better. When you knew me, I was just some silly kid who didn't know what I was doing!" In the interim, says Rich, he'd learned how to do "the big-time deejay Boss Jock stuff."

"The trend at the time," explains Taylor, "was for jocks to adopt an affected presentation, and it just took away all his spontaneity."

Taylor wasn't kind and Rich was devastated, but decided to take his advice. "Gary told me to listen to some of my old tapes and to compare them to what I was doing."

So, he did. "I noticed that when I talked to people on the phone I sounded like a real person, but when I strapped on the headphones, I became Johnny Jock." To fix the problem, Rich says he laid his headphones on the floor, so they'd be "loud enough for me to hear what was going on, but not so loud that I'd fall in love with the sound of my voice."

He even tried holding the phone up to his ear every time he opened the mic.

"Finally, I broke myself out of it," he says.

•

Rich decided to quit his job at KSTT. He sold all his worldly possessions, bought a Winnebago and hit the road. He says he wasn't worried, even if his destination wasn't KJR. It was going to be an adventure. "I thought to myself, 'I'll get a job. All I've got to do is find the right place.' "

As it turned out, WMYQ/Miami wasn't it. He joined the station to do the night shift but, after only four months, he decided it wasn't what he wanted to do, so he quit and headed north to join his friend, John Long, at WAVZ/New Haven. The station's consultant was Paul Drew, the newly appointed Program Director of KHJ/Los Angeles, and its Program Director was Long. "I did all the promos and a high energy, screaming afternoon show," says Rich.

We didn't talk about his New Haven social life, but it was the early '70s, he was in his twenties and, given his hours, there's no reason to believe he'd be an early riser or welcome an early morning phone call.

"There are only two reasons I'd call and wake you up," John Long told him, when he phoned. "One is to say, 'Come in to cut a promo. And, the other is to tell you that you're going to KHJ."

Rich, still asleep, only heard Long say "promo."

"OK," he replied, "I'll be there in twenty minutes."

"No, man, really," insisted Long. "You're going to KHJ."

Rich's reaction wasn't over the top. "I knew it was an important station, but it wasn't like somebody said, 'You're going to KJR.' If that had happened, I'd have gone crazy."

Ten minutes later Drew called from Hollywood. "Bobby," he said. "We're going to pay you $25,000."

That's what shot Rich to the moon.

KHJ *was* KHJ, but it still wasn't KJR and after a while Rich discovered doing nights, even on a world-famous radio station, didn't rock his boat.

So, after a year in Los Angeles, Rich headed south to San Diego to become Program Director off KFMB-AM. When he arrived the format on KFMB's FM station was beautiful music. But, Rich had other ideas and, in February of 1975, he introduced San Diego to a brand new station that called itself B-100. B-100's target audience was teens and young adults and although it took three years to accomplish, by 1978, B-100 was the #1 radio station in San Diego, a feat that didn't go unnoticed by the national radio press.

As a result, Rich was offered a job he couldn't turn down: the Program Directorship of WXLO/New York City, an RKO Broadcasting station. From the beginning, New York rubbed him the wrong way. "It felt like a foreign country to me," he says.

WXLO's ratings increased under Rich. But, after about six months the tide turned when WKTU launched its disco format. Rich, who's had years to think about it, says there was nothing he or the station could do to fend the disco station off. "WKTU was an overnight success," he says, "and we were an overnight failure."

Rich left the east coast and landed in Los Angeles as the new Program Director of KHTZ, but it was clearly a time of transition for him. He left KHTZ, joined Drake-Chenault to consult (and engineer a big money giveaway) but quickly realized he missed the day-to-day radio station life and got a job at KFI/Los Angeles as Assistant Program Director.

What he remembers most about his time at KFI is that he re-discovered how much doing a morning show meant to him.

•

Bobby Rich returned to B-100 as Program Director in 1985.

One of the first things he did was begin to tinker with the music. His goal, he says, was to create a music mix that would appeal to both teens and younger adults. He threw out all his preconceived notions and judiciously, based on sound, began to pick songs from both the Top 40 and the Adult Contemporary charts. It was one of the first attempts at creating what the trade magazines dubbed *Hot Adult Contemporary*.

On the air he created "The Rich Brothers B-Morning Zoo," a morning show that dominated San Diego ratings from 1985 to 1990. During these years Rich was named Program Director and Personality of the Year three times by "Radio and Records" magazine.

In 1990, his decision to become a General Manager took him to KMGI/KIXI/Seattle. It was this experience that led him to think he might like to own a radio station of his own and, two years later, in 1992, he went to Tucson, AZ. Rich will tell you that his ownership experience isn't a pretty story. But, he'll also say that he fell in love with the desert and decided to stay.

Today Rich presides over the #1 morning show in Tucson. It doesn't appear he's going anywhere. He's found a station and a home, all a radio man could wish for.

He is a rich man.

CHAPTER 42

STEVE RIVERS: THE PRESIDENT
OF PROGRAMMING

Almost four decades ago an eighteen-year old kid named Carl Douglas left Lexington, Kentucky.

He was driving a blue and white Delta 88 crammed with all his earthly belongings and heading to Kansas City to begin his first major market radio job. He was both nervous and excited, and he was traveling alone. He arrived in KC, checked into a hotel the radio station had booked for him and went up to his room. He set his bag down, took a deep breath and called the station to let them know he'd hit town.

He left a message, but the call wasn't returned. The next day he called again; again, he got no response. By the third day he was starting to sweat. He sat in his room listening to the radio, to WHB – the big Kansas City AM Top 40 station. He knew it was the one to beat. From time to time, he also listened to KBEY-FM, the station he was going to work for, but it was still an album station and a little too "freaky" for him and, along with all the other things going on, listening to it made him nervous.

Finally, the phone rang. "Sit tight," said his boss, Chris Bailey. "Everything's fine."

But, everything wasn't fine for the DJs who were still working at KBEY. KBEY was an early '70s, free-form, progressive, underground FM radio station and its owner, desirous of higher ratings and more advertiser revenue, had decided to change the format. Bailey, fresh from success at KCBQ/San Diego, the industry's newest Top 40 darling, planned to blow the hippie DJs out, bring in a new, high energy air staff, including Douglas, and re-name the station KBEQ, with an emphasis on the Q.

In a better world, the owners would have told the departing jocks what they were doing and would have made the transition palatable. But, this was a top secret format change and the owners, frankly, didn't care.

The new Top 40 staff camped out several floors below KBEY's main studios and secretly began to dub their music library onto audio cartridges. Two floors above, the underground progressive DJs began to sense a disjointed future; I don't know how they knew something was going on, but they did. So, with no warning, the entire staff went on the offense and walked out, leaving the radio station with no bodies and dead air. This was problematic because the new Top 40 format wasn't ready to debut. "So, we had to go on the air earlier than expected," remembers Douglas. "And it was strange, because most of us didn't really know the music." I know this sounds strange, but these guys were AM Top 40 disc jockeys who'd probably never played an album on the air before and were only familiar with Top 40 hits. "So, we kept playing album cuts as if nothing had happened, but we decided to not use our names," Douglas says. It was about not wanting to sound stupid.

When the new Top 40 KBEQ-FM finally hit the air the first song it played was *I Want You Back* by The Jackson Five. (Imagine how that freaked out an audience raised on the Grateful Dead.) But, the Top 40 jocks and station management weren't concerned. They knew the hippies would never stick around once Karen Carpenter came out of their speakers.

The New Q was built around a very short playlist, a shotgun jingle and a group of high-energy, mostly teenage disc jockeys, who lived and breathed radio. "Our whole world revolved around it," says Dan Mason — the Dan Mason who would become President of CBS. Mason says he still remembers all the hours he and Douglas spent listening to tapes of other Top 40 stations. "We loved KCBQ/San Diego and used to sit around the apartment and imitate them."

But, it wasn't all fun and games and the two baby DJs say they never got past feeling insecure. "We were always worried about getting fired," says Mason.

Finally, the pressure and the uncertainty took its toll and both Douglas and Mason quit. "Carl went back to Lexington, to WLVK, and I went to WKLO/Louisville," Mason says.

They would unite again, but not before Carl Douglas was forced to change his name. "Steve Rivers was a house name at WIFI/Philadelphia." explains the man who was Carl Douglas. "When I arrived at the station they already had jingles singing it. That's how I got my name."

(Sorry. I know you expected something more dramatic.)

•

In the mid 1970s, Jerry Clifton was programming Miami's 96 X, where Rivers did the night shift. Clifton, who Rivers credits as being a big inspiration, had his staff hopping. A typical day meant four hours on the air, two hours in the production studio and two on the streets. "I got stuck with Palm Beach County, because I did nights," says Rivers. "I'd drive all the way up there, do a few van hits (personal appearances in the radio station van) and then drive back to Miami Beach, where the studios were."

Perhaps — and I didn't pose the question — it was during these nocturnal runs that Rivers came to the conclusion that he'd never be a "big jock" (his words). Or, maybe it was simply seeing Clifton in action and seeing himself in the role. Either way, Kent Burkhart suggests that after 96X it was the right time for Rivers to take hold of his career. "I thought Steve was very intense about the radio business and had a HUGE motivation to do well. He had that certain intangible 'thing' that all great programmers have and he's serious about his craft.

He did not disappoint me, or the industry."

The station was WGNG/Providence, Rhode Island. Burkhart was consulting and Rivers was the new Program Director. Gary Berkowitz, across town at WPRO, says he remembers competing. "Rivers had that little station sounding killer. Great audio, jocks and music. It was quite impressive!"

"We tried to make as much noise as we could," says Rivers. "The most amazing promotion we did was tied around a group called Klaatu."

In 1976, a writer for the "Providence Journal," Steve Smith, wrote an article suggesting that a recording act named Klaatu was really The Beatles.

**"COULD KLAATU BE THE BEATLES?
MYSTERY IS A MAGICAL MYSTERY TOUR."**

Rivers read the story, called Smith and brought him to the station to be interviewed. "We cut up the interview and used it on the air as the ratings period promotion. I had the General Manager record special promos saying, 'Listen Thursday morning for the missing Beatle tapes.' "

The station played Beatle and Klaatu songs side by side, even played some of them backwards. "We milked it for all it was worth," Rivers says. "I even called Capital Records in Los Angeles and asked the receptionist for information on Klaatu. I still remember she said, 'I have no idea what you're talking about.' "

The phones at the station were burning up and Rivers did his best to fan the flames. "We created havoc in the community," he says. "That little five hundred watt radio station had never seen such intensity."

Hold it! Only five hundred watts?

"Oh yeah!" says Berkowitz. "But Rivers took advantage of every one of them!"

When the ratings came out, WGNG had doubled its audience.

Now, with a programming success to point to, Rivers was ready to move up the ladder.

•

WAPE/Jacksonville sat next to a highway in Orange Park, Florida and the first thing you saw from the road was a swimming pool. Once owned by Stan and Sis Kaplan and programmed by Jack Gale, it was a fifty thousand watt AM flamethrower that could be heard all along the coast for at least five hundred miles. But, despite the grand signal, WAPE was still an AM station at a time when FM was coming in to its own.

Rivers say that FM stereo versus AM mono was an issue, but a bigger problem was WAPE's heavy commercial load. The Ape, he says, sounded like *all* it played were commercials and this was particularly true when compared to the eight minutes per hour cap rival WIVY-FM had in place.

But, WAPE wasn't all bad. Rivers had two secret weapons. One, an owner who believed in big promotion and, two, a morning man named The Greaseman.

They called their big promotion "The Big Ape Treasure House" and the winner, whose name would be drawn by the Mayor of Jacksonville, would win a fully furnished new home, PLUS a car, a boat and every tool in handyman heaven. The buzz was on and tens of thousands of Big Ape listeners registered to win — each having toured the house in advance to see what their dream home looked like. But, when the winner was announced on the air, he arrived at the station with an announcement of his own. "Don't want the house," he said. "It's not as nice as what I've already got."

Jacksonville went crazy. As the winner, an African American employed by the city, publicly pondered selling the house or, maybe, just giving it to his son, the press jumped on the racial angle and made the story bigger than it really was. "Let's just say the Civil War was being fought again," explains Rivers.

Meanwhile, back at the station, The Greaseman reacted in his own way. He walked over to the winner, looked him directly in the eye, and said, "Jeez, what a slap in the face."

Things eventually calmed down, but Rivers says (with not just a little satisfaction) that talk continued long after the promotion was over. "It was great publicity for us."

He was learning that, in rock radio, you roll with the punches.

•

FM penetration was the measurement of the number of people listening to stations on the FM dial relative to those still listening to AM. The tipping point — when FM listeners outnumbered AM listeners — came in 1978. Rivers, ready to leave the AM dial forever, reconnected with his Kansas City roommate, Dan Mason. "When Charles Giddens was General Manager of KOPA-FM/Phoenix and I was First Media's National Program Director, we hired Steve to take the station Top 40," says Mason.

Historically, Phoenix had always been a great radio town. During the '60s, the Top 40 battle between KRIZ and KRUX was legendary, and the '70s and '80s were, as it turned out, proving to be equally exciting. Initially, KOPA-FM went after the AM Top 40s. Then, once those skirmishes started to lean his way, Rivers took aim at KDKB-FM (Album Rock), KUPD-FM (format of the day) and KZZP-FM (another FM Top 40). When the smoke cleared, KOPA and Rivers were on top and that's the way it stayed until 1984.

Then, during River's sixth year at KOPA, a new General Manager arrived and with no promotion and no call letter change, he decided to make KOPA an Adult Contemporary station. "And the numbers just tumbled," says Rivers.

The station remained AC for almost a year. To hear Rivers tell it, it sounded as bad as the air staff felt about it. "Finally, I convinced the company that it wasn't working and that we needed to go back to Top 40."

Rivers says he stayed long enough to get KOPA back on track, but he was no longer emotionally invested in the station. Besides, he had the seven year itch. "So, I got the hell out of there."

He went back to Florida, this time to Tampa.

"First of all," says Rivers, "You can't jump into Scott Shannon's shoes. But, going to WRBQ gave me a chance to learn *from* him without actually *having* him in the building." What he means is that virtually everything at WRBQ (Q105) was in place with Shannon's name on it. What Rivers brought to the party, he says, was "a little science." What he got in return, by absorbing Scott Shannon's "voodoo," was what he called a graduate degree in programming.

Modestly, Rivers explains that his job at Q105 was to simply keep things running. "And that's what I did," he says.

After two years at WRBQ/Tampa, Rivers traded one city by the bay for another.

•

The legendary San Francisco Top 40, KFRC-AM was no longer playing music. Instead, under consultant, Walter Sabo, it was dallying around with its short-lived Game Zone format. The city's dominant FM Top 40 was KITS and its competitor was KMEL. When Nick Bazoo, KMEL's program director announced he was leaving, Rivers applied to be his replacement, got the job and inherited a great staff.

"Honest to God," Rivers says, "I'd had great teams to work with before, but these guys were very special. We were busting records left and right."

In the end, KMEL won the San Francisco Top 40 battle, KFRC changed formats again — eventually finding its niche as a home for Sinatra and friends — and KITS dropped Top 40 to become an alternative station.

That's when Rivers got the call from Hollywood.

Looking back, Rivers admits going to KIIS-FM/Los Angeles was frightening. Still, he says, he'd always wanted to work for Gannett Radio and long admired Gerry DeFrancesco and Jay Cook, the guys who ran Gannett. "The biggest challenge at Kiss was fighting the ghost of that 10 share," he says.

Four or five months before Rivers arrived in Los Angeles, Emmis Broadcasting's KPWR (Power 106) turned the city on its ear with a musical format, urban based, that appealed to whites, blacks and Hispanics in LA. "And, they cleaned Kiss's clock," Rivers says, matter-of-factly. Prior to this, Kiss had been on top, with an incredible and unheard of ten share. "A lot of that number," says Rivers, "came from Hispanic listeners, but when Power hit the air, it was like driving a Mack truck through a mall."

Despite his feeling that a 10 share could never happen again, after arriving and listening for a while, Rivers decided that he thought Kiss was still in good shape. "It just wasn't the station it had once been," he says.

(For the record, former Kiss GM Lynn Anderson, the manager who hired Rivers, says, "That ten share was a once in a lifetime accomplishment. Never been done before or since on FM in LA. Great bragging rights, but 12+ numbers are little more than 'ego share' — which is to say, nice to have, but not as monetizable as owning top requested demos. Steve built and solidified sellable demos that transcended the broad strokes," says Anderson. "Our billing increased exponentially every year (he was there), even as our 12+ numbers declined. What's not to value about that?")

He went to work.

To his surprise, Rivers discovered the job took more than stamina and determination. "Corporate was across the hall and it was like being in a fishbowl. I just put on the blinders, kept my head down and did what I thought was right. I just let the chips fall where they'd fall."

He remembers an incident with Michael Jackson. "He'd just put out an album and his manager called and said, 'Michael doesn't think it sounds right on the air. He thinks your audio chain needs to be adjusted.' "

Rivers says his response was direct. "If Michael Jackson wants to come down and adjust the audio on the station; well, he's welcome to do so."

When Scott Shannon left WHTZ/New York and came to LA to launch Pirate Radio, "Everyone in town was concerned," says Rivers. "Scott was a mentor to me and I knew how deadly he could be."

On the morning Pirate launched, Rivers was glued to the radio. "When he did the sign-on with *Welcome To The Jungle* by Guns and Roses, I can't tell you how relieved I was. I remember thinking, 'Thank goodness he didn't sign on with Madonna.' "

But, by the spring of 1989, Rivers felt Kiss had come to a crossroads. He called Anderson and Cook and told them he believed the station no longer had the luxury of being all things to all people. He argued Kiss needed to focus on its strengths and that the station had no choice than to be what it really was — a true, straight ahead Top 40.

His bosses agreed and Rivers did the fine-tuning he thought necessary. When the summer ratings were released, Kiss was #1 12+, 18 to 34 and 25 to 54. By then Rivers had been at the helm of Kiss for close to three years and was starting to feel burned out. It was no wonder. He'd been in six cities in fourteen years, each a step up and each with a new lesson to be learned. Still, in 1989, when Rivers stepped down at KIIS-FM/Los Angeles and announced he was going to WZOU/Boston, there were many who wondered if it was a mis-step.

It wasn't.

•

When the 1990 Boston spring ratings book was released, WZOU had beaten perennial Top 40 leader WXKS-FM. Across town, in the offices of Kiss-108, there was some concern. After some conversation,

Gerry DeFrancesco, working in Philadelphia for Kiss 108's parent company, Pyramid Broadcasting, was asked to make a call.

"Gerry called me and asked if I had any interest in crossing the street to program KISS," says Rivers. "I told him 'no,' that it really wasn't my thing."

"Why don't you at least sit down with John Madison?" said deFrancesco. "What could it hurt?"

WZOU had never asked Rivers to sign a non-compete contract and for a year he'd been working with a letter of agreement and dragging his feet on more formal documentation. "I really didn't know whether I wanted to stay in Boston," he admits. "My wife was homesick for Seattle and, for a while, I kinda thought I'd get a couple of books out of WZOU and then move out west and start a consultancy."

Still, one Kiss meeting led to another and, by the end of the year, it was agreed that Rivers would take over as Program Director of Kiss-108 at the beginning of 1991.

"That was really something," he says, "because it was the first time a PD change had occurred at Kiss since Sunny Joe White had signed the station on years before."

•

WZOU hired Steve Perun to replace him. Rivers says he began to listen for changes in the station's programming, but Perun kept WZOU sailing in the same direction Rivers had plotted out.

Then something unexpected happened. Perun quit and WZOU named a new PD, Sunny Joe White. "So, Sunny and I basically ended up trading places," says Rivers.

To understand the dynamics of this competitive dance, you need a sense of who Sunny Joe White was. Sunny Joe was a Boston institution and, until Rivers showed up, he'd been the only PD Kiss had ever had. The station, owned by Richie Balsbaugh, had signed on in 1979, two weeks after New Year's day. Licensed to Medford, MA, a suburb north of Boston, the station was called

Kiss-108 Disco and, for the times, it was "spot on." During Kiss-108's first ten years its staff included, among others, Sunny Joe, Dale Dorman, J.J. Wright and later, Matt Siegel.

By the late 1980s Kiss-108 had morphed into a mainstream Top 40, albeit one with some strange little musical twists. "It was Sunny's nature to reach for the extreme," says Rivers. "He'd have had no problem segueing from a Liza Minnelli record into Steppenwolf." But, upon arriving at WZOU, Sunny Joe basically stuck to the plan Rivers (and Perun) had laid out the previous year.

Meanwhile, back at Kiss-108, Rivers says he did nothing with the air staff except appreciate them. "They were wonderful," he says. Instead, he set his sights on fine tuning the music and learning what the audience wanted. "All I did was add some research and tighten it up," he says.

Rivers makes it sound like nothing, but by his second book, the one reflecting radio listening in the fall of 1991, Kiss-108 was #1 among all age groups. "It was a clean sweep," he says.

"Yeah, it felt pretty good."

With the win, came lots of trade attention, because he'd essentially beat himself.

•

The Telecommunication Act of 1996 changed the face of American radio. William Kennard, the Chairman of the FCC, explained it this way: "The fundamental economic structure of the radio industry is changing from one of independently owned operators to something akin to a chain store. I don't think anybody anticipated that the pace would be so fast and so dramatic."

In a flurry of activity, Pyramid Broadcasting, Kiss-108's parent company, was sold to Evergreen Communications, which then began a series of acquisitions that included Chancellor Broadcasting. Then, the new company, re-named Chancellor, merged its assets with Capstar to become AM/FM and, eventually, part of Clear Channel.

As all of this was happening, Rivers corporate responsibilities grew; first at Pyramid and then with the principals of Evergreen. "Scott Ginsburg and Jimmy deCastro gave me a chance to prove myself," he says, referring to the launch of WKTU/New York. (In the late '70s, WKTU had been a very successful New York disco station and, by the middle '90s, according to Rivers, there was a notion that those call letters might be of value again, if used on a rhythmic contemporary station.) "There were a lot of people involved with WKTU," Rivers says. "Me, Jimmy deCastro, Guy Zapolean and Bev Tilden.' "

The station launched during the tail end of the winter book, in late '95/early '96 and by summer, WKTU v2.0 was a New York #1. "From the beginning Guy and I knew that 'KTU was going to be a home run," Rivers says.

Next Rivers took on the Corporate PD role at AM/FM – his title was Chief Programming Officer — and the personal challenge of moving from Boston to Seattle. "Jimmy was very accommodating and simply said, 'You're going to be on a lot of airplanes.' "

He was. In fact, during his last year with the company, when AM/FM was putting on "Jammin' Oldies," Rivers flew over 300,000 miles. "We ran hard for five or six years, buying stations left and right and, while there was always too much to do, we had a lot of fun."

But, when AM/FM was eventually sold to Clear Channel, Rivers had a decision to make. "For a number of reasons, I didn't really want to deal with the Clear Channel thing. So, I started looking for something different to do."

In hindsight, Rivers says he knew what was happening."At AM/FM," he says, "we were building the last truly great radio company."

•

Just before the millennium, Rivers and Radio Ink's Eric Rhoads, caught in the buzz of internet possibilities, formed Radio Central.

Based in San Francisco, the idea was to build internet radio stations for non-radio companies. "We did ten or twelve stations for Earthlink, some for Lycos.com and A&E Television also signed on. But, we were five years ahead of ourselves." By this, he means streaming costs were prohibitive and the RIAA was beginning to raise its head on licensing issues. In 2002, faced with more questions than answers, the venture capital guys told Rhoads and Rivers to "shut it down."

Rivers returned to Seattle to launch the consultancy he'd long talked about. But, within a short time, he was offered and accepted the position of President of Programming at Infinity Broadcasting. Sadly, given the politics involved, the position didn't provide the opportunities he'd hoped it would, and after a short stay, he opted to leave the company and go into business with his old friend, Richie Balsbaugh, one of the principals at Pyramid Broadcasting. They decided to call their new venture PyramidRadioInc.com, and explained their core business would be to design "in store radio stations" for commercial businesses. Think big retail chains. Based in Los Angeles, it was another idea ahead of its time.

In 2007 Rivers returned to Seattle, the place he and his family call home. He'd accepted a job programming CBS's KBKS-FM, Kiss 106. The move back to front-line, hands-on programming wasn't surprising to those who know how Rivers thinks. They say he's always up for a challenge and enjoys rolling his sleeves up. Rivers says he still believes that the type of opportunities he was offered early in his career still exist for someone who wants to program. "At least I hope so. But, if you want to program," he says, "you have to be willing to go anywhere, learn what you can and then, when you've stopped learning, be ready to move again."

In an industry with a propensity to eat its young and exile its elders, Steve Rivers has proven to be an innovator and a survivor. According to his old Kansas City roommate, Dan Mason, it's because he's a master of radio programming principles.

"Steve has an incredible amount of experience and his knowledge of the history of programming has served him well."

The book on Mr. Rivers is still being written.

CHAPTER 43
ART ROBERTS: THE ABCs OF ART ROBERTS

Even with a degree, he didn't think his prospects were hot — not back then, not in the sweltering summer of 1953. Air conditioners were so scarce that breathing was like swallowing hot cotton candy, and he wasn't warming up to the idea that he'd have to drive a truck to make a living.

I'm writing about Elvis Presley, but just as easily I could be describing Art Roberts because, except for the city and a couple of changes, in 1953, their situations were identical. Elvis was eighteen and fresh out of high school, when he got behind the wheel for Crown Electric in Memphis, and Roberts, who'd just graduated from Southeastern College in Hammond, Louisiana, had just accepted a truck driving job with Jackson Brewing Company, a beer distributor in New Orleans. His father wasn't excited.

"You went to college for four years and now you're going to drive a truck?" he exclaimed.

•

Roberts grew up in New York City, but unlike other New Yorkers I've written about, the city didn't get into his blood and, once he left, he wasn't drawn back to it. Radio was no attraction, either. In fact, he had no favorite announcer and didn't particularly like the pop music of the day. "I listened to jazz," he says, "and loved country music."

His first taste of radio came in college. "We had a job board," he says, "and there was a note posted that read:

PART TIME ANNOUNCER NEEDED

When no one else applied, the job at WIHL/Hammond was his and, in that hot summer of 1953 when he graduated, Roberts decided to pursue a radio career. "I sent tapes out, but didn't get one call back," he recalls. "Nothing."

Discouraged, he got ready to truck to New Orleans, but he wasn't jazzed about it. "Then I got a call from Atlanta," explains Roberts. No, not Georgia – Atlanta, Texas, a speck on the map, about an inch south of Texarkana. "Half the money, but it sounded better than driving a truck."

The decision made, he headed to Texas. It was the beginning of a journey that would lead to KLIF/Dallas, WKBW/Buffalo and then, back to the Midwest and ten years at "The Big 89" — WLS/Chicago.

•

Atlanta, Texas was a one-horse town. When Roberts reported to work, the Program Director sat him down. "I want you to try to sound like you're from around these parts," he told him.

Eager to please, Roberts slowed his New York pace to a crawling drawl. "But, one day this guy walked into the studio," he says.

"You know," the stranger said to him, "we like the music you're playing, but you're tryin' awful hard to sound like you're from around here. And, look, everybody knows you're not."

In other words – that dog won't hunt.

"It really taught me a lesson about being myself," Roberts says. It was a lesson that would serve him well.

•

In 1954, Roberts headed for KPBB/Tyler. The station's format was a mish-mash, and like today, the station wasn't about the music, it was about sales and the money. Roberts still recalls the manager's mantra: "If two squirrels want to mate on the air, we'll broadcast it, if you get a sponsor."

1954 was the dawn of the rock age, Tyler was a stones throw from Dallas and Roberts was developing a taste for gospel and rhythm and blues. It all came together for him when he got a call from Gordon McLendon.

"KLIF still had a rather loose format," says Roberts. It was so loose, in fact, that he'd walk into the studio at night with a box of blues records and play whatever he pleased. "I always considered KLIF my master's degree in radio," he says. "McLendon was a flat-out genius, a master of illusion."

By 1956, Elvis Presley had left truck driving behind and Roberts, like many of the McLendon jocks, was coming in to his own, too, and getting offers to program. Station owners, he says, knew McLendon had a format and they wanted it. The road led to Shreveport. "The first thing I did was throw a parade for Elvis," says Roberts. "No, Elvis wasn't there; it was just a parade *for* him. What amazed me is how many people believed they saw him."

Three months later, he was off to Dayton, Ohio.

His plan was to play rhythm and blues records on the radio at night, and to make extra cash doing record hops. It sounded like a good idea until the station's owner, Ronald B. Woodyard, objected to the hops.

With no hops to do, Roberts left Dayton for Akron. It was there that Roberts first met the soon-to-be legend, Dick Biondi, and developed the contacts that would take him from Dayton, to WKBW/Buffalo and, ultimately, in October of 1960, to Chicago.

•

WLS/Chicago was owned by ABC and, in April of 1960, the station went Top 40. "Mort Crowley was doing mornings, Jim Dunbar followed him, Gene Taylor did afternoons and from nine to midnight it was Dick Biondi," explains Roberts.

At first Roberts pulled the mid-day shift. "They didn't really tell us what to do or how to do it," he says. "By the time you got to Chicago, they figured you should know what you're doing." So, he made up his own contests and played the music he wanted in the order and rotations he wanted. Freedom! "That's what made us sound different. There were no two of us on WLS that sounded alike."

In February of 1963, as WLS's Music Director, Roberts added a record called *Please, Please Me* to the station's playlist and, by doing so, WLS became the first station to play The Beatles in the United States.

Later that year, when Dick Biondi left the station, Roberts moved to nine to midnight. "The first night I was on the air, I told the kids I was going to do a different show every night."

Art Roberts did nights at WLS for five years, until 1968. With a 50,000 watt signal, he had listeners in two-thirds of the nation. "I listened on the sky wave in Pennsylvania," says former WLS PD, John Gehron. "The things Art and WLS did shaped my radio philosophies. Art captured the pulse of Chicago."

Roberts was everywhere and, seemingly, connected to everything. "Art crammed a ton of stuff into his program and never sounded cluttered," recalls Lee Abrams, who, as a kid, was a fan. "Art defined big city personality radio."

•

In 1970, after ten years, Roberts left WLS and headed to KNBR/ San Francisco. But he was missed in Chicago and, when WCFL made him an offer he couldn't refuse, he returned to the Windy City to do mornings and to be the station's Program Director. "But it was the wrong time, the wrong place.," he says. Besides, you can never beat yourself."

During the '70s, '80s and '90s Roberts programmed and managed stations in suburban Chicago, Shreveport, Milwaukee, Dallas and San Antonio. He also consulted and started a radio trade magazine, "The Music Programmer's Guide."

"We did the first research column," he says proudly.

On March 6, 2002 Art Roberts had a stroke. When he died, radio lost a true pathfinder.

"Art's show was a theater of the mind masterpiece," say Abrams. "He'll be long remembered, appreciated and loved by the industry and by millions of Americans he blew away with years of truly amazing radio."

(Art Robert's website, with links to audio, is still online at www.artroberts.com).

CASEY KASEM

LARRY LUJACK

ART LABOE

GORDON
MCLENDON

ROBERT W. MORGAN

BILL MACK WITH LEANN RIMES

PAT O'DAY WITH JIMI HENDRIX, 1968.

PAT O'DAY (RIGHT) WITH LISA GANGEL(LEFT).

TODD STORZ

KEVIN METHENY

BRUCE MORROW

ALL PHOTOS COURTESY OF RADIO & RECORDS UNLESS OTHERWISE NOTED

Fred Winston at WYFR (L) and WLS (top right).

Bobby Rich

Gary Owens (right) with Howard Hesseman (left).

DICK PURTAN

ART ROBERTS

STEVE RIVERS

DR. DON ROSE

JOHN SEBASTIAN

ED SALAMON

ALL PHOTOS COURTESY OF RADIO & RECORDS UNLESS OTHERWISE NOTED

JOHN ROOK

WITH PETULA CLARK

RICK SKLAR

TOM ROUNDS

SCOTT SHANNON

MICHAEL SPEARS

RUSTY WALKER

Courtesy of Jerry Del Colliano

GARY STEVENS

JERRY DEL COLLIANO, TODD WALLACE AND GARY STEVENS

CHARLIE TUNA

CHARLIE TUNA AND LARRY LUJAK AT THE MARCONI AWARDS.

WOLFMAN JACK (C) WITH JERRY WEXLER (L) AND PAUL DREW (R).

ALL PHOTOS COURTESY OF RADIO & RECORDS UNLESS OTHERWISE NOTED

Chapter 44
John Rook: Checkmate

This reads like the beginning of a bad novel.

It was a rainy, cloudy, Sunday night in Chicago. John Rook walked to the hotel window, sighed and glanced out at the lights of the city. "God," he thought. "Here I am."

Five years earlier, Rook had left KQV/Pittsburgh to take the programming reigns at WLS/Chicago and quickly snatched the ratings back from WCFL. For the next five years, WLS stayed on top of Chicago's rock and, in fact, the mountain of ratings he notched up for ABC, including knocking out WGN, was the impetus that had thrown him into consulting.

Now, it was 1972 and he was back in the Windy City, working for WCFL. "Ok, you better do it," Rook told himself. He picked up the phone and booked a limo for three a.m.

Just before dawn the next morning, Larry Lujack, the morning man at WLS, found Rook waiting for him at the curb. Rook says they chatted a moment and he convinced Lujack to meet him later that day.

"So, we met for lunch that afternoon," says Rook. "I told him, 'You're too great a man to have to get up so early. I can pay you more to do afternoons.' "

Mr. Lujack agreed and, in 1972, he resigned from WLS to join WCFL and a fierce and spirited battle between the two stations began.

WCFL won.

•

In 1956, the movie "The Girl Can't Help It" was big for more reasons than Jayne Mansfield. Unlike most early rock 'n' roll flicks, the film was shot in ravishing color and Little Richard, like Ms.

Mansfield, was pert and posed, and gave a startling performance.

What you may not remember, however, is the appearance of a little known American named Eddie Cochran, singing a song called *Twenty Flight Rock*. Cochran, of course, would made rock 'n' roll history with his song, *Summertime Blues*. But, it was *Twenty Flight Rock* that knocked John Lennon's socks off, particularly when Paul McCartney taught him how to play it, on July 6, 1957, the day the two boys first met.

It was about the same time that Rook met Cochran at the singer's home in Bell Gardens, a community south of Los Angeles. Rook had only been in L.A. a short while. He'd graduated from high school in Chadron, NE, and immediately headed for Hollywood, where he found work at a Sears store in Santa Monica. "Three weeks into it," says Rook, "I went down to the beach; lo and behold, I ran into Burt Lancaster."

How or why the two became friends isn't important to the story. What is key is Lancaster convinced Rook to join the Pasadena Playhouse and before long, the teenager was hanging out with Hollywood's young elite: Natalie Wood, Sal Mineo — even James Dean. These contacts led to TV and movie roles. "I was in the Wild Bill Hickock series because I knew how to ride," says Rook. "And then I was in "My Man Godfrey" with June Allyson and David Niven."

He changed his name to Johnny Rho and pursued acting. But, as a sideline, he took on Cochran's career. "I did everything I could to get him started," says Rook, "and we became close friends."

•

The suggestion came from Cochran and Tennessee Ernie Ford: Rook should try his hand at radio.

"I went back to my hometown in Nebraska, but couldn't find a job," Rook says. "So, I headed up to Wyoming."

He found work at KASL/Newcastle, where he was given a twelve-hour shift and a pile of polka records. Rooks says he wanted to play Eddie's records, or tunes by Elvis or Chuck Berry, but was told he couldn't play that "jungle bunny" music until the sun went down. Yes, that's exactly what his boss called it. It made Rook furious. It still does.

He changed his name again, this time to Johnny Rowe. He jumped from New Castle to KALL/Salt Lake, and from there east, to KTLN/Denver, where he jocked for two years. Then, in 1963, he was unceremoniously fired by a new PD, who Rook remembers as being "right out of the payola era with some friends he wanted to bring in."

Ken Palmer was across town at KIMN and, when he couldn't hire Rook because of a KTLN non-compete, he let ABC's Hal Neal in on his find and, in January of 1964, John Rook joined ABC at KQV/Pittsburgh.

It was just in time to welcome the British Invasion.

•

KQV's manager was named John Gibbs and the Top 40 radio battle in Pittsburgh was between KQV and KDKA. Because of his relationship with Cochran, Rook had an "in" with the manager of the Beatles, Brian Epstein, and Rook was determined that KQV would be the station to present The Beatles to Pittsburgh. Epstein said fine, but he had a condition. "Brian also wanted us to bring in the Rolling Stones," says Rook.

America, in 1964, despite the Beatles, was still about crew cuts, white socks and penny loafers. "And along came these guys who looked like they had snot dripping from their hair," explains Rook. The morning after the Stones rolled into Pittsburgh, Gibbs summoned Rook to his office.

"There was this picture and terrible review in the paper," Rook recalls.

Gibbs threw the paper down on his desk. "John," he said, "don't ever subject us to this type of thing again."

Uh, uhm, sure, boss.

"Then, when we brought The Beatles in, Gibbs said, 'My God, do you know what this is going to do to us? We'll be dead, we'll be ruined.' " But, of course, it didn't happen that way. Instead, KQV beat KDKA. Shortly thereafter consultant Mike Joseph tried to lure Rook to WFIL/Philadelphia, but when ABC got wind of the plan, Rook got a call from Hal Neal and was told "get his tail" to New York. "Neal took me into Leonard Goldenson's office (The President of ABC) and explained to him what a brilliant programmer I was," says Rook.

"The next thing I knew, I was the Program Director of WLS/ Chicago."

•

In 1967 WCFL, under PD Ken Draper, had soundly beaten WLS. Rook's job was to fix the problem.

"You go in and look it over," he says. "You see if you've got any good parts; scrub up the ones that are good and put the other ones away."

Rook moved Clark Weber to mornings and made Art Roberts music director, moving him to mid-days. He kept Larry Lujack in afternoons. The station began to click and, after beating WCFL, things got even better. Before long Rook was able to boast, "We even beat WGN, and they had the Cubs!"

The ratings gains came because everyone at WLS worked hard and because Rook was very demanding. "He listened twenty-four hours a day," says Tom Bigby. "I'll never forget my first night on WLS. I was a kid, scared to death of fifty thousand watts going to thirty-eight states and I mispronounced the word *resume*. Right after midnight, he called me." Rook and the hotline were *so* connected at the hip that, when he left WLS in 1972, the staff ripped the phone off the wall and gave it to him as a going-away present.

During the five years Rook was at WLS, the station was a solid #1. "Not just teens," says Bigby, "but adults, too. When WGN had a twelve share, WLS had an eighteen."

"Rook understood the importance of doing every thing right," says former ABC exec Bob Henabery. "He was a masterful Top 40 programmer."

•

There's more to John Rook's story, of course: consulting, Bill Drake, KFI and KABC/Los Angeles, station ownership, ambition, risk-taking, unbreakable bonds of friendship and the changing role of radio and media in the 21st Century.

For now; however, let's leave it this way. "John Rook is the greatest programmer of our time or any time," says Larry Lujack.

(If you'd like to know what Rook is doing and thinking today, visit his website — www.johnrook.com.)

CHAPTER 45

Dr. Don Rose:
The First To Say "Good Morning"

She was a single mom at the end of her rope who lived with her kids in a tiny one-room flat in San Jose. The room had no stove, so she cooked over Sterno. It wasn't a pretty picture. "I decided the world would be better off without me," she wrote.

Her plan was simple: Get in the car, hit the accelerator, close her eyes and ram into a freeway overpass.

The streets were slick in the Bay Area that morning. "Just makes it easier," she thought. Then, for some unknown reason, she doesn't know why, she turned on the radio to 610/KFRC/San Francisco. "And you said something that snapped me out of it," she wrote to Dr. Don Rose. "I don't remember what, but it gave me the strength to keep trying."

As he told me the story in 2001, Rose was very low key. "A couple of things like that make it all seem worthwhile," he says. He spoke very softly. It may have been his recent surgery. I prefer to think it was his humanity.

On April 1, 2005, "The San Francisco Chronicle" reported this news:

> Dr. Don Rose, the last of the great Top 40 disc jockeys, died in his sleep Wednesday at his Concord home after months of fighting pneumonia. He was 70.

This is Dr. Don's story.

•

Buffalo Bill and Don Rosenberg had one thing in common: They were both from North Platte, NE, where hitchhikers hold up signs that say, "Anyplace but here." (Dr. Don's line, not mine.)

Rosenberg was fifteen and needed a couple of hundred dollars to go to a Boy Scout National Jamboree in Valley Forge, PA. The local newspaper, looking for a reporter to tell the jamboree story, had a contest and Rosenberg won. Not to be outdone, North Platte's local radio station, KODY, announced that *they* wanted part of the action and gave him a choice: write for the paper or for the radio station.

"I was a terrible speller," he says, "So, I decided to go for radio. I swear that's the only reason." (At the jamboree, Rosenberg interviewed Dwight D. Eisenhower, just before he was elected President.)

After high school Rosenberg headed off to the University of Nebraska in Lincoln to study accounting and to look for a radio job at a local station. But, after auditioning there were no offers and he spent the next two years working at the campus station, KNUS. (Rose says he was the only person to notice that KNUS spelled backwards was SUNK.)

In the middle of his junior year, Rosenberg's friend, Al Canyon, scored a real radio job in Lincoln. Canyon *had* been working for KWBE/Beatrice, a small station in a little town forty miles outside of Lincoln, and when Rosenberg applied for Canyon's job, he was hired. "Al had a very unfortunate habit," said Rose. "When he came to a word he couldn't pronounce, he'd just jiggle the microphone switch."

Eventually KLMN/Lincoln, where Canyon worked, caught on to his game and fired him. Again, Rosenberg was his replacement.

Then, in 1955, a few hours short of college graduation, Rosenberg was offered a job by Chick Crabtree, the Program Director of KOIL/Omaha.

He accepted in a flash. "Four years, but no degree," he explained.

•

Don Burden, KOIL's owner, told Crabtree he was crazy to hire the kid and, sure enough, four weeks later, they fired him. As a parting gift, Crabtree gave the young man some advice. "Look," he said, "Your name is too long. Shorten it to Rose and, gee, since your initials are D.R., why don't you call yourself doctor? Dr. Don Rose."

The details are sketchy here, but Rose told me he was hired next by Don Keyes, Gordon McLendon's right hand man, and sent to KTSA/San Antonio. But, one month into the job, McLendon heard Rose on the air, didn't like him, and instructed Keyes to fire him. Rose was distraught, and with his tail between his legs, he went home to Nebraska.

Once there, he decided, somewhat ambitiously, that he wanted to work for the Storz Organization in Omaha. But, Bill Stewart, Storz's right hand man told him he just wasn't ready. Instead, Stewart helped Rose get a job at KRNY/Kearney.

"It was really a big step backward," said Rose. Fifteen months later, he was fired again.

It would be the last time it ever happened.

•

Rose couldn't find work. For a few months he pounded spikes for the Union Pacific Railroad. His parents didn't say a word.

When he finally found a job in radio, it was at KWMT/Ft. Dodge, Iowa, where he was named Program Director and given the morning show. After a while, he says, he began to settle in and attract an audience. "Did you wake up grouchy?" he'd ask on the air. "Or, is she still in bed?"

Rose was in Ft. Dodge for a year and it's where he met his wife, Kae. But, before long, he moved to KUTL/Tulsa. "I hoped it was close enough to Oklahoma City and KOMA that someone at Storz would notice," he said. "But, they didn't."

So, in 1959, he accepted a job at WEBC in Duluth, MN. "Kae was watching the weather on TV when I called to tell her," said Rose. "In Duluth, it was forty below zero."

•

Don and Kae Rosenberg settled in (and for) Duluth. "They were tough years for my wife," Rose told me. "But, professionally, they worked out well for me."

He was a Program Director again and, after having no luck finding a morning man, he decided to do it himself. He went on the air and told corny Finlander jokes. He got a cowbell and was generally crazy. His show started getting better and better and zanier and zanier. Before long, word began to spread about "that guy in Duluth."

That's when he got the call.

Kent Burkhart and Paul Drew invited him to join WQXI/Atlanta. Rose had been in the frozen tundra for three years; the warm climate and the big city sounded pretty damn good. He bought himself a white Buick convertible, packed up and headed south.

•

The job at WQXI was the mid-morning shift, nine to noon. One day, when a technical mishap required Rose to ad lib himself out of a difficult situation on the air, he rose to the occasion. Burkhart says he sat in his office listening and laughing. Later that day, Burkhart told Rose he was being moved to mornings.

"I was up for the challenge," Rose says.

The new show had reverb and energy, and was goofy and funny. In short order, like a Sherman tank, Rose conquered Atlanta, got headlines in radio trade magazines and was offered a big job in Philadelphia by WFIL.

WFIL's only direct competition was WIBG, the city's long-time Top 40 leader. But, by '68, WFIL had been in format for two years and WIBG had taken some big hits, which is to say that WFIL was making some inroads. Jim Hilliard, WFIL's PD, allowed Rose time to fit in and room to grow. The plan worked. "I'm not sure that I ever got to be a solid #1," said Rose, "but WFIL *was* the #1 *music* station in Philadelphia."

Then, Don Rose had a heart attack. "Open heart surgery and some pretty horrible complications," he told me.

He was out from October 1972 until June of the next year. When he returned to the show, listeners noticed he had a different take on things. "Instead of the rapid-fire, move-move-move thing I'd been doing," said Rose, "sometimes I'd just stop and say, 'You know, we have to talk about this.' "

He began talking about his life at home. He started a tradition of celebrating his family's Christmas on the air, with presents being unwrapped, carols being sung, and voices saying, "I love you."

"I started to be more Don Rosenberg and less Dr. Don Rose."

•

In 1973 Dr. Don was named Best Disc Jockey of the Year by "Billboard" magazine.

While in Los Angeles to accept the award, he ran into Paul Drew, the Vice President of Programming for RKO. When Drew discovered Rose wasn't married to WFIL (Lin Broadcasting, it turns out, hadn't been thrilled by the eight months he was off the air recovering) Drew flew into action. Shortly thereafter, Dr. Don Rose became the morning man at KFRC, and the people of San Francisco fell in love with him.

"I don't think it's the zaniness that people remember about me," Rose told me. "I think it basically one line that I used to say every morning."

I'd never heard the line, so I waited.

"If nobody's said it to you," Dr. Don Rose said over the phone, "I'd like to be the first. Good morning!"

Sometimes, it's that simple.

CHAPTER 46
TOM ROUNDS: THE TALENTED MR. ROUNDS

Their blood was racing. Competition does that to young men. In 1959, Tom Rounds was a novice newsman at WINS/New York and Rick Sklar, who'd gain fame at WABC the next decade, was still a struggling assistant in the station's programming department.

On this particular day, Peter Tripp, the crosstown WMGM/New York disc jockey who called himself "the curly headed kid in the third row," was engaged in a feat of endurance, a Wake-A-Thon, staged to benefit the March of Dimes. He'd been awake for over eight days. Rounds and Sklar, the self proclaimed WINS anti-promotion squad, decided enough was enough.

"We sent him some bean-and-bacon soup laced with seconal," admits Rounds, adding that such competitive pranks were endemic in the radio business back then. The soup never got to Tripp, though Rounds does remember one of Tripp's producers took a nap almost immediately, and that Tripp crashed and burned after 201 hours.

"By the way," says Rounds, "I mentioned this story just to prove Randy Michaels didn't invent dirty tricks."

•

Jock Fearnhead — not a made-up radio name — was General Manager of WINS. As the '50s ended, the stress of New York — the weather, traffic, throngs of people — was beginning to take its toll on him. When he decided that he'd finally had enough, he chucked it all, bought a radio station in Hawaii, and convinced Tom Rounds to go with him. The day Rounds left New York the city was wrestling an ice storm.

The trip west, routed with bartered tickets, seemed endless to him and, when he finally arrived in Hawaii, he was beyond tired. But, when he awoke, he says he discovered he was in paradise. "I still dream about it," he says.

One of the things Rounds remembers most fondly about Hawaii is his time at KPOI/Honolulu. He was a newsman; that's what he'd been hired to do. But, from time to time, he pulled a few weekend disc jockey shifts and when Ron Jacobs, KPOI's PD, heard him, Jacobs said, "You ought to be one of the guys. And, to introduce you, I'll dream up a promotion." What Jacobs came up with was a Wake-A-Thon.

"Your active, rational mind goes after about forty-eight hours," says Rounds. At two hundred and two hours, he surpassed Peter Tripp's record and then, awash in lights and sirens, he was squired to the hospital where he slept for an entire day.

"The final thing," he says, "was the headline."

ROUNDS SLEEPS, HE'S A CHAMP

"And, there I am zonked out on the front page of 'The Honolulu Advertiser.' "

•

In 1962, Jacobs left for the mainland and Rounds was named the Program Director of KPOI, where he stayed for the next four years. By 1966, Jacobs was at KHJ/Los Angeles and when the PD job came open at sister station, KFRC/San Francisco, Jacobs told RKO consultant Bill Drake to call Rounds. Drake did and Rounds, ready for a change, accepted the job.

Peace, love, flower children — you should have been there. The whole thing only lasted a short while, but when it was happening, San Francisco was the center of the universe. In the spring of 1967, about the same time Tom "Big Daddy" Donahue launched underground KMPX/San Francisco, Tom Rounds begin preparing to do something that had never been done before – put together a pop festival. Six months of planning went into "The Magic Mountain Music Festival." The idea was to make it a KFRC promotion featuring great music in an outdoor venue and to involve the entire community. Twenty-thousand tickets were sold, at two bucks a head, but somehow, someway, over twice that many people showed up. "It was very successful and quite wonderful," recalls Rounds. "We had The Jefferson Airplane, The Dead, The Doors and even The Fifth Dimension."

June of 1967. Mark it down as the beginning of The Summer of Love. Four months later, on October 18th, Jann Wenner published the first issue of "Rolling Stone" magazine. On the cover was a picture of John Lennon, and alongside, to the right of Lennon's picture, were the words:

ROUNDS QUITS KFRC

Yes, it was that big a deal.

•

The New Year of 1968 found Rounds in Los Angeles running a new video production company, Charlatan Productions. His partner, long-time friend Peter Gardiner, had worked on Channel 9's "Boss City" and had also helped create the psychedelic effects for Peter Fonda's movie, "The Trip." Fifteen years before MTV Rounds and Gardiner saw a future in video, and some of the hipper record companies saw it, too. "Charlatan was very busy, but we (we includes KHJ PD Ron Jacobs) also got back into the concert business and entered into a joint venture with Drake-Chenault to produce concerts in all their markets."

The first step was The Miami Pop Festival. Talent was lined up, contracts were signed and then, at the eleventh hour, Drake-Chenault pulled out. "They were financing it and since we were already committed, we were stuck for an investor," says Rounds.

Trouble. To the tune of a quarter of a million dollars. Enter Strawberry mogul, Tom Driscoll.

"Miami didn't make money," admits Rounds, "but it didn't lose any either."

So Rounds, Jacobs and their new partner, Driscoll, made plans for more outdoor concerts, including one scheduled to happen on a farm outside of Woodstock, NY. "I remember going in a limo from New York City with Bill Graham and Michael Lang to look at sites," says Rounds. There was mud as far as the eye could see. "It was spring and it had been pouring rain all day."

Rounds says he and his partners dropped out of Woodstock "because we thought there was no way they could draw a half a million people."

They were wrong and Woodstock lasted three days, from August 15 to August 18, 1969, forever changing the way concerts were done. "It pretty much ended it for everybody," says Rounds. By this he means that expectations about what a concert is should be changed.

With the concert business over and the film company no longer active (Gardiner had died, unexpectedly, earlier in the year), Rounds found himself at a crossroad.

What to do next?

•

It was a new decade.

Tom Driscoll decided to invest in Rounds and his creative partners and, by the beginning of 1970, they had their hands in lots of pots. "We'd already built recording studios on La Cienega," explains Rounds, "and we had a music-publishing company and a management company, too."

Jacobs brought the new company a project called "A Child's Garden of Grass: A Pre-legalization Comedy" and, after producing the album, which was based on a book by Jack Margolis and Richard Clorfene, the work was distributed by Elektra Records. Next, Jacobs thought up the "Cruisin" series, which, according to Rounds, was conceived as a new way of packaging oldies compilations.

They decided to call the new venture Watermark. "And then Casey Kasem came to us with an idea to do a countdown show."

"American Top 40" launched in the United States on July 4, 1970 with only seven affiliates. I don't have to tell you the rest of the story, do I?

"The original purpose of Watermark," says Rounds, "was to get production work." It became more than that. "Everything was geared around creating new and exciting products," says former Westwood One Vice President, Gary Landis, who worked at Watermark during the late '70s. "It was as pure a creative environment as I've ever been in."

By 1982, the year Watermark was sold to ABC, the company was producing over twelve weekly programs, including "American Top 40" and "American Country Countdown."

Rounds stayed at Watermark's helm until September 1985 and then, sensing an international market for American radio programming, he founded Radio Express, a company that does business today with over seventy-five countries around the globe. One of Radio Express's premier products is "The World Chart Show," developed by Rounds and Jacobs in 1994-95. By Christmas day 1995, the program was heard on three hundred and sixty stations in fifty-four countries, with co-productions in twenty-seven different languages.

The future?

"The play is clearly a combination of terrestrial and internet broadcasting," says Rounds.

The man, as usual, knows what he's talking about.

I know because I asked him the question over a dozen years ago. Sometime in the last century.

CHAPTER 47

ED SALAMON: THE WISDOM OF SALAMON

In Pittsburgh, during the middle '60s, Top 40 radio station, KQV, was making noise and its disc jockeys, Chuck Brinkman, for one, were making extra coin doing record hops. The draw was the djs spinning 45s and signing autographs, but the kids also craved a live band, which was no problem since Pittsburgh was alive with three chord wonders.

One local group featured a singer/guitarist so tall and skinny that Brinkman dubbed him Pittsburgh's answer to Mick Jagger. It was a joke, of course, but still when pushed on it, Brinkman insists "Eddie looked a lot like Mick. He had the hair and the build."

"Eddie" was Ed Salamon and while he loved rock 'n' roll, with no Andrew Loog Oldham to guide their fortunes, his group's only recording (a demo of *Money* and *Little Latin Lupe Lu*) went nowhere. When the band fizzled out Salamon headed off to college.

Fast forward through the years.

This rock 'n' roller became a seven-term President of the Country Radio Broadcasters Association and, among other things, made a country station, WHN/New York, a winner in a town where conventional wisdom had it that listeners wouldn't cotton to country music. He also became one of the nation's leading network executives, mentored some of radio's best and brightest and, finally, putting a cap on his career, went to Music Row in Nashville. Who'd have thunk it?

The answer is Mr. Karmizan.

In 1995, Mel Karmizan spoke at the Country Radio Seminar. "What's going to happen is more and more stations are going to look to the Ed Salamons of the world for programming and guidance."

He's right, of course, but there is only *one* Ed Salamon.

•

Salamon was a radio fan but, apart from a teenage fascination with KQV, he hadn't a clue about how to get into the business or even what kind of jobs might exist. But, when he graduated from The University of Pittsburgh in 1969, he got lucky and was hired by KDKA/Pittsburgh. KDKA was legendary. Owned by Westinghouse Broadcasting, it was the first radio station to broadcast in the United States, beginning in November of 1920.

While Salamon's title, Director of Marketing Research, sounded like more than it really was, the job opened his eyes. "It was basically a sales-support position," he says. "Westinghouse was in the vanguard of radio research, and I did a lot of sales presentations on reach and frequency." In 1970, radio research wasn't far removed from voodoo; demographics was a word shrouded in mystery and programming decisions, more often than not, were based on "gut."

Salamon spent his first year at KDKA preparing for the station's 50th anniversary. In the process he was exposed, not only to the workings of one of America's great radio stations, but also to what it took to keep the station in motion. He decided he wanted to do more. "I went to the General Manager, Bill Hartman, and offered to do the music for free," he says.

Today, handing responsibility for a radio station's music over to a rank beginner seems bizarre, but KDKA was personality-driven — lots of talk, news, etc — and the music was always a secondary consideration. So, the station let Salamon play with it. "KDKA's demos leaned older, and I felt I could change that by playing a younger mix."

He started by adding music questions to the call-out research already being done to support the sales department. "I don't recall when, but at some point we started testing particular songs." In 1972, testing music was a new and cutting edge concept; Bob Pittman was doing his take on it at WDRQ/Detroit, and John Sebastian and Todd Wallace were dabbling in the arena, too. "So, we started sharing information," reveals Salamon. "From my perspective, that's how the whole music research thing got started."

For his inventiveness KDKA paid Salamon the princely sum of $13,000 a year. When management suggested the salary would never go higher, an off-the-cuff remark to WEEP/Pittsburgh's GM led to Salamon's first programming job. WEEP was country. "The biggest thing I did, at least in the very beginning, was demand the call letters be said (by the disc jockeys)," says Salamon.

Then, using Top 40 techniques, he shortened WEEP's playlist. "It's not good enough to be a good country station," he told 'Radio and Records.' We have to be a good radio station."

By the time Salamon was approached about programming WHN/New York, WEEP was a solid #2 in Pittsburgh. Salamon had only been in radio five years.

•

Charlie Warner was the General Manager of WPEZ/Pittsburg and to get a call from him, says Salamon, was a big deal. "I was nervous when I picked up the phone." Warner was calling to tell him NBC was taking WMAQ/Chicago country. "At first, I thought he was calling to offer me the job," Salamon says. But, no. "Bob Pittman's going to be my PD," Warner said. "I was wondering if you'd spend some time with him before he leaves for Chicago."

Salamon agreed to the meeting. Sometime later his payback came when Warner recommended him to Neil Rockoff, the GM of WHN/New York. WHN had been doing country for two years, but was floundering. The challenge, a difficult one, was how to make country acceptable to New Yorkers. So far the station hadn't figured it out, but Salamon had some ideas. "One of the smart things we did was put listeners on the air," he remembers. One of the station's listeners happened to be Dodgers' Coach/Manager, Tommy Lasorda, and Salamon and his ace Promotion Director,

Dale Pon, did everything they could to turn Lasorda's love for country into a home run for WHN. Yes, lots of Lasorda audio hit the air.

To attract further attention WHN scattered bus and cab cards all over town. And, on the air, they gave visiting recording artists free reign. "They read commercials, did traffic, whatever we could do to link them to the market," Salamon says.

It was all about building a country identity in a city not used to the lifestyle. Live broadcasts became part of the game plan. "Ronnie Milsap, Willie — the big artists at the time — all played the Lone Star Café, and we broadcast them live on WHN."

On July 4, 1976 "The New York Times" wrote:

> "Suddenly the New York station is flying. It's skyrocketed to the #2 position among competitors, second only to (Top 40) WABC."

Quoted in the article, Salamon said, "Country music has true mass appeal." He was right.

In 1976, WHN was named "Billboard" magazine's Radio Station of the Year. The following year the station won the honor again and, this time, Salamon was named Program Director of the Year. To this day WHN still holds the record as the-most-listened-to-country music station in history. (This is disputed by John Sebastian, who says the honor goes to KZLA/Los Angeles.)

•

Storer Broadcasting named Salamon its National Program Director and between 1978 and 1980 his attention was focused on WHN and stations in the company's other major markets. In 1981, when Storer sold WHN to Mutual Broadcasting, Salamon says he began to think about the advantages having a network to distribute programming might bring. "I'd produced 'Live from The Lone Star Café' for WHN and, so, I started doing specials for Mutual. His first effort, "The Johnny Cash Silver Anniversary Special," was awarded Billboard's 1981 Special of the Year.

But, network radio was changing. "Dick Clark, Nick Verbitsky and I thought that entertainment programming was a growth area," says Salamon. So, the three approached Mutual with their concept, but the company wasn't interested. Undeterred and with financial support from Clark, the trio decided to form their own company. They called it United Stations. "Our first product was "The Weekly Country Music Countdown," says Salamon.

During most of the '80s, Salamon spearheaded the programming for the company and, when it merged with the Transtar Radio Network in 1989 and became Unistar, he was named President/Programming. Salamon set his sights on innovation and created and produced live national radio events featuring big stars like Willie Nelson, Alabama and beginners like Garth Brooks. If you walk into Salamon's living room today, you'll find the cover of one of Brooks's albums inscribed with these words.

> Thanks for the start, Ed. I'll always owe you.
> Garth

•

By the early '90s, mergers were common among radio networks, and Salamon, through a series of moves and acquisitions, was named President of Programming at the Westwood One Radio Network. Salamon transferred to their twenty-four hour format headquarters in Valencia, CA, where he stayed until being transferred back to New York around 2000.

Then, in 2002, Salamon was drafted to become Executive Director of Country Radio Broadcasters, a non-profit organization based in Nashville. Salamon had been involved with the organization since 1976 and the opportunity to lead it was thought by many to be the perfect combination of talent and timing.

Today Salamon works out of an office on Music Row. When he's not planning ways for country radio to prosper during these challenging times, he's an adjunct professor at Middle Tennessee State and Belmont University, passing on what's he learned and leading a discussion on how media is changing in the new century.

"We're all reading the same book," says Salamon's protégé, McVay Media's Charlie Cook. "But, Ed's always been a few pages ahead of everyone else."

Ed Salamon was inducted into The Country Radio Hall of Fame in 2006.

CHAPTER 48

JOHN SEBASTIAN: THE ONE WHO'S
DONE IT ALL

"**This is no** joke," says John Sebastian. "My father raised me to be President of the United States. I, however, wanted to play professional baseball. And later, when it was obvious I was better at basketball, that's where I focused my attention. I was going to play at the University of Oregon, go to law school and find a way to satisfy my dad."

Then Sebastian broke his back.

At first, he says he ignored the pain and played through it. The doctors soon put the kibosh on that. "If you keep this up, you're going to be paralyzed from the waist down," they told him. "So, I had spinal fusion," he says.

He was in a body cast for six months. Dreams of college ball and sports scholarships were dashed; all he was left with was time to think. "During the darkest hours I decided to do the most radical thing I could think of — become a disc jockey."

It was a whole new ballgame and his father, dare I say, wasn't happy. Radio. Why radio?

•

In June of 1963, KISN/Portland named a new Program Director. The man came from KXLY/Spokane and, within two years, he'd be in Hollywood. His goal was to contemporize KISN, to give the station a little "show biz sizzle." He put himself on the air from three to seven p.m. and broadcast from a studio, with a big window overlooking a busy street, where anyone who wanted to see him could. In 1964, as a promotional stunt, he announced he was running for President. His name was "The Real Don Steele."

"Steele was berserk, and I was captured by his energy," says

Sebastian. "I remember thinking to myself it would be a dream come true if it was ME in that window."

Sebastian was ambitious and talked himself into a job at KPAM/Portland. For little pay he played tapes on the overnight shift and, to supplement his income, he flipped burgers, sold fire alarms and managed a local putt-putt course. "Basically I didn't sleep," he says. His father finally put his foot down.

"That he did that was a good thing," Sebastian concedes, "because it forced me to start sending out tapes, which led to my first full-time gig at KACI/The Dalles."

Sebastian's job at KACI required he do everything. He opened the station before dawn, swept the floors, made coffee and when eight-thirty a.m. came around, he'd hit the phones to sell advertising time. By two p.m. he'd be exhausted, and that's when he'd go on the air.

Sebastian's on-air presentation reflected the station owner's wants. This means the personality he projected wasn't what he might have done had he been left to his own devices. But, when the station signed off — it was a daytimer — he returned to the studio and did the show the way *he* wanted. His only audience was a tape recorder. Sebastian's practice paid off when KPAM hired him back to do afternoon drive. It was a great job and opportunity, he says, but what he wanted — what he dreamed about — was sitting in Don Steele's chair, in the studio in front of KISN's window to the world.

When KISN finally called about the job, Sebastian says he began to believe that what you envision can come true. "But, first you have to envision it," he told me.

Not a bad lesson for a twenty year old to learn.

•

In 1971, Todd Wallace brought Sebastian to Phoenix to do nights at KRUX. It was a big market move for the young man, and one of the first things Wallace did was give him a new name: Gary Stevens. Normally this wouldn't mean much, but ex-WMCA/New York disc jockey, Gary Stevens, had just been named General Manager at crosstown competitor, KRIZ, and Wallace was determined to have some fun at Stevens' expense. "It drove Gary bananas," Sebastian says. "He'd introduce himself at agencies and they'd stare and say, 'Yeah, we heard you on KRUX last night.' "

When Wallace arrived in Phoenix, KRIZ and KRUX had been running neck-and-neck. But, within one ratings book, KRUX had an eleven point nine and KRIZ was down to a 3.0 share. Wallace, quickly, became the topic of national radio conversation. What had he done? How had he done it?

Across the street at KRIZ, GM, Gary Stevens, began making telephone calls. His mission was to get Wallace out of town. At the time Wallace says he was naïve and didn't know that's how the game was played. But, when he got a phone call from KTSA/San Antonio with an offer worth twice what he was making, he says he couldn't turn the job down.

So, Wallace left for San Antonio and Sebastian stayed parked at KRUX.

Seven months later, Wallace was being celebrated for turning KTSA around. In the radio press, Gary Stevens was quoted as saying, "If Todd Wallace can't fix a station, it can't be fixed." After such a testimonial, no one was surprised when Wallace returned to Phoenix to take over the programming reins at KRIZ. Once inside the building, Wallace told the real Stevens he wanted to bring (the other) Gary Stevens over from KRUX. "OK, but you gotta change his name." The name they decided on was John Sebastian. Yes, after the lead singer of The Lovin' Spoonful.

When the next Phoenix ratings were released, KRIZ was up over three points — from a 6.1 to a 9.3. (Statistically KRIZ was the last Class IV local station [1,000 watts, days; 250, nights] to be #1 in a Top 100 market.)

With this success, Doubleday Broadcasting transferred Gary Stevens to Minneapolis/St. Paul to manage KDWB. Stevens invited Sebastian to join him and, eventually, he did. But, getting there was convoluted.

•

Stevens named Buzz Bennett Program Director of KDWB. It was the political thing to do at the time, but Stevens says he always had Sebastian in the back of his mind. "I told John he'd be PD of KDWB at some point, and that I wanted him up there," he says. But, it was easier said than done because Stevens had promised the company that he wouldn't "steal" anyone from KRIZ. So, the men devised a plan.

Stevens told Sebastian to quit KRIZ and to say he was going back to Portland. "Then, after a couple of days at home, I told John to speak to Todd at KRIZ and tell him things hadn't worked out. So, John did exactly that and Todd told him, 'Well, I'd love to have you back, but I don't have anything.'

And, John was on the next plane," says Stevens.

Buzz Bennett didn't stay at KDWB very long; it wasn't expected he would. Then, as promised, and despite objections from some of the older jocks, Stevens made John Sebastian KDWB's Program Director. Sebastian had been preparing for this opportunity all his professional life.

He remembers executing his plan one step at a time. One of his first moves was to establish a means of testing music. This, at the time, represented radical thinking. "Gary let me develop a research department," says Sebastian. He brought Steve Casey up from KRIZ and, together, the two young men computerized the call-out data they'd collected. Stevens signed off on the idea as mainly a gesture of faith and it paid off. KDWB took off like an explosive rocket ship. "Gary gave me the confidence to be as expansive, broadminded, contrarian and 'out of the box' as I could be," says Sebastian. "We didn't stop until we had double digits."

Stevens became a winner, too. As a result of KDWB's success and the powerful program Sebastian and Casey had come up with, doors were opened for him at other Doubleday stations. When Sebastian's success led him to Los Angeles, Stevens was named Doubleday's Senior Vice President of Research.

•

It was the job offer of job offers and it came from KHJ/Los Angeles. Sebastian couldn't say no.

In 1978, FM penetration in LA was close to 70% and KHJ, an AM station, was on its last legs. The first thing Sebastian did was to cut talk on the station to a bare minimum — something morning man Charlie Tuna found problematic. Then, Sebastian attacked the music library. He decided KHJ should play a tight mix of music reflecting the best of "hip" Top 40 tunes and the best album cuts. (Later this would be referred to as playing "top tracks.")

When the ratings came out, KHJ, with less talk and hit records being played in high rotation, increased its cume and posted a 3.0 share. "It wasn't a Ron Jacob's number," says Sebastian, "but it was pretty damn good." Sebastian knew, however, that music on the AM band had little future and, figuring he'd done all he could for KHJ, he left Los Angeles and returned to Phoenix to program KUPD, an AM/FM combination. (In the fall of 1980, KHJ, at the height of the Urban Cowboy movement, switched from Top 40 to Country.)

At KUPD, Sebastian continued his music experimentation by merging the sensibilities of AOR with Top 40's tight rotations. Explaining his thought process, he says, "I applied research, ears and instinct. It was just common sense, but I was among the first to try it."

•

What happened next sounds like a game of musical chairs. When the PD slot at KLOS/Los Angeles opened up, Sebastian began to salivate. General Manager Bill Sommers heard Sebastian's pitch, but gave the job to Tommy Hadges, Program Director of WCOZ/

Boston instead. When he heard the news, Sebastian immediately called Boston about replacing Hadges.

Sebastian got the job and flew to Boston. "The first thing I did at WCOZ was to take everything out of the control room (he means every piece of music) except the albums I knew wouldn't kill us."

This move was unprecedented because Album Radio was supposed about tonnage; album stations were *supposed* to play lots of music. But, Sebastian didn't care. As he took dozens of albums from the studio, he saw the look of disbelief on the DJ's face. WCOZ's air staff ran screaming to the press and "The Boston Globe" described Sebastian as "a hatchet murderer from the west."

"It wasn't fun, but I stuck to my guns," says Sebastian.

When the ratings came out, WCOZ was in double digits and Sebastian, already a hero to his bosses, became the most talked about programmer in America. Everyone in the know, including Jimmy deCastro, the Sales Manager at crosstown WXKS/Boston, told him to consult, to grab the money while he could. Sebastian agreed.

During the first half of the '80s he and Steve Casey consulted album rock stations all across America, becoming road warriors as they competed for clients with Burkhart/Abrams, Pollack Media and other lesser-known rock radio consultants. But, by 1985, Sebastian was motel and road weary, and distressed that his new format concept, EOR (Eclectic-Oriented-Rock) hadn't been embraced by the industry. For the record, EOR pre-dated and suggested formatic nuances that would characterize and define the Adult Alternative format.

•

The bells of deregulation rang in the mid '80s and Sebastian, tired of travel, jumped into ownership in Sante Fe, but before the decade was over he'd returned to Los Angeles to "fix" KTWV-FM, the much heralded "new age" station that was the prototype for the "smooth jazz" format but needed to be more than a jockless jukebox, its original incarnation.

Then, after a return to Phoenix – where he always goes to recharge – Sebastian returned to LA, in 1996, to program KZLA-FM, a country station. (Historically, Sebastian is the only programmer to have led three LA stations in three decades: KHJ in the '70s, KTWV in the '80s, and KZLA in the '90s.")

Apart from a quick fling with Jack-FM/Chicago (another "jockless" franchise that CBS asked him to "mature"), for the past few years Sebastian's energy has been focused on country radio in Lexington, Nashville and Dallas. "I sincerely believe country radio can be the most mass appeal and successful of all the radio formats," he says, today.

Many of his peers bemoan the state of 21st Century radio, but not Sebastian. Now at WWQM/Madison, he remains enthusiastic about the future and his place in it. "I'm convinced I'm as good as or better than I've ever been. And with the way radio has "devolved" my brand of programming can be more successful than ever."

"John knows how to win and takes programming very seriously," says Todd Wallace.

We all continue to watch.

CHAPTER 49
SCOTT SHANNON:
PROGRAMMER OF THE CENTURY

WHTZ-FM, Z-100, wasn't going to be a New York City radio station. New Jersey, Long Island, Westchester — those were the targets. They didn't even talk about New York on the air and when the press caught on, the reviews weren't good. The Daily News wrote, "I hope this punk, Scott Shannon — whoever he is — has a round-trip ticket back to Tampa, because this station is never going to make it."

WHTZ signed on August 2, 1983 and, before ninety days had passed, "hot-rockin,' flame-throwin' Z-100 — the little station that could — owned New York. In the process, it almost single-handedly re-invented Top 40. More than three hundred "Morning Zoo" shows popped up around the world.

This was good news for Michael Scott Shannon, Z-100's PD. He'd only bought a one-way ticket.

•

By the time it rained in Indianapolis in the summer of 1965, he was long gone. "Like a moron, I quit school," he says. He'd run away from home to become a disc jockey. He says the night he snuck out of the house, he was so pumped and ready to hit the future that it didn't matter that he'd never driven on a highway before. "I was seventeen. I had forty-five bucks, half the clothes I owned, fifty of my favorite records and a battery-powered record player."

He crossed the Illinois state line, then Missouri — call it James Dean/Jack Kerouac gutsy. When he hit Arkansas, he aimed his car toward Little Rock. He figured there'd be enough traffic that his out-of-state license plates wouldn't be noticed.

Shannon needed money. He delivered dentures door-to-door, worked at a bakery called Oscar's and talked his way into a radio station — KAJI/Little Rock — where he hung out, pulling commercials and records for the afternoon disc jockey, Rolls Royce, The People's Choice.

He says the radio station didn't pay him anything, but it wasn't about the money. When a Sunday morning shift opened up on the station, Shannon fibbed about his experience. The station probably didn't believe him, he admits today, but Sunday morning shifts on radio stations were about warm bodies, not experienced voices. "I sounded horrible," says Shannon.

Still, after only three months, he decided he was ready for Los Angeles — for KHJ. So, he headed west. "I never even got through the door of that place," he admits.

Instead, he got an offer from Uncle Sam

•

Some guys sweat the Army, others finesse it. "I told them I didn't want to go to Vietnam because I was in show biz," laughs Shannon.

As hard as it may be to believe, the Army bought it. After basic training, Shannon was sent to Fort Bragg in Fayetteville, NC, where he quickly marched into a part-time radio job. "It didn't take me long to realize that Fayetteville was probably a better fit for my talent than Los Angeles," he allows.

But, Boss Radio was still on his mind. "I had three role models," says Shannon. "Bill Drake, The Real Don Steele and Robert W. Morgan. I loved Steele's energy and Morgan's coolness and efficiency of words."

When the Army sent Shannon, by then a sergeant, to Columbus, GA, he found part-time work at WCLS and began to think about life after the military. "I ran into a fellow named Jim Taber and asked him to listen to my aircheck," he says. Taber, from Dallas

— the same Taber that influenced Ken Dowe — liked what he heard and suggested Shannon get in touch with Bernie Dittman, the owner of WABB/Mobile. Shannon took the advice.

"He sent me a little dime-store tape with a note written in pencil," said Dittman. "It said,

> Dear Mr. Dittman,
> I understand you hire inexperienced DJs. Cheap.

Two weeks later, Shannon drove his blue '55 Ford to Mobile. He did the all-night show for two nights and then Dittman slid him into the seven to midnight shift. "He wanted me to do six to ten," Shannon remembers. "But, I said, 'Nope, it's not enough time.' "

"He was unbelievable," Dittman told me. "He must have stayed up all night thinking, 'What can I say tomorrow?' "

By the time Shannon left Mobile for Memphis, he'd taken WABB from #12 to #1 and had an unbelievable 73.0 share.

•

Wild, fast, obnoxious and passionate — that was Shannon on the air. He was also street smart and related to the kids who listened. "Top 40 was playing some pretty interesting stuff back then," he says. "The new progressive stuff — Hendrix, Cream, Credence — but we also had Donny Osmond." His last hour every night on WMPS/Memphis was called The Super Shan Power Hour. "I was Davey Jones's (of The Monkees) best friend until eleven o'clock," Shannon says. "Then I went into the heavy metal 'Super Shan' and would play the long version of *In-A-Gadda-Da-Vida*."

Joe Sullivan, PD of WMAK/Nashville — two hundred and ten miles to the east — lost his night guy. "Johnny Walker got drafted," he says. "I hadn't found anyone to replace him yet and started to hear from record folks about Scott Shannon, so I called him."

Shannon's aircheck, truth be told, didn't float Sullivan's boat, but everyone kept telling him, "Shannon's the guy." "So, I went to

Memphis and drove around and listened," Sullivan says. "When I heard him live, I understood. Anything the competition did, he did twice as well. He out-promoted and out-programmed and it was clear that he was very competitive."

Super Shan loved being on the air — he lived it, breathed it — but after he'd been in Nashville for a while Sullivan resigned and Shannon decided he wanted the job. Sullivan says Shannon was promoted "because he was going to work harder, get up earlier, stay later and out-hustle the competition."

"I took what I learned from Bill Drake and added what Joe taught me about personality," says Shannon.

Under Scott Shannon's leadership, WMAK/Nashville became one of the hottest Top 40 stations in the south.

•

It's said that WQXI/Atlanta was the model for the television show, "WKRP in Cincinnati." Shannon says it's true. "Jerry Blum was the Art Carlson character, and I was Andy." (You can picture it, can't you? Particularly the hair.)

It only took eighteen months for Scott Shannon to turn WQXI around, but, strangely, the day after the winning ratings were released he was fired. "I never figured out why," he says. "The weird thing is, the entire staff that I'd brought in stayed; so, it must have been something about me."

He was at a cross-road. 'Radio and Records' Publisher, Bob Wilson, offered him a job at R & R and he took it. "I started *Street Talk*," says Shannon. But, once in Hollywood, he was offered another job; this one came from Neil Bogart at Casablanca Records. The offer included a Mercedes, an unlimited expense account and a chance to fly across America.

"I said, 'That's me. Sign me up," says Shannon.

His heart, however, belonged to radio. In his future were WPGC/Washington, WRBQ/Tampa, WHTZ/New York, KQLZ/Los

Angeles, and his current and long-standing home, WPLJ/New York. He had no idea how big it was going to get.

•

On the morning of August 2, 2001, my telephone rang. It was 7:40 a.m. PDT, and three hours later in New York. "There's some kinda funky mojo magic going on here," Scott Shannon said. "You know, it was eighteen years ago today that we signed Z-100 on."

"Really? What can you tell me about that morning?" I asked, as I spilled my coffee.

"We only had two microphones in the place, one in the control room and one in production, so J. R. Nelson, my sidekick, had to hook the production room mic to a card table." He's silent for a moment, remembering something else. Then, he starts to laugh. "We didn't even have phones. I had to close the request lines when we opened the office because New Jersey didn't have choke lines."

Z 100 started simply. "We opened up with a playlist of thirty-five to forty records and just pounded them," says Shannon. "The format was salt and pepper – one white, one black, one white, another black." Yes, he says, there were lots of complaints about the repetition. "We went on the air and said, 'Our Music Director, Michael Ellis, is going to run down to Tower Records — we've got a little money — so if you have anything you want to hear, let us know, or if you have some songs you want us to play, send them to us, because we're a little short.' "

The audience loved the candor. "They'd say, 'Tell your music director to pick up a few new songs so I don't have to hear that damn *Every Breath You Take* another twenty times today.' "

Z-100 turned its lack of promotional bucks from a negative to a positive. "We had the homemade sign contest," Shannon says. "You'd be driving through Yonkers and see an apartment building with three or four 'I Love Z-100' signs on sheets hanging out of windows."

You know what happened next, don't you? Z-100 went from worst to first in seventy-four days and, suddenly, Scott Shannon was the only person the radio industry was talking about. Bob Pittman called from MTV to discuss a new video channel, VH-1, and, for two and a half years, Shannon was a cable star. "It was really weird. There were places where I was recognized on the street and others, where VH-1 had no penetration," he says.

National radio syndication followed. Norm Pattiz, Chairman of Westwood One, approached Shannon about a Top 40 countdown show, the show that would become the "Rockin' America Top 30 Countdown." "What made that show unique were the production values and the show's attitude," says Gary Landis, Westwood One's VP of Programming, when the countdown launched. "It was as much about Scott's personality as it was about the music." "Rockin' America" was a mainstay on over 150 of America's most prominent CHR stations for close to five years. Westwood One made money. So did Shannon, and Pattiz approached Shannon with another idea.

"What if I bought you a radio station in Los Angeles?" Pattiz proposed.

The idea intrigued Shannon and, besides, he was ready for a new challenge. So, he threw out a number and Pattiz agreed.

"Welcome to the Jungle."

•

On Saint Patrick's Day, 1989, Pirate Radio, 100.3/KQLZ, signed on. "It was a magic day, and if you want to hear their launch, it's all over the Internet," says Landis. "I still think it represents one of Scott's finest hours."

"I loved working for Norm, loved Los Angeles radio," says Shannon. "It was just financial. The real sticky wicket that's never been discussed is that, at the completion of my two-year contract, I was going to become a part owner. That really made the deal lopsided. So, along about twenty months, Norm pulled the plug on me."

Shannon says he and Pattiz are still friends. "We still talk. He more than made the trip worthwhile."

•

September 11, 2001. Not a normal day.

"We were coming out of a stopset, around 8:45-8:46, when one of our listeners, who was across the street from the World Trade Center, called to say a plane had just rammed into one of the buildings."

Scott Shannon's voice is low and somber. "At first, it was surreal and difficult to comprehend. We had TV monitors in the control room and were watching Channel 7. We didn't have time to think about what we were doing. It was all instinct, minute-to-minute, and we basically started doing play-by-play."

"As events unfolded," he says, "there was a point when we realized that it was a large airliner and how it ran into a building on a clear day was kind of a mystery to us. While we were discussing that, we spotted another plane coming around the left side of the screen." I said, 'There's another plane coming into the picture.' When it hit the second building, Todd Pettengill said, 'Oh my God, this isn't an accident, it's an attack!' "

"Those words rang through the speakers like a knife," says Shannon.

"We were talking to someone in the towers when another guy called and, as he was talking, he stopped and said, 'There's people jumping out of the building. Oh my God.' And then he started crying."

"The worst moment for all of us was when we saw the first building collapse. We described it, but we didn't honestly believe it. It was difficult to grasp."

Penn Plaza was evacuated, but The WPLJ morning crew — Scott, Todd Pettengill, Patti Steele — along with their three staff producers and weatherman, Bill Evans — stayed on the air for thirteen hours straight. "When we finally walked out that night, it was one of the strangest sights I've ever seen," says Shannon. "The streets were deserted. No traffic, a few people walking. The look on their faces was chilling. There was all this white soot that looked a little bit like snow, and there was this horrible, horrible smell in the air.."

"It was difficult to sleep that night because of the complexity of this horrible event. Who did it? How did they plan it? How'd they get away with it? What did the people in those buildings have to go through? What about the people in those planes who knew they were over the city, flying too low, heading towards a building?"

"The next morning was even more difficult," continues Shannon. "We started getting calls from wives and husbands whose mates hadn't come home the night before, and they still hadn't heard from them. It was just draining."

On September 11th, and in the days that followed, WPLJ wasn't a news station, a Top 40 station, or a talk station. "We were just a New York people station," says Shannon. "What we had to do was crystal clear, and I have to say that I'm so proud of everyone involved with our show. We lived through it together and were the eyes and ears of millions of people in NY who didn't have television."

"As long as I'm walking the face of the earth," Shannon says, "September 11 is a day I'll never forget."

"Scott's true love is being on the air," says Tom Cuddy, WPLJ's former Vice President/Programming. "I have yet to meet an air talent who has a heart bigger than he does."

Some days make the point even more than others.

(Scott Shannon, as of this writing, is the Program Director and co-host of the morning show at WPLJ/New York, where he's been since

1991. In 2000, trade magazine "Friday Morning Quarterback" — FMBQ — named Shannon Program Director of the Century. Three years later, he was inducted into the National Association of Broadcasters Hall of Fame, and The National Radio Hall of Fame honored him in 2006.

In addition to his work with WPLJ, Shannon is the creator and host of True Oldies, a twenty-four hour oldies format syndicated by The ABC Radio Network.)

CHAPTER 50

RICK SKLAR: A CONSPIRACY OF ONE

The young Program Director was beside himself.

He'd been invited to join Rick and Sydelle Sklar at the New York premier of Neil Diamond's new movie, "The Jazz Singer." When he got to the table, he was greeted by the Sklars and introduced to their friends, Neil and Leba Sedaka. Then, to his surprise, they introduced the other person at the table — Neil Diamond's mother.

He was taking it all in, acting nonchalant, when he noticed that the table number was seventy-seven, WABC's frequency. "Being the petulant twenty-something Program Director of WNBC/New York," says Kevin Metheny, "I refused to sit down at a table numbered seventy-seven."

This caused a bit of brouhaha, but Sklar remained calm and thoughtful. "If I were he," said Mr. Sklar, finally, "I wouldn't sit here either. But, if you can arrange it, I would be delighted to join my young friend at table sixty-six."

Yes, sixty-six was WNBC's frequency.

By 1980, the year Metheny joined WNBC, Sklar had been promoted up the ABC corporate ladder and was no longer involved with the day-to-day decisions at ABC. But, there was no doubt that he was the Dean of New York Programmers. "Rick was the first to point out to me that the club of successful practicing and former New York PDs was a small one, and it was a privilege to be a member," says Metheny.

•

The $55 a week paycheck Rick Sklar earned at WPAC/Patchogue didn't stretch very far, so he moonlighted over a typewriter, writing pulp fiction under the pseudonym, Victor Appleton II. "I still have a copy of "Tom Swift and His Giant Robot," laughs Sklar's daughter, Holly.

WPAC, on the South Shore of Long Island, was no final destination but for a kid from Brighton Beach, who was just out of college and had no experience, it fit the bill. Besides, it was close enough to New York to see the daily papers. In his autobiography, "Rocking America," Sklar wrote, "One day I noticed a blind want ad in "The New York Times" that simply read:

'COPY/CONTACT – RADIO.'

Sklar answered the ad and was surprised to hear back from WINS/ New York and even more surprised when he got the job writing commercials. He worked in the dead of night, he says, and during the day collected cash from "hapless sponsors."

Then, in 1954, Alan Freed arrived at WINS. With him came rock 'n' roll. "Freed had four hours to fill and he put the show together according to his personal likes and dislikes," Sklar wrote. (Allowing disc jockeys to select their own music was the way it was done during the '50s, but Sklar thought it was problematic because each show was different and subject to the jock's mood. He began to think about it.)

By September of 1957, WINS was gaining ground on its main competitors, WMCA and WMGM, but Sklar thought it could be better. "What if we control the air exposure of each piece of music, basing its repeat plays on the current popularity of the song?" he asked. At the time, this was revolutionary thinking.

•

"For music, news, time and the weather, keep your dial where the tens come together: Ten-Ten-WINS/New York."

On the strength of his jingle writing ability (the lyrics above are his), Sklar was named the Assistant Program Director of WINS. At the time, the station's identity revolved around its personalities — A Smith Named Irv, Jack Lacy and Alan Freed and, later, Murray the K – but there were other elements that helped to define the station's sound. "I produced every second of WINS features for excitement and ratings," wrote Sklar. "Even the newscasts were introduced with 'ear-splitting sensationalist effects.' "

By October 1957, WINS was #1 in New York. The next spring, when the government of France was crumbling, the news editors at WMGM were looking for a way, any way, to steal the limelight from WINS. Someone decided getting General Charles de Gaulle on the phone might be the ticket. At 10:30 that morning, WMGM newsman, Bill Edmunds, hit the air, promising the long distance call was being arranged. "So," he said, "stay tuned for first hand information from France."

Edmunds finally received word that the trans-Atlantic call was ready. Once on the line, General de Gaulle insisted that he go on "live." He didn't want tape delay, he told 'MGM. Finally, through the static, in heavily accented English, de Gaulle began. "Err, monsieur," asked the General, "can you tell me who I am speaking to?"

"My name is Bill Edmunds," said the newsman. "I'm one of the Minute Men here at WMGM, a radio station in New York City."

"I see," replied le General. Then his accent disappeared. "Well, of course, everybody knows that the best station in New York is WINS. Viva la France!"

By that afternoon, the story was all over town. "It was front-page news," wrote Sklar, "with 'The New York World-Telegram' saying it all."

WHO HAD DE GAULLE TO CALL WMGM?

WINS was on top of the world and so was Sklar. "I was happy at my typewriter ten hours a day, knocking out contests, jingles and promotional ideas," he wrote. But, behind the scenes trouble was brewing. It was spelled P-A-Y-O-L-A. Then, as if that weren't enough, the American Federation of Television and Radio Artists (AFTRA) went on strike. Although the strike provided the entrée at WINS for an unknown DJ from Brooklyn named Bruce Morrow, it was decidedly the beginning of the end for WINS dominance in New York City.

In 1960, WINS was sold to Westinghouse Broadcasting and Sklar was named Program Director of WMGM/New York, a station owned by the Lowe's Corporation. It wasn't his first choice and, in fact, he'd already had some discussions with Hal Neal, the ABC executive brought in from Detroit to take over WABC, but they'd led nowhere.

Sklar knew that the job at WMGM wasn't going to last forever. Part of the reason was that Lowes, controlled by Bob and Larry Tisch (who later controlled CBS) sold the station to Storer Broadcasting and, when the new owners took over, they announced the station's call letters would revert to what they'd been in the '30s, WHN, and that the format would change to "easy vocals."

Sklar and his assistant, Art Wander, worked at WHN for a few more months but, when a new manager arrived from Philadelphia, he brought a new program director with him, and Sklar found himself out of a job.

•

On July 11, 1962, Rick Sklar went to work at WABC/New York. He wasn't named Program Director – that position hadn't been approved by ABC corporate yet. Instead, he was named Production and Community Affairs Director.

Regardless of the title, it was a tough job. WABC was burdened by commitments to the ABC Network, like Don McNeil's Breakfast Club, that made competing with WMCA difficult. From the start; however, Sklar was nothing if not tenacious. "He persuaded his bosses to give him the budget for better personalities, more jingles and promotions like 'The $25,000 Button,' " says Bob Henabery. "He was an uncorrupted man, self-contained to the point of being called a 'conspiracy of one.'

And very, very intuitive."

It took Sklar six years to do it. But, in 1968, WABC finally became the #1 radio station in New York. "My father was very methodical, but he was also a showman," says Holly Sklar. "I think of him as sort of the PT Barnum of radio or maybe Ziegfeld. WABC was the stage where he and some very talented people got to put on a show everyday."

On June 22, 1992 Rick Sklar, a marathon runner, died prematurely from anesthesia complications during surgery to repair a tendon. The radio industry was shocked.

Kevin Metheny, his young friend from WNBC, speaks for many, when he says, "I loved Rick Sklar and I miss him."

In 1993, Rick Sklar was inducted, posthumously, into the Radio Hall of Fame.

CHAPTER 51
MICHAEL SPEARS: A REMEMBRANCE

The message from Ken Dowe was dated October 25, 2005 and time stamped 3:37:32 PM Dallas time. "Sad news, guys," he wrote. "Michael Spears died a few minutes ago ..."

Even though the message wasn't unexpected — when someone's got cancer, you're always waiting — it hit me like a ton of bricks. I won't lie to you. Michael and I weren't bosom buddies, but we had spent considerable Texas time together and, more than once, had shared a Christmas party and our common birthday, June 23rd. In the days following Michael's death, my e-mail was flooded by remembrances — some professional; most, deeply personal.

•

Michael Spears, who used the air name Hal Martin until the early '70s, was raised in Dallas under KLIF's mighty shadow. Anyone who's ever listened to the stations he programmed would know it, because Gordon McLendon, Bill Stewart and (later) Ken Dowe, were all there in the method, mix and execution. But, if you're reading this and never actually heard one of Michael's stations, know this: the shading, the nuance and the momentum came from Michael alone.

"Michael always understood that winning is in the details," says Dowe.

Perhaps that explains why Spears won Billboard's PD of the Year Award twice, and why his stations were named Station of the Year three times.

By the way, even before radio, Michael Spears was a winner. In 1963, he was named the best magician in the State of Texas.

•

When Ron Chapman was still calling himself Irving Harrigan and the #1 station in Dallas was still KLIF, Spears took to hanging out in the studio, begging Chapman to give him advice. "After about six months of me playing him my tapes, Ron told me, 'Get out, quit bothering me and go get a job,' " said Spears.

He sent out over a dozen tapes. Finally, a call came in inviting him to KAND/Corsicana, a Corvair trip away from Dallas, but a million miles from the Mighty 1190. "The microphone hung from the ceiling on chicken wire," Spears remembered. His next job, at KDOK/Tyler, got him closer to Dallas. "Tyler was like the minors, a proving ground for Dallas." (He's right. KDOK alumni include Bill Young and Steve Lundy [KILT/Houston], Jimmy Rabbit [KLIF and KMET/Los Angeles] and Larry Thompson [Thompson Creative].)

Then lightning struck when KLIF, his dream station, invited him home. "Going back was amazing," said Spears. "Lots of fun, incredible promotions. But, it was barely a format. Now, don't get me wrong. There were guidelines — we had jingles to play and all — but, you know, we kind of put our shows together our own way."

Spears stayed at KLIF for three years; think of it as radio graduate school. When his friend, Charlie Van Dyke, was named Program Director of CKLW/Windsor-Detroit (Bill Drake consulted), Spears headed to the frigid north. He was 21 and had never lived outside of Texas. "I'd never read a weather forecast with a one digit temperature before," he laughed.

Job one at CKLW was to immerse himself in the Drake format. "I was intimidated for a while," Spears admitted. "It was like the Marines: very regimented, no deviation and it had to be executed perfectly."

Spears was in Detroit for close to eighteen months, but, after Van Dyke left and was replaced by Paul Drew, Ken Dowe called and offered him his first programming job at McLendon's WYSL/Buffalo. The version of the story Spears always told was that he got out of Detroit just a moment before Drew "chopped his head off."

(Drew is kinder with *his* version.)

Buffalo was cold and the heat under his first-time PD's chair was uncomfortable. WYSL's signal was awful and Spears, despite his best efforts, made a lot of beginner mistakes. Dowe, his boss, was patient and understanding, and chalked it all up to a learning curve.

Did I mention Buffalo was cold? Or that when Van Dyke called from KGB/San Diego with another on-air offer, the beaches and the sun sounded ever so appealing? KGB/San Diego and KFRC/San Francisco were stepping stones to KHJ/Los Angeles — the pinnacle of Bill Drake's stations. Spears was jazzed. He accepted the job at KGB on the condition that he could start at the station, take time out to get married and go on his honeymoon, then return to live happily ever after as a newlywed and new-born Boss Jock.

He was still caught up in the afterglow of his honeymoon as he drove into San Diego. When he got within range of KGB's signal, he tuned in the station and, after a while, realized that the staff he'd been hired to join wasn't on the air. That night, over a bottle of wine, Van Dyke spilled the story. Drake, said Van Dyke, was embarrassed because rival KCBQ had cleaned KGB's clock; so, the order had come down to fire the entire staff.

Spears, looking back, said he, Van Dyke and the rest of the staff were never given a chance. "New people, jocks — everybody was canned," he explained.

He didn't have a job, but he did have a new wife, a car full of wedding presents, and time on his hands. He sat on the beach and listened to KCBQ. "Might as well figure out how they beat us," he thought. As it happened, Spears was only out of work for forty-five days. For a very short time, he returned to Detroit, and CKLW. But, it was just a way of killing time until he could get back home to Texas.

•

In 1972, when Gordon McLendon sold KLIF/Dallas for ten million dollars, it was the most money ever paid for a radio station. During last-minute negotiations, McLendon turned to the buyers and asked them if they'd like to "buy his little FM, too."

"How much?" they asked.

"I don't know. How about $150,000?"

According to the story — I swear it's true — the buyers declined, explaining they'd stick with KLIF, the cash cow. Yes, there was a no-compete clause in the sales contract. But, get this — it only applied to the AM band. Walking from the meeting, Ken Dowe, Executive Vice President of McLendon Broadcasting, says McLendon asked him what he thought they ought to do with the FM. (By the way, the FM was an automation machine operating out of a closet near KLIF's main studio and playing a very loose album rock format.)

The next day, Dowe returned with a plan to take the station Top 40 — with some album cuts thrown in — and told McLendon that he wanted to bring Spears back to Dallas to program it.

"Michael had done a good job for us in Buffalo and so I brought him home," says Dowe.

KNUS-FM hit Dallas like a Texas tornado. "We went on the air at 8 p.m., May 6, 1972," Spears said. Gordon McLendon, himself, was on the air doing local election results. As he wrapped up the voting totals and his comments, McLendon paused. Then, majestically, he said, "Ladies and Gentlemen, I am launching a new format here in Dallas."

•

Contests, instant winners ("Rip me off for a Grand Funk LP!") — the city had never heard anything like KNUS. To be more precise, Dallas hadn't heard anything like it *on* FM before. Within months KNUS was the #1 station in town, and when KLIF fumbled, stumbled and tumbled, McLendon only smiled. (In the middle '80s, under new owners, KNUS became KLVU and then KLUV. The station today is worth ... well, let's just say it's worth a lot more than $150,000.) Shortly thereafter, Spears got a call from Pat Norman, the General Manager of KFRC/San Francisco. He was twenty-five and being offered his third programming job.

"Mom, Daddy," he told his parents, "You're not going to believe this, but I'm going to work for Bill Drake in the most beautiful city in America."

•

Michael Spears was the Program Director of KFRC/San Francisco for four and a half years and, during that time, he hired a stable of talent that many in the radio industry believe was unequaled by any other Top 40 station of its era. Among the names are Chuck Buell, John Mack Flanagan, Marvelous Mark McKay, Mucho Morales, Big Tom Parker, Dr. Don Rose, Dave Sholin and Shana — just to name a few.

Promotionally, Spears ran a ship like no other — perhaps it was the McLendon influence. According to Michael Hagerty, a TV producer in Phoenix (quoted in a column written by David Ferrell Jackson in "The Bay Area Radio Digest" on October 26, 2005), "Spears's first promotion was giving away Mick Jagger's Morgan Plus 8 Roadster. Then there was "The Grand-A-Day-Giveaway," "The-Car-A-Day," and "Hawaii-A-Day" contest."

During our mutual birthday talks, Michael often mentioned how he loved his years in San Francisco. At times, he was even exuberant in the telling of stories, but never (as I recall) as over the top as this posting I found on Beau Weaver's website:

> "Ah, the good old days of the Patty Hearst Kidnapping, streaking, and Tower of Power records. At twenty-one years of age I had the honor of doing morning drive on KFRC (for about fifteen minutes)...warming up the chair for Dr. Don Rose. Sitting in the control room at KFRC was like flying a 747. I never had more fun on the air than I did doing nights in San Francisco. Michael took an already hot station and built it into, unquestionably, the best Top 40 station ever! There was magic in those rainbow painted walls."

They don't make them like that anymore.

In 1977, Spears turned thirty and turned his attention to KHJ/Los Angeles. It was, after all, the one station all the RKO Program Directors were supposed to aspire to. Paul Drew, RKO's National PD at the time, says he was out of the country when he heard about the move and wondered what Michael was doing. Charlie Van Dyke, the exiting KHJ PD, echoed the same thoughts. "It's not going to be as easy as you think," he told Spears. "You're going to be in the fishbowl."

But, Spears had an ulterior motive. "A couple of partners and I wanted to buy a radio station and we reasoned that I would be more valuable as a person to raise money if I was running the (RKO) flagship. So, I accepted the job."

But, Spears never liked Los Angeles. "Too many corporate people buzzing 'round and too much politics," he said.

His on-air staff included Machine Gun Kelly and Charlie Tuna, and he brought some of his favorites from KFRC along with him. But, the radio station Spears inherited was a mere reflection of its former 1960's self. "So," he explained. "I really wanted to do something different with the station." His goal was to revamp the station, to prepare it for the future.

"I was even working with Jim Long at TM on a new jingle package that would actually mean we were going to drop the Drake logo."

The new KHJ melody Michael proposed incorporated the notes in the song, *Hooray for Hollywood*, but it never got on the air. "Right up until the 11th hour, we were ready to do it. But, I guess, it wasn't meant to be," he confided. "It was a very difficult time."

Before a year had passed, Michael's RKO ride was over. He'd been wildly successful in San Francisco and wildly frustrated in LA. Now, he and his partners decided it was time to throw their hats into the ownership ring.

•

His goal had always been to own a station by the time he was thirty. He was running a bit behind, but KHJ had been a valuable detour, so he figured he was still pretty much on schedule. "We looked at Seattle, Sacramento and, finally, identified Tampa," Spears told me.

The station they chose was a two hundred and fifty watt AM daytimer, at 570 on the AM dial, doing Album Rock. "We had assurances that we could take it full time and, because "60 Minutes" was huge, we thought a talk station made a lot of sense."

At the time, Tampa didn't have a talk outlet and the call letters Michael selected were WPLP which, he said, stood for "people listening to people." WPLP was modeled after KGO/San Francisco. Spears put a news block on in the morning and a psychologist named Dr. Lois Miller on in afternoons. And, for a while, it appeared that the station would make a mark. But, in 1982, there was a partnership dispute. (Spears went off the record here and only allowed that it was a tough time and that he lost his family's fortune and his inheritance.) "I left Florida penniless," he said. "I didn't even have a suit."

More than twenty years after the partnership fell apart, memories of it, and what transpired afterwards, were still vivid to him. "I never want to enter a courtroom again," he said.

•

He left Florida, and thanks to his friend Ron Chapman, connected with Fairbanks Broadcasting. "I bought a new suit," said Spears, "and moved to Indianapolis to replace George Johns as the group's National PD."

But, Indiana was a far cry from California or Texas, and the job, as it turned out, wasn't a job made in heaven. Six months later, Spears was back in Dallas interviewing for a job programming an urban station, KKDA-FM. During the interview with KKDA's owner, Hyman Childs, Spears says he brought up his lack of experience with a black format.

"What's to know?" replied Childs. "Just different records."

Spears was still skeptical. KKDA's physical plant reminded him of his station in Florida — not a good thing. "It looked like a massage parlor in the middle of a cornfield; orange shag carpeting, no sign, a screen door in front and weeds everywhere."

"Can you, uh, afford to pay me what I'd need to come down here?" he asked.

Childs said "Yes." KKDA would match his Fairbanks salary and, on top of that, offered an incentive plan based on ratings.

"And so, we were off to the races at KKDA," said Spears.

Little did he know that the tiny concrete building would become the home of one of America's greatest and most enduring radio stations.

•

The staff at KKDA (K-104) was surprised by how much he knew about their music; no one commented about him being white.

K-104's direct format competitor, KNOK, had a 5.6 when Spears arrived at the station and, in his first rating book, Spears posted a 5.3. Next, it was a 5.6 and then another 5.6. "I'd never seen an identical share," he told me.

He was starting to get rattled. When the next book showed KKDA with a 5.9, he thought, "Crap. I can't figure out how to make this thing move."

A year passed. Then another six months.

Spears had cleaned up KKDA and knew the station sounded better than KNOK, but it didn't seem to matter. One day, while stopping for gas in Ft. Worth, Spears asked the attendant why he was listening to KNOK, instead of KKDA.

"I don't know," the man replied. "They play more music, I guess."

Today, with all the research available, the more music position would be one of the first things a PD would look at. But, back then, particularly in urban radio, research wasn't in wide use. Spears quickly commissioned a research project and the results only served to confirm his gas station hunch. "So my job was to convince the audience that we had more: more music, more contests and more fun."

KKDA began to play its songs in clusters of ten-in-a-row. "We called the campaign, 'KKDA Gives You More,' and, yeah, it really was that simple."

When the next book came out the station's ratings were up over a point — to a 7.1. This was remarkable because it made KKDA second only to KVIL, the # 1 radio station in Dallas. Eventually, KKDA hit a 10.6 and beat KVIL. For his work at KKDA/Dallas, "Billboard" Magazine named Michael Spears Black Programmer of the Year. (Yes, he thought it ironic.)

•

My guess is that well over two hundred and fifty people attended Michael's memorial service. It was a mix of radio people and civilians. The non-radio folks heard radio industry stories and laughed politely, although I'm sure most of them had no idea what we were talking about. And the radio people heard stories about his tremendous faith and spirituality, traits he'd kept mostly to himself.

In a career that lasted over forty years, Michael Spears lent his talents to radio stations from Corsicana to Los Angeles. He consulted or programmed over thirty stations in five different formats (including Top 40, News/Talk, AC and Urban). In the '90s, after leaving K104, he started a television company and wrote over one hundred and fifty episodes for a half hour syndicated program for Fox Television, and co-produced a youth news magazine series for the USA Network.

Back in Dallas, while programming Infinity's KRLD, he helped develop The Amber Plan, an instant radio alert system designed, in conjunction with law enforcement, to alert the public to missing children. In 2002, the NAB honored Spears with the Distinguished Service to America Award and, in 2004, he was inducted into the Texas Radio Hall of Fame.

•

One more thing.

At the church, we radio people learned something about Michael that only his friends in the congregation knew. Several months before he died, when the effects of cancer were obvious for all to see, Michael ended the service by inviting the members of the church to take a walk with him.

He exited the building — a throng of people followed — and headed down the street. After a few blocks, they all stopped in front of a house. There, Michael turned to his friends and explained. "I read in the paper that the people who live in this house lost a son last night in a drive-by shooting."

He continued. "So, I thought maybe we should come by and see if we could help."

Chapter 52
Gary Stevens:
The Five Billion Dollar Man

I don't know much about the French I took, but I do know *savior faire* when I see it.

In the early '60s, Gary Stevens, already a major market talent at WIL/St. Louis, had his sights on the Big Apple. "Ron Lundy and all the guys at WIL wanted to go there," he says. "So I did, too. New York was like the Holy Grail."

In 1964, despite the fact that he'd already accepted a job at WKNR/Detroit, Stevens was still sending out tapes and working the phones, determined to land a job in New York. "Ruth Meyer, at WMCA, was receptive to my contact, but I wasn't interested in the all-night show," he says.

Still, he *was* willing to audition. "In those days, they auditioned you in a studio," Stevens explains. "Talk about being intimidated."

Inside the booth, an old, rusty engineer stared him down. "Whadda ya need, kid?" Outside, a crowd gathered to watch. It was nerve-racking! Adding insult to injury, his headphones weren't right. "No processing!" he said.

He felt left-footed. When he didn't get the job, he figured that was all she wrote. "I'm done. One shot and I blew it."

He headed back to Detroit, dejected.

WKNR (KeeNeR) was only supposed to be a place to hang his hat until something better came along. The job, in fact, was considered so temporary that his family never fully unpacked. "But, then the station did really well. There were three rockers in Detroit: CKLW, WJBK and WXYZ, and we knocked 'em all off. So, we took to the market and stayed."

Before he knew it, he'd been at WKNR long enough to take a vacation. "My wife and I went to Europe," says Stevens, "and, for a schmooze, I sent Ruthie Meyer a postcard from Paris." A week later he got a telegram from WMCA, asking if he wanted to audition again.

"I told Ruth, 'If you wanna hear me, you gotta hear me in my natural habitat.' " In other words, come to Detroit.

Meyer snuck into town a day early. Not knowing she was listening, Stevens says he just screwed around on the air. The next morning Meyer called.

"Well?" asks Stevens.

"I was here yesterday."

"Oh, shit!"

"And you broke every format rule in the book."

"Uh, huh?"

"And it was great," said Meyer. "I loved it."

•

Eight Days A Week, by The Beatles, was all over the radio, but what Stevens remembers most about flying into New York City were the lights of Manhattan. "I'd never seen anything that big all lit up at night." He remembers looking out the plane's window and thinking, "My God, there are eight million people out there."

In the spring of 1965 Gary Stevens replaced B. Mitchell Reed on WMCA/New York. It was a disc jockey dream come true. He had no way of knowing his future was going to be less about playing records and more about making deals.

•

Don't hold me to exact details, but here's what happened next: Reg Calvert, the owner of Radio City, a pirate radio station that broadcast from a World War II fort off the coast of Kent, England, was gunned down by Oliver Smedley, the owner of rival pirate ship, *Radio Caroline*. The British press, particularly the tabloids, had a heyday and the Parliament, conscious of the outcry, quickly passed "The Marine Offences Act," which made it illegal to provision the pirates and to broadcast a radio signal into Great Britain from offshore. For all intents and purposes the age of British Pirate radio was over. But, not before Stevens got a chance to play.

He still did nights on WMCA, but during the day he recorded an hourly show, at the Brill Building, for "Swinging Radio England," a Top 40 station that only operated for six months — from May until November of 1966. It skirted the law by having its offices in London's West End, its studios in the North Seas several miles off of Frinton-On-Sea, Essex, England and by being represented by a company that also handled ABC Radio and TV in Europe. "I visited the ship once when it first signed on," he says. "We went out and back on a Dutch tender from Felixstowe."

But, pirate radio was never about smooth sailing and, by February of 1967, Stevens was disillusioned. "It was a wonderful couple of years," he says, "but we got caught up in protests and the Vietnam War, and then the music started changing."

Being on the air wasn't fun anymore.

So, just like that, he and his family moved to Europe. "I sold film, mutual funds, had a really good time." But, by 1970, he was ready to come home. He was going to get a programming job, right? "Nope," he says. "I went looking for a job as a General Manager."

•

He interviewed at KRIZ/Phoenix, a station owned by Doubleday Broadcasting. Halfway through the job interview, he was offered the job and accepted. But, on the day he was supposed to leave Europe he had second thoughts. "My wife took me to the airport three times before I caught the last plane out," he says.

Stevens settled in at KRIZ and stayed for four years, working with, among others, programmers Buzz Bennett, Todd Wallace and John Sebastian. Then, in 1974, Doubleday transferred Stevens to KDWB/Minneapolis.

What you probably don't know is the research systems John Sebastian and Steve Casey set up at KDWB opened doors for him at the other Doubleday stations. "Their systems became a power base for me, and I was named Senior Vice President of Research," says Stevens.

On December 7, 1977, Gary Stevens was promoted to President of Doubleday Broadcasting.

•

He'd been the President of a major broadcasting group and was known in New York. When the first round of deregulation began in the early '80s, Stevens says he realized asset based investment bankers didn't understand the radio business. By this time Doubleday had sold most of its stations and Stevens knew he was going to be out of work. "If you're leaving a job, it's got to look decent," he says. He decided he had to market himself to the industry. "The notion of Stevens going to Wall Street — well, I kinda liked that."

Since 1986, The Gary Stevens Company has orchestrated radio station sales worth more than five billion dollars. I don't know about you, but I think that's called *savior faire*.

CHAPTER 53
TODD STORZ: THE FATHER OF TOP 40

Monday, June 4, 1956, when the #1 record on Billboard's Hot 100 was *Moonglow and Theme from Picnic* by Morris Stoloff (conducting the Columbia Pictures Orchestra), the editors of "Time" published these words:

> "The fastest-rising figure in U.S. radio is Omaha's R. (for Robert) Storz, 32, whose low estimate of listeners' intelligence is tempered only by his high regard for their cupidity."

Calling Storz, "the King of Giveaway," the magazine wrote,

> "...This cash-and-Harry formula is so popular with listeners and advertisers that Storz in six years has run a $20,000 investment of his own, plus $30,000 from his father, into a $2,500,000 network."

The editors were sarcastically complimentary of the young man's accomplishments. Between the lines, however, was a generation gap, and one can only assume that the New York based journalists, chomping on cigars and sipping lunch-time martinis, had no idea what Storz was doing.

It was called Top 40.

•

Either you believe the story, or you don't. The bar wasn't much to speak of, but it's where they figured it out. Todd Storz, the owner and General Manager of KOWH/Omaha, and Bill Stewart, his Program Director, were having a few pops after work, when they noticed a young girl feeding the jukebox. Each time she put a coin in, the box burped back the same song. It happened again, and again, and again.

"Why are you playing that song over and over?" they are said to have asked.

"It's my favorite," she supposedly answered.

According to legend, the two men began to wonder that if a radio station did the same thing — that is, play people's favorite songs over and over — it might gain an audience. It was the early '50s and radio was desperately trying to reinvent itself.

It was a far simpler time, but don't think for a moment that broadcasters had it easy. Radio station owners, like Storz and Dallas-based Gordon McLendon, were faced with adapting to the changing times and technology. Their response was to devise a musical format centered around the most popular hits of the day, and to promote it aggressively.

"Todd Storz has the music part down," says Ken Dowe, Gordon McLendon's protégé. "But, Gordon came up with the promotions and marketing ideas that made Top 40 fly."

By the way, the bar story may not be true.

•

Storz came from money.

His grandfather, Gottlieb Storz, founded the Omaha Brewing Association in 1891. Twenty-six years later, in 1917, prohibition came to Nebraska, but the brewery was able to survive by manufacturing ice and non-alcoholic beverages. "Near-beer" was a product brewed by Omaha Brewing.

When prohibition was repealed in Nebraska in 1934, the company was back in business and, before long, the brewery was making 150,000 barrels of beer a year.

In 1949, when Todd Storz was twenty-five, he and his father bought a local Omaha radio station, KOWH. Storz wasn't new to radio; before buying KOWH, he'd been on the air and had sold radio time. In 1952, according to Richard Fatherly, a former Storz programmer based in Kansas City, Storz got his ideas about tight playlists and repetition from a University of Omaha research paper.

The paper exists (consultant Walter Sabo sent me a copy a few years ago) and it indicates that music was one of the main reasons people used the radio.

Regardless of where the concept came from — the bar or the university — Storz took all the network programming off KOWH and replaced it with music, news, and lots of promotion. Within two years the station was #1 with forty-eight point eight percent of the afternoon audience.

What Storz first created in Omaha and then took to New Orleans (WTIX), Kansas City (WHB), St. Louis (KXOK), Minneapolis (WDGY), Oklahoma City (KOMA) and Miami (WQAM) had never been done before. Interestingly enough, the Top 40 format Storz developed — one that plays the best of all popular music regardless of genre — can no longer be found on the radio.

•

Robert Todd Storz died, from a stroke, on April 13, 1964. He was only thirty-nine.

Along with Gordon McLendon — who always agreed that Storz was responsible for coming up with the principles of the format — Todd Storz is considered one of the Fathers of Top 40.

"Todd didn't ask, 'Who else is doing it?' " says Sabo. "He asked, 'What do the people want?' He trusted his instinct, the research and had the courage to act."

Storz was inducted into the Radio Hall of Fame in 1987.

CHAPTER 54
CHARLIE TUNA:
"YOU'RE A GOOD MAN, CHARLIE TUNA"

Boston was buried under four feet of ice and snow the morning he flew out of Logan Airport.

When he landed in California, it was sixty-five degrees — balmy to him. He was met by Ron Jacobs, the Program Director of KHJ. Jacobs started their conversation by complaining about how cold it was. Tuna says he just stared at the man and thought, "How bizarre."

Later that night, Jacobs returned the stare. "So, tell me, what is it you do on the air?"

Tuna says the specificity of the question caught him off guard and he scrambled. "I said, 'Well, I'm quick with drop-ins and sound effects, I run a tight board and, uh, try to be real topical.'"

It was 1967. At the time Tuna was doing afternoon drive at WMEX/Boston, but he was a hot property and his future was in play. In fact, WABC/New York had expressed interest in him for the overnight shift and he was beginning to think it might be a good move.

But, one evening, as he was getting off the air, someone told him there was a call from Los Angeles holding for him. Tuna says he picked up the phone and heard Ron Jacobs' voice for the first time. "Listen, man," said Jacobs, "I just got a tape of your show in Boston, heard three breaks, and I'd like to offer you a job at KHJ in Los Angeles."

Tuna was floored.

He knew all about KHJ and had even listened to a few airchecks of the station. "It was the fastest thing I'd ever heard," he remembers.

But it had never occurred to him that he'd ever work there. After all, it was only two and a half years since he'd left Kearney, Nebraska. So, anyway, there he was in Los Angeles, sitting in Ron Jacobs' living room, and they're talking about him becoming a Boss Jock. He thought it was very strange.

Jacobs and Tuna talked into the evening. Around eleven o'clock Tuna began peeking at his watch; his plan was to catch a redeye back to Boston. Jacobs thought otherwise. "You know, man, you look kinda tired. Why don't you crash on the couch and we'll book you another flight in the morning?"

Tuna slept like a baby that night. When he woke up the next morning he was jazzed. "KHJ," he thought. "Wow!" He turned on the radio to listen to the Robert W. Morgan Show and that's when he heard the news: the TWA flight he was supposed to have been on the night before had crashed during a rain storm in Cincinnati.

Forty-five people had been killed.

•

Charlie Tuna's real name is Arthur Ferguson and he's from Kearney, Nebraska.

"When I was five years old, there was a disc jockey in Kearny, a very creative guy named Jack Lewis," Tuna begins. Lewis worked for KGFW and caught the boy's ear because he announced the school closings, had a daily dressing race ritual — the boys against the girls to see who could get dressed faster — *and* he talked about UFOs. "Jack was one of the first to ever talk about flying saucers," Tuna explains.

UFOs were exciting stuff for a five-year old, and he says he couldn't help but think that Lewis had the greatest job in the world. So, he decided he wanted to be a disc jockey, too. His parents bought him a seventy-eight rpm record player for eight dollars and sitting in his bedroom and pretending to do a radio show became a ritual.

By his early teens, Tuna decided he was ready to show off.

"I went into the DJ booth during a Junior High hop and started playing some records. After a while, I decided to let the kids see what I could do."

He was a hit. "The kids all said, 'Hey, you're pretty good.' "

'I oughta be,' thought Tuna to himself. 'I've been practicing for nine years.' "

So, announcing the local teen dances became a regular occurrence and his friends encouraged him to apply at KGFW, to get a real radio job. But, he was shy, so it was his father who made the overture to the station.

"Listen," his dad said, "My kid's doing this thing at the youth center on the weekends, but he'd really like to get into radio. Can you give him a shot?"

The audition went well enough, but it didn't land him a job. "Not bad," KGFW's Station Manager told him. "But, we don't have any openings."

Six months later something opened up. "They put me on at night," says Ferguson. "I worked from ten to one in the morning." But, thirty days later opportunity knocked. "One night the morning man had too much to drink at a party and, while worshipping at the porcelain throne, he lost his dentures."

Tuna filled in that morning and, for reasons unexplained, stayed in the slot. (Maybe the morning man never found his dentures. More likely, the young DJ was paid less.) "All of a sudden, I'm a sixteen-year-old high school kid doing the morning show on the station I grew up listening to." And, when he wasn't working or going to school the young man listened to another station, the big one in the sky — the one he dreamed about at night — 50,000 watt KOMA/Oklahoma City.

•

A boyhood friend, Don Williams, convinced him to send a tape to

KLEO/Wichita. Wichita was a big jump from Kearney and when the station hired him for $350 a month, Ferguson decided to buy himself a brand new 1964 Mustang. It wasn't the only change he made. "I figured I had to have a radio name in a bigger market," he says. "So, in Wichita, I used the name Billy O'Day."

One hundred and fifty miles away, in Oklahoma City, there was a man named Chuck Dann who wasn't very happy. Dann was a KOMA newsman, a *journalist* — not a disc jockey. But, when the entire KOMA crew got sick, he was drafted to do a weekend dj shift. Dann was reluctant. Playing records, he insisted, would hurt his credibility as a newsman. Desperate for a substitute, management suggested he simply come up with another name. "Anything," they implored. "Just pull the shift."

"As the legend goes," says Tuna, "Dann was sitting in front of the TV the night before, a six-pack of Coors in him, saw the Star-Kist commercial and thought, 'Ah hell, I'll be Charlie Tuna.' " The name got tremendous reaction and, by the time Art Ferguson arrived at KOMA, it had been decided that *he* would become the permanent Charlie Tuna. It was January 22, 1966. In less than two years Tuna's life would be incredibly different.

•

Larry Lujack had been working for Pat O'Day in Seattle at KJR, but in 1966, when he was offered more money to do afternoon drive at WMEX/Boston, he couldn't say no.

The drive from Seattle to Boston, about twenty-five hundred miles, took him days. Lujack says he doesn't remember coffee or restroom breaks, but does recall hearing a great disc jockey on KOMA and, when an opening came up at WMEX, Lujack suggested the station call Oklahoma City and ask for a guy named Charlie Tuna.

•

Thanksgiving Day, 1967, Charlie Tuna was on the air at KHJ/Los Angeles.

That morning Robert W. Morgan preceded him and, opening his microphone, the first thing Tuna did was to thank Morgan for "warming up the audience." According to insiders, Morgan, wasn't pleased.

Still, three years later, Tuna was the heir apparent when Morgan left to go to WIND/Chicago. Tuna took over Morgan's KHJ shift and didn't miss a beat. On his first day, he told a knock-knock joke.

"Knock, knock."

"Who's there?"

"Robert W."

"Robert W. who?"

"How easily we forget."

•

But, Morgan never liked Chicago and, when he decided he wanted to come home to KHJ, the station welcomed him with open arms.

This time it was Tuna who wasn't pleased. He figured he'd earned the right to keep the morning slot, and when KHJ said "no" and tried to keep him on board by offering him another shift, he also said "no."

Instead, he accepted the morning show at KCBQ/San Diego, just as the station was launching Jack McCoy's historic Last Contest promotion.

Then, for close to a year, Tuna drove roundtrip from Los Angles to San Diego every day.

•

Charlie Tuna has been a constant presence on Los Angeles radio for over forty years. Besides KHJ, he's worked for KROQ-AM, KKDJ, KIIS-AM/FM, KTNQ, KHTZ, KRLA, KODJ-FM, KMPC, KLAC and KBIG-FM. In February of 2008, Tuna joined KRTH, LA's Oldies station. In many ways, K-Earth is a 21st century version of

KHJ and, for Tuna, it must have felt a little bit like coming home.

Charlie Tuna has a star on the Hollywood Walk of Fame, is a member of the Nebraska Broadcasters Hall of Fame and, in July of 2008, was inducted into the Radio Hall of Fame.

And, in Los Angeles, a long way from Kearney, he is recognized as one of the Top 10 L.A Radio personalities of all time.

In case you don't get it, Charlie Tuna is a very big fish.

Ooops. Sorry, Charlie.

(Charlie Tuna is syndicated on "Classic Top 40" by Thompson Creative and United Stations.)

CHAPTER 55
RUSTY WALKER: THE MAN FROM IUKA

They were heading southeast into Florida from Florence, Alabama. On the landscape were seedy motels, fast food palaces – not many, though; franchised America was still in the early thralls of sprawl — and scores of sun-bleached billboards bragging about low-price gas.

Sam Darwin says he didn't stop or even notice.

It was 1976, the year the south won the White House for the first time in decades and when a song about citizen band radios, called *Convoy*, topped the charts. Darwin, in his seventh year in radio, had his foot to the floor and was barreling down the highway racing toward his first big time radio job: mornings at WQYK/Tampa.

The Program Director at 'QYK, during their conversations about the job, had suggested Darwin change his name, but when Darwin came up with the moniker, Pomegranate Jones — "…if there can be a Rhubarb Jones," the PD indicated he was less than impressed. This left Darwin and his wife on the road rocketing towards a nameless future. The truth was, he couldn't come up with anything, and his wife was at the end of her rope. Finally, in exasperation, she told him to stop futzing around. As the white lines passed, they both stared out the window, hoping for inspiration. And so it was, at seventy miles an hour, that they grabbed a name out of the air — or more precisely, off a billboard. "It was for Walker's Hardware and said something about rusty nails," Darwin recalls.

Hard Nails didn't pass the road test, but the name Rusty Walker did.

•

Corinth, Mississippi. Call it the middle of nowhere if you want, but if you were born there it holds a revered place in your heart because it's close to Tupelo, Elvis's birthplace. "It's about eighty-five miles southeast of Memphis, where the blues were born and

Sam Phillips helped rock 'n' roll go through labor," says Walker.

He got addicted to radio, particularly Top 40, early on. "I spent my days listening to WHBQ and WMPS/Memphis and at night it was WLS/Chicago, when I could get them," he says. And, on nights when the atmosphere was right, he also picked up Buffalo's WKBW, where he could "listen to some Jackson Armstrong."

But, in 1969, Rusty Walker was flipping burgers at Byrd's Dixie Queen and dreaming of a future in music, not radio. "I'm a percussionist," he says, "and played string bass in high school. I was going to be a junior college or community college band director. But, I knew a guy at WWTX named Ron Morgan, and he knew I had some interest in radio, so he gave me the number of Doug King, the station's Program Director."

That night, Walker made the call. The next day, after school, he showed up at the station, a combination sales office/studio, equipped with a microphone, a turntable and a cart machine. "King had me read the front page of the newspaper and, apparently, the audition must have gone OK because, by five o'clock, I was sitting in a single-wide trailer learning the control board."

•

Imagine it: he's sitting in a trailer, with a big tower behind it. He's 15 miles out of town, in the middle of nowhere. "The first song I intro-ed was Nat Stuckey's *Sweet Thang and Cisco,* and I called him Nat STOOKEY," he says. "You know that embarrassing feeling you get where your face flushes and feels hot? Well, for the rest of the time that I was on the air that night, my face never felt cool again. The cool thing about it is my mother, and the other person listening that night, didn't care."

WWTX was a country station, but it was the jocking, not the music, that appealed to Walker. In fact, Rusty Walker's next five jobs, at WTUP/Tupelo, WTIB/Iuka, WAJF/Decatur, WOWL/ Florence and WQLT/Florence – were Top 40 gigs. But then, in 1975, while visiting his mother back home in Corinth, he discovered something that changed his life and his career. "I realized that my mother and I had the same favorite song, Willie Nelson's *Blue Eyes Crying in the Rain*. He says he thought it was weird that they'd like the same music and began to think there was might be something to this country thing.

Back in Florence, at WQLT, Walker set his sights on getting to a larger market and working at a contemporary country station. He and his friend, John St. John, poured through the trades and found a classified ad advertising a job at WQYK/Tampa. St. John applied for the job and was hired, and after he arrived at the station, he recommended Walker to the PD who was looking for a morning man.

Now, we've come full circle. We're back on the highway to Tampa, looking at billboards.

•

By 1980, Walker had thrown his hat into the programming arena. His first PD job, after leaving Tampa, was with Marshall Roland, the owner of WQIK/Jacksonville, who had bought a little station outside of Macon and asked him to help out.

"Then, Dick Ferguson recruited me to come up to WZZK-FM/ Birmingham," Walker says. Ferguson, who retired from Cox Broadcasting in 2006, says, "Rusty created an adult contemporary radio station that played country music." Today, that sounds tame, but in the mid '80s, country was an AM format and many "wise old radio guys" didn't believe it would ever transition to FM.

"WZZK debuted with a thirteen share of the audience," says Ferguson, and it went on to have a fifty-five or sixty share. It was a fun, warm, exciting, vibrant, credible place on the radio dial."

Walker remembers the time fondly, too. "The station just went KABOOM!" he says.

In 1983, Sconnix Broadcasting called. They wanted him to come to KFKF/Kansas City.

"No thanks," Walker responded. "I'm happy here in Birmingham."

But, Sconnix was persistent. Walker, they insisted, could continue to work with Ferguson and Katz; what they wanted was for him to consult KFKF. Walker and Sconnix signed an 18-month deal and Rusty Walker Programming was born. Within a year, the company was a going concern.

Today, Rusty Walker's fingerprints are on close to 5% of the country stations in America. "He's a strategist, but he never lets the science and discipline get in the way of the magic," says Ferguson. "He's as honest as the day is long; a good, solid person. I just love him." Walker, named "Country Radio Consultant of the Year" by "Billboard" magazine seven years in a row, and "Country Programmer of the Century" by "Radio and Records," remains grounded and appreciative!

If you're in radio, take these words with you as you go to work tomorrow. "I believe the most important people in the world are program directors of radio stations," says Walker. "It's the most gallant position you can aspire to."

In these tumultuous times it's a thought to reflect and hold on to.

CHAPTER 56
TODD WALLACE: THE FATHER OF
CALL OUT RESEARCH

One day in the late '60s, a young disc jockey from Wichita, Kansas approached his boss, one of the most-respected radio programmers in America, with an idea that would change the nature of questions that radio stations asked record stores when they made their weekly calls. Oh, you don't remember this archaic practice? Well, here's the deal: Hit-oriented stations would call records stores to see what was selling. Often, the titles were hyped (a record guy would give some pimply-faced gnome free albums, beers, etc. to file false reports) or there just wasn't enough data gathered to make the effort anything but an exercise in futility.

So, anyway, the young Turk wrote a memo to the revered programmer: "In addition to checking on what songs are being bought, we should also ask what OTHER songs they would buy, if they had enough money. And, which songs we're playing that they don't like and which songs they're tired of hearing."

It was a concept ahead of its time. The PD said so, thanked the kid for caring so much, shoved the memo aside, and moved on to the next item on his desk.

At this point the idea had nowhere to go.

•

Building a career as a disc jockey doesn't happen the way it used to; the aura of a distant station isn't as glorified as it once was because, well, nobody listens to far-away radio stations anymore. But, forty years ago, if you were a DJ and any good, your early years were all about market climbing and money, with the market jump — moving up in market size — much more important than the money.

Todd Wallace was a tenacious teen. Not knowing what he didn't know, he applied for work at every radio station in Wichita, his hometown. He had a voice, he was bright and he was motivated, but even *he* didn't know how lucky he was when he landed a part-time job at the leading Top 40 station, KWBB. It was 1963, he was a self-described "teenage DJ" and his life would be lived on the road for at least the next ten years. "The early years of my career were spent working my way up the DJ food-chain, leap-frogging every few months from one Top 40 station to another."

He's not exaggerating. He left Wichita in 1964 to do afternoons at KLSI/Salina. The next year, enamored by the power and regional influence of WNOE/New Orleans, he joined its sister station, KNOW/Monroe, LA. But, once he got there, he was shocked by what he discovered. "The headquarters of The Klan was located nearby," says Wallace, "and (they) had a major influence on our programming."

What he means is the station didn't play any black artists, an unusual move for a Top 40 station back in the day. On top of that, he says, "KNOE wouldn't even play any songs by Bob Dylan, because he wrote *Blowing In The Wind*, nor would they play any songs by Peter, Paul and Mary, because they sang it!" It was a different time, but it still didn't sit well with a kid raised in integrated Wichita. Before the year was out he moved again — this time to Ft. Smith, Arkansas, which got him within earshot of the Mighty 1190, KLIF/Dallas.

•

Like anything else, it's *who* you know, then *what* you know. "Big Jim O'Brien, who would eventually program CKLW/Windsor-Detroit and KHJ/Los Angeles, was doing afternoons at KLIF," says Wallace.

KLIF was like a magnet to Wallace. He'd been listening to it for years, so getting PD Johnny Borders to give him a weekend job — just because Big Jim said he was good — was a big coup. But, it was only part-time, so when a full-time job popped up at KSEE/ Santa Maria, California, Wallace was forced to head west. He had his traveling shoes on.

Towards the middle of 1996, Wallace accepted an invitation to return to Texas to do PM drive at KDOK/Tyler. "My intention," he says, "was to also work weekends at KLIF, but while waiting for a part-time gig to open up, I got an offer to do the all-night show at KBTR, the #2 Top 40 station in Denver. He took it (his *fifth* job that year).

From the outside it may have looked like he was crazy, but he was doing exactly what he'd set out to do. "I knew I wanted to make it to the BIGS," says Wallace, "and that became my primary goal."

•

He couldn't buy a beer yet, or even vote for President. He didn't care. He drove out of Tyler, heading west and, eventually, crossed the border into New Mexico. Then he turned north, motoring towards Colorado and his destination, Denver, and a full-time gig in a major market.

Never mind that it was an all-night show, and never mind that he hadn't put down any roots yet. It was nothing to be ashamed of. By the way, did I mention that his show at KBTR/Denver was broadcast from a bowling alley? Or, did I say that the show from Celebrity Sports Center had to be loud, and that between screams and squeals, and a soundtrack that must have included *Wild Thing* and *Summer In the City*, Wallace, the new kid in town, had to keep things rocking? "I'd be right in the middle of a front sell," he says, "and someone in the background would yell 'STRIKE!' It took some getting used to."

He began at KBTR with good intentions. But, at the end of his first week, he heard that KIMN's midday jock had abruptly resigned. KIMN was the #1 Top 40 station in Denver.

What happened next involves the fickle finger of fate. "One night," says Wallace, "KIMN PD Ted Atkins; MD Hal Baby Moore; and PM-drive DJ Chuck Buell all came out to the bowling alley while I was doing my show." It may have been coincidence, but probably not. After a few hours of conversation, Atkins offered Wallace the all-night show at KIMN.

"Only one hitch," Wallace explains. "I didn't have a first ticket (1st Class FCC Radiotelephone License), but Atkins said it wasn't a problem. He told me I could do noon to three until January, at which time they'd pay for me to go to Elkins Institute in Dallas to get the license."

Wallace stayed at KIMN for two-and-a-half years. "At nineteen, I was the 'baby' of the station, always asking questions, always looking to learn." One of the lessons he learned was about competing. "KBTR announced they'd give away a new '66 Ford Mustang and that listeners could qualify to win ten times a day over the next month." KIMN's owner, Ken Palmer, responded. "He went down to a car dealer on East Colfax and said, 'I'll take them all.' " (I'm sure there was trade involved, but that doesn't diminish the power of the story.) "The dealer was taken aback and asked what Palmer meant. According to Wallace, Palmer replied, "All ninety-five of them."

And so, while KBTR was soliciting listeners to qualify to win *one* car, KIMN was giving away *ten* Pontiac GTOs a day. Wallace says it was a great lesson in how to make your competitor look small.

•

KIMN was like college for Wallace. But, by 1969, he was ready for grad school. That's when he got the call from KILT/Houston. Once the sister station of KLIF/Dallas — when Gordon McLendon had owned it — the station was now part of Lin Broadcasting, managed by Dickie Rosenfeld and programmed by Bill Young. By the time Wallace arrived in Houston, KILT had been the market Top 40 leader for over a dozen years.

"The morale at KILT was the best I'd ever experienced," says Wallace. In part, this may have been due to the monthly "Sock It To Me" parties Rosenfeld threw for the staff. "At most of them, he gave across-the-board raises to EVERYONE," Wallace remembers.

KILT was about promotion and, shortly after arriving at the station, Wallace did something that made him a household name in Houston, and throughout the radio industry. "To commemorate man's first walk on the moon," he explains, "KILT staged a contest giving away $5,000 to the first person who could guess how long I could live on the top of the Houston Astrodome." On the air Wallace vowed to stay on top of the dome "until it hatched." Local television stations, normally reluctant to glorify anything a radio station ever did, covered the event like a blanket. Newspapers did the same.

After three weeks, Wallace had enough, but that wasn't the end of it. "My Astrodome exploits didn't go unnoticed in the radio community," he says. At the time, there were changes going on at the RKO stations, consulted by Bill Drake. Jim O'Brien was leaving CKLW/Detroit to take the programming reigns at KHJ (replacing Ron Jacobs) and his interim replacement, Frank Brodie, was urged to talk with Wallace, who'd quickly become the talk of the industry. Encouraged by his friends Michael Spears and Steve Hunter, Wallace went for the interview and decided to take the job. "I had planned to stay at KILT for several years," he explains, "but I was so intrigued by what I could learn by working at an actual Drake station that I made the decision to accept the all-night DJ position."

As it happened, Frank Brodie didn't get the programming job at CKLW and, within a month of arriving in Detroit, Wallace had a new PD to deal with.

His name was Paul Drew.

•

Drew was a button-down, no-nonsense executive with a very definite idea of how he wanted things done. Wallace, CKLW's new all-night guy, was the young thinker who'd written a memo containing some thoughts about what would later be labeled "call-out research." You'll recall Drew thanked Wallace for the memo, but noted there was no budget to do it, and suggested that some of the ideas were "ahead of their time."

So, Wallace had tucked his idea away, saving it for a brighter day. Then, one night, he found a reason to write Drew another memo. "At CKLW we had board ops," explains Wallace. "Anyway, I gave the wrong cart number to my board op and ended up playing a record, an oldie, that had been played earlier in the day."

The bat phone—the hotline—rang. It was Mr. Drew, who apparently never slept. "You played a song that played four hours ago."

"Yeah," laughed Wallace. "My mistake. I gave him the wrong cart number."

Drew, according to Wallace, was not amused and instructed him to take the cart in question, break it in half and put it under his office door. Wallace chewed on that idea for a while. When he got off the air at six o'clock that morning, instead of breaking the cart, he sat down at a typewriter and wrote Drew a two-page memo.

"It was my mistake and I won't do it again. But, let's not deprive listeners of a hit just because I made a mistake. I hope you understand why I didn't break the record, even though I did think about it. But, also hope you understand what I had to say."

Wallace was proud of what he'd written and equally sure Drew would be impressed by the time and effort he'd put into to.

The next night, he arrived at work to find a large envelope in his box. "And in it," says Wallace, "was the broken cart with a note attached that said: Always follow instructions.

He'd been market climbing for seven years, the amount of time scientists tell us it takes to shed all our skin or, said another way, to respond to an itch. As a disc jockey, most of his career had been nocturnal, but like anybody with ambition, he knew that doing a morning show provided a chance for stability, respectability and, at the very least, more money. Besides, he reasoned, the nights were cold in Detroit and the sun would he warm in Phoenix.

"KRUX/Phoenix was one of the better 'fake-Drake' stations," Wallace says. By this, he means that everything on the station — formatics, jingles, features, etc. — was copied from (or at least modeled after) the "real" Drake stations — the ones actually consulted by Drake and his team at Drake-Chenault.

In 1970, when Wallace reported for mornings at KRUX, there was a ferocious Top 40 battle going on between the station and its nemesis, KRIZ. (Interestingly enough, although "Billboard" never made a big deal about it, both AM stations had small signals, which meant that what they lacked in strength and coverage had to be made up with smoke and mirrors. Think David vs. David.)

Wallace was excited about doing morning drive and convinced himself that it made up for Phoenix being smaller than Detroit. However, three months into the job, he got a call inviting him to Los Angeles — or, to be precise, Anaheim, in Orange County, near the stars and on the edge of Disneyland.

He says he couldn't say no. "My obsessive goal to move up the market ladder led me to KEZY, who offered me afternoon drive.

•

KEZY had great local ties with Disneyland and the park's marketing machine was in its infancy. As a result, KEZY jocks, mainly because of their proximity to Disneyland, were chosen to be the parade announcers for the Disneyland Christmas Parade." For a kid from Wichita, it must have been like a dream come true. And, of course, there was the connection to the stars that came with being in Southern California. "Singer Jose Feliciano lived in Orange County and invited all of the L.A. jocks to a Christmas party at his home," says Wallace. "For some reason, he liked my jock style and one of my prouder moments was when Jose, while jammin' with other musicians in his large backyard, began an impromptu song about 'listenin' to Todd Wallace on the radio.' "

Today, Wallace laughs and calls this event a cheap thrill. But, at the time — in front of big-time L.A. personalities he admired, like Robert W. Morgan, the Real Don Steele, Gary Owens and Dick Clark – the evening became something he would never forget.

Then his phone rang. It was KRUX, and this time they wanted him to become Program Director. "PD gigs didn't grow on trees," says Wallace.

As he was packing to head back to his valley, the San Fernando earthquake hit. It was February of 1971.

•

He was a first-time programmer, but he knew what the job called for and he dug in. KRIZ and KRUX were running pretty much neck-to-neck but, within one rating period (there was no continuous measurement back then) KRUX had an 11.9 share and KRIZ was down to a 3.0.

What happened next and how fast it occurred may surprise you. Gary Stevens, the GM of KRIZ, wasn't a happy camper and decided to get Wallace out of town. Fast. He called his friend, Bernie Waterman. Waterman owned KTSA/San Antonio, a station that was losing to crosstown KONO. "Bernie was famous for paying big money in those days," says Wallace. "So, it was an easy decision for me to join KTSA for twice the salary I was making in Phoenix."

"When I arrived in San Antonio, KONO was winning the Top 40 battle in the Arbitron ratings — 14.0 to 9.0. Within one book, we reversed the trend. KTSA jumped to 13.0 and KONO fell to a 9.0

share." One of the reasons for the win, says Wallace, was the size of his playlist: He cut the KTSA list of fifty-five records down to only twenty-five. "The record promoters went ape-shit," he says.

Eight months later, Wallace's second ratings book at KTSA came out, and the station was on top again. This didn't go unnoticed back in Phoenix, where Gary Stevens had started to refer to him as "One-Book Wallace." After a testimonial like that, no one was surprised when Wallace returned to Phoenix to take over the programming reins at KRIZ. In short order, he took the ratings from a 6.1 to a 9.3.

Now, he thought, it's time to move on up.

•

By now radio trade magazines were watching Wallace's every move. In 1974, when it was announced he was leaving Phoenix and heading to Dallas, the news made headlines:

"WALLACE NEW KLIF PD" and "PLAYLIST MAY SHRINK TO 15 RECORDS."

"Once again," says Wallace, "I was in a situation where I needed to drastically cut a station's playlist from over fifty songs to just fifteen or twenty."

Dallas's record community got upset, but Wallace didn't care; he thought what was going on in Dallas radio was off balance. "Dallas record promoters had convinced local PDs to add songs quickly and to take them off fast, thereby making room for even more unproven new songs." The result, he says, was that Dallas charts were weeks ahead of the national charts.

With the benefit of call-out research, he implemented hyper-tight music rotations (songs classified as "powers" were played every ninety minutes) and created a "Gold" universe of only two hundred records. "In other words," says Wallace, "every song KLIF played was a proven hit."

KLIF's primary competition was Gordon McLendon's FM, KNUS. One of the nation's first FM Top 40s, KNUS had beaten KLIF just as Wallace was arriving in Dallas. A book later, KLIF jumped two points, then another point-and-a-half. Final score: KLIF 8.8, KNUS, in the mid 5.0s.

But, things were about to take a nasty turn. According to Wallace, the Dallas record community revolted and, when a new General Manager came to KLIF, they demanded Wallace be fired. If not, they said, they'd pull all their advertising. The ploy worked and, within days, the record guys threw a "Todd Wallace Going Away Party." Wallace wasn't invited.

With Wallace no longer at KLIF, the station elevated a secretary to Music Director and she implemented an eighty-song playlist. When the next Arbitron ratings results arrived, KLIF had taken a nose dive, from an 8.8 to a 3.6. The glory days of KLIF/The Mighty 1190 were over.

•

Because the Arbitron Ratings Company didn't offer continuous measurement in 1975, a radio station's success (or lack thereof) was judged only twice a year during month-long rating periods conducted in the spring and the fall. (As you'd imagine, this led to some stations "pimping up" for their thirty days in the spotlight, then becoming something else when ratings weren't going on.)

Wallace thought the lack of information was dangerous and, when he was invited to deliver a keynote address at a Swanson Broadcasting Programmer's Conference, he suggested a novel concept. "There are virtues," he said, "to knowing what your ratings are year-round AND advantages in knowing how diary keepers feel about every song you're playing."

This caught the ears of Ken Greenwood and Gary Swanson, the executives who ran Swanson. "One thing led to another," says Wallace, "and in September of 1975 Ken and Gary became investors in the company incorporated as Radio Index. Their financial backing enabled us to expand quickly and move our offices into a high-rise bank building in the uptown Phoenix corridor. Before that, we operated out of my converted garage. By that time, we had computerized all of our proprietary formulas, so we were poised to expand quickly."

It was the middle '70s. FM penetration was beginning to be a factor, Hooper and Pulse ratings had gone out of business, and Radio Index, along with competitor, MediaStat, were the only alternatives to the Arbitron ratings. "This led to amazing growth," says Wallace. "At our peak, we were delivering weekly ratings to 54 different markets, including a Who's Who of America's biggest stations: WNBC/New York, KHJ/Los Angeles, WLS/Chicago, WFIL/Philadelphia, WTAE/WXKX in Pittsburgh and KILT/Houston.

•

Wallace's success as a statistician — not many programmers could execute, much less envision the nuts and bolts of Radio Index — appealed to owners and managers and, by the end of the '70s, Wallace was also consulting stations on their programming.

During the '80s and '90s, he quietly kept working at his craft and growing his business. His client list featured many of the legendary stations we've all heard about; yes, multi-formats and great call letters, like WGCI, all the Kisses you know about, and all the players you've read about: Steve Rivers, Jay Cook, Sunny Joe White, Gerry DeFrancesco, Donnie Simpson, Ken Dowe, Al Brady Law ... the list goes on and on. One of the reasons Wallace, and Todd Wallace/Associates, has been so successful over the years is that ninety-eight percent of the stations he consults win. (Can you say "One-book Wallace?")

In case you didn't know, Wallace virtually invented international radio consulting, with a multitude of clients in Australia, New Zealand, The Philippines and the U.K. "Todd is internationally recognized as the founding father of call-out research," says Steve

Rivers. "He's one of the pioneers of modern radio programming and format theory."

"Radio Index," Wallace told me, "still conducts about forty or fifty surveys a year. Over the past thirty years we've conducted over five million interviews with adults in over three hundred radio markets worldwide (and) produced over fifteen hundred research reports for over five hundred radio stations."

By the way, he reads every report.

"He always gives his 'A' game, and he expects as much from any station manager smart enough to have him on board," says Ken Dowe. "Character, tenacity and talent. That's Todd's legend. He's as good a consulting gunslinger now as he's ever been."

Amen.

CHAPTER 57
FRED WINSTON: THE SINGLE ENTENDRE

Fred Winston was scheduled to begin his new job at WLS/Chicago on a Monday, but first he needed to do a practice run to get the lay of the land. So, Mike McCormick, the PD of WLS, arranged for him to sub for Kris Erik Stevens two days before his grand debut. It was a Saturday night.

Winston remembers driving with McCormick into the city seemed to take forever. Finally, they turned onto Michigan Avenue. "I remember craning my neck, looking at the size of the buildings," he says. "I was in awe and not just a little scared."

The car radio was on, of course, and he couldn't help but notice the guy on the air — "a big-voice legend." His stomach started turning. "Holy shit," he said to himself.

All he wanted to do was run and hide.

WLS was in the Stone Container Building, where the world famous London House stood guard on the main floor. Winston and McCormick walked into the building, took the elevator up to the 5th floor and were greeted by glass doors. Fred Winston says he stood there looking at the large two-foot block letters that spelled out WLS — ABC Radio. For the second time in as many minutes he thought to himself, "Holy shit." Young Mr. Winston had arrived. He was twenty-five.

•

When his voice changed at eleven, Fred Winston's friends nicknamed him "The Frog." When he spoke up, strangers would stare and say, "Kid, you ought to be on the radio — be a morning newsman." Never mind that he didn't know what a morning newsman was. What did matter was that he loved music and the old radio shows. And, because his parents were musicians and radiophiles to boot, he'd grown up with a radio playing in his house all the time.

Still, when he told them he'd gotten a job at a radio station, they didn't believe him. "You're going to be ... what!?! You mean you're going to come out of the radio speaker?"

"Yes."

"Oh, I don't believe that," his father replied.

"It's true," insisted young Fred. "And, you're going to have to give me a ride to the radio station on Sunday morning."

•

He remembers his first time on the air. "I was so terrible that the Program Director, Jolly Raleigh Fowler, told me he never wanted to hear my voice again."

Fowler pre-recorded things for Winston to play so he didn't have to speak. "But naturally," admits Winston, "I didn't play them."

Such defiance didn't make for job security and Jolly Raleigh jettisoned ready Freddy. But young Winston wasn't discouraged. "I wanted to talk on the radio, but I was young, and I didn't have the stones to say that what I really wanted to do was be a rock 'n' roll star behind a microphone."

So, he drifted into the newsroom.

•

KBOX, in Dallas, had been the only station broadcasting live from the motorcade when President Kennedy was shot. This, says Winston, gave its news department a certain cache, and it was one of the reasons he left Syracuse at eighteen and headed for Texas. He was still ignoring his inner voice — the one imploring him to become a disc jockey — and, by 1964, he'd carved out a promising career as a newsman.

But, he was a young man on the move and, for the next three years, he didn't plant his feet in one place for very long. "From Dallas, it was on to the Starr stations," he told me. First, he went to KOIL/Omaha, then east to WIFE/Indianapolis, then west to KBTR/

Denver. He was still Frederick Winston, newsman, but the jester, the DJ on the sideline, was beginning to gain emotional yardage. That's when Ted Atkins makes a cameo appearance.

At the time, Atkins was the Program Director of KIMN/Denver and Winston was across the street at KBTR. "I did news," says Winston (lowering his voice when he hits the word, NEWS), "Monday through Friday and, on Saturday, I did a morning shift as a disc jockey."

Winston's secret identity dj name was Bill Fortune, and his on-air persona — inspired by screamers of the day: Dick Biondi, Barney Pipp, et al — was a radical departure from his news approach. So, when Atkins called inquiring whether Bill Fortune might like to work at KIMN, Winston's response knocked him for a loop. "I told him I had a full-time job as a News Director and that the Saturday shift was only a part-time thing that allowed me to indulge my disc jockey fantasies."

By 1967 his fantasies were taking over. Like having to decide which girl to marry, he had to make a choice. "So, I ended up in Dayton, Ohio," says Winston, "because I, uh, got a jock job." This meant giving up a news career that, according to his mentors, could have led him to stations like — well, for example, WLS/Chicago. But, Winston was determined. "It was as if the sirens of radio disc jockery were calling me," he says.

Over the next five years, he paid his dues all over again.

•

Now, suppose you wanted to be the best disc jockey in the world. First, you'd have to know what that meant and have some idea what it sounded like. You'd have to be smart enough to be able to break it all down into easy-to-absorb, not-hard-to-swallow bites that, when applied, didn't make the execution sound mechanical. You'd think, study and practice, try a few bits here and there — mostly stolen from other jocks you admired and thought you could copy without getting caught — and, then, after a while, it'd start to become natural. That is, if you were lucky. And, then, after a while, you'd find your on-air voice and become YOU. Of course, you'd have to have some talent, too. Fred Winston, disc jockey, had it all, and he was in a hurry to get to the big time, to make up for lost time.

In Dayton, at WING, he did afternoon drive and was the station's Music Director. It was during his time there, he says, that he began to find his groove. "I mixed and matched styles and borrowed a little bit from everybody to create what I call the Frankenstein monster behind the mic."

Then he wanted to move up. As a kid from Syracuse, he might have been expected to aspire to WABC/New York or, maybe, WBZ/Boston. But, no — he had his sights on Miami and WFUN. "Nice weather, pretty girls," Winston explains. But Lee Sherwood, WFUN's PD, wouldn't give him the time of day so, instead, with a little push from Ted Atkins, he ended up two hundred miles northeast of Dayton, working for NBC in Cleveland. "My first big job was at WKYC, Power Radio, Heavy 11," says Winston.

But, in his mind and at the heart of his ambition, despite an infatuation with Miami, it was always about Chicago. He didn't know how he'd get there — he didn't know when, didn't even know who to reach out to — but, he was determined. That's when he got the call to come to someone's rescue.

•

The highway sign, slightly obscured by rain, was pointing the way to Cleveland. The driver, Mike McCormick, had already traveled ten hours and more than a thousand miles, when he heard an unwelcome sound coming from his engine. Ever so slowly, the car began to lose power. He probably sighed, maybe swore, then opened his door and was greeted by pelting rain. He didn't know where he was, what to do or who to call. Then, after a moment of concentrated reflection, a smile probably crossed his face. He walked to the nearest phone booth (no cell phones back then) and his call was answered by a live human being.

A little while later, he watched a car approach. A man got out, yelled "Hello," walked over and grinned. Then, the two hugged and pounded each other on the back, like men do. They hadn't seen each other in a while, but from that day on, at least for a few years, their futures would be tied together.

"Mike had been the PD at KOIL when I was still a newsman, before I went to Dayton," Winston explains. "He was a former military guy and back then, hearing that I was a 'handful,' he did military camp on me by keeping me on a short leash — on and off the air. Mike helped me find the courage and discipline I needed, to give up news and pursue my disc jockey dreams. So, that night in Cleveland I went out in the rain and rescued him."

As things happened, a conversation began — about what Fred wanted to do, about ABC and about Mike's vision for KQV/Pittsburgh, the station he just been hired to program. KQV had been sculpted by John Rook, who was leaving to head the charge at WLS/Chicago. Fred Winston was twenty-two and KQV would be his third disc jockey job. "So we moved to Pittsburgh and I began my career with ABC," he says. "It was destiny." He planted his feet in Pittsburgh and stayed for three years.

At KQV, Winston was the Production Director, worked mid-days and did character voices for the morning show.

Then, in 1971, WLS's afternoon drive talent, Scotty Brink, decided to head west to KJR/Seattle. Winston's phone rang again. Again it was Mike McCormick. But this time, it was Winston being thrown a line.

"Would you like to come to Chicago?"

•

Winston started at WLS in 1971, doing afternoon drive, but when J. J. Jeffries arrived, he moved to mid-days. Then, at the end of his second year, he replaced Charlie Van Dyke in mornings.

On the air, Winston says he was "irreverent, brash and sometimes even a bit arrogant." But, if you were a listener, he was also clever, funny, topical and always prepared. Hearing an aircheck from the mid-'70s, you can't help but get the feeling that he was a bit of a bad boy, willing to cross the line for impact or just for attention. No, I'm not implying Stern or the Greaseman, but it's safe to say that Fred Winston's irreverent act influenced many younger jocks in the Midwest.

As if to illustrate the point, Winston tells me that at WLS he was "The King of the Single Entendre."

"OK, I'll bite. What's a single entendre?"

"A burp!" he tells me, and laughs out loud.

And so, for five years, everything was almost perfect. But, like many young entertainers who read about themselves in the trades and believe their own press, Winston got too big for his britches. "In 1976, I had a vacation in Jamaica scheduled," he says. "I had airline tickets, hotel — it was all planned. Anyway, the weekend before I was supposed to leave, John Gehron (WLS Program Director) pulled me aside and told me, 'Bob Deljorno is starting on WIND, and I want you here.'"

Winston wasn't happy. "It's all planned," he told Mr. Gehron, "and I'm going!" He says he had a great vacation planned, thank you very much. When he got home, he says he was relaxed, ready to get back on the air and kick some butt. But, instead, ABC kicked his butt right out the door.

It was, Winston admits, the first time he understood that the needs of a big company could trump the needs of talent. But he still had trouble believing it could happen to him.

He packed up his stuff, took the elevator down from the 5th floor and went home. He was convinced big offers were going to fly in, but the phone didn't ring and things were as quiet as dawn on New Year's Day.

He did take a few calls, notably Charlotte and Kansas City, but they were of little interest to him. ("Kansas City?!? HAH!")

Today, with the humility and perspective that comes with age, Winston says WLS gave him exactly what he deserved. "What do you mean you go on vacation when the boss asks you not to? That was so stupid!"

So, he was left with a lot of time to soul search. One of the decisions he made was to stay in Chicago.

•

Bob Pittman was the PD of WMAQ/Chicago, one of America's most listened-to-Country stations. He decided to come to Winston's rescue.

Winston was humiliated by what happened at WLS, but he wasn't humbled and, for damn sure, he wasn't going to pretend to be a yahoo just because he was playing country music. At least that's what he told himself. "I figured I could move right in and, you know, be me.

So, I'm on the air, chirping away, and I say, 'Wow, you sure can feel the heat from Merle Haggard's neck today ... Ha, ha, ha (jingle out/record) ...' "

Later that day, in the NBC cafeteria, Pittman saddled up next to Freddy and, in the Mississippi accent he was famous for, softly said, "You know, don't say anything like that about Merle Haggard's neck. Just say, 'This is 'MAQ. Hi, I'm Fred. How are you?' "

Before long Fred and Bob were singing D-I-V-O-R-C-E. Winston crossed the street to do mornings on RKO's WFYR — the station that would become the market's first FM Adult Contemporary. From there he joined WCFL; then, in 1983, he was invited back to WLS, where he stayed for the next seven years, until the station switched from music to talk in 1990. ABC execs offered Winston a shot at joining the new talk line-up, but he declined.

During the first half of the '90s Winston was all over the dial in

Chicago. He worked for Michael Spears at WPNT, an AC that never set the city on fire. He took a turn with a group that tried surrounding the city with low-power simulcasts, but that, too, was short-lived. Besides all that, and going to WJMK to do oldies, he and his friend, Lorna Ozmon, collaborated on talent coaching.

•

On the day WJMK/Chicago became Jack FM — a format created with no disc jockeys — not even the PD had been given much warning. It was about 2:45 in the afternoon. WJMK's midday jock was still on the air and, as Winston walked by the studio, Charley Lake motioned to him to come in. "I've gotta talk to you," said Lake.

Winston gave him a look that said: What? Now? Do you know what time it is? What he said was, "I gotta go on the air."

"You're not going on the air," said Lake. "They're dumping the format."

"Cut it out," responded Winston, shaking his head. "Really, I gotta go."

Lake stood firm, insisting it was true. CBS, he said, has decided to flip formats.

When?

"At three o'clock."

"And I was supposed to go on the air at three," Winston explains. "They'd been working on it for a while and hadn't told anybody. Not even Charley, the PD."

As you might imagine, emotions in the room were running high, and Lake and Winston, grizzled old vets that they were, started to laugh.

"Here we go again," they thought.

When the General Manager arrived, Winston was told he had three options: one — he could stay and run the control board (for the jockless Jack); two — he could stay and do WJMK's format on the Internet, or three — he could leave and they'd buy out his contract.

He remembers his response. "Well, shit, I'm in for the ride. Let's go, let's stay with 'JMK."

So the oldies ride continued, from WJMK's showplace studios, no less; at least for a while. Then the Program Director of Jack FM, John Sebastian, decided Jack FM should have the big studio. This left WJMK, a once-glorious radio station broadcasting daily from an 8' by 10' closet, with no windows and only a monaural console. "And the audience," says Winston, "shrank from seven million a week to about twelve hundred." Poof, it was gone.

"I did have a regular caller from Fair Hope, Alabama, and another guy emailed me regularly from China, where I was apparently a morning man in Beijing, but ..." But, it just wasn't the same, and it wasn't what he signed up for.

So, ok — CBS was going to keep on writing him checks and abiding by the language in his contract. But, after over 35 years in Chicago as a media commodity, he began to wonder if broadcasting from a closet was the best way to market the Fred Winston brand. He started asking himself if broadcasting to an Internet and HD audience was really doing himself a disservice? He rationalized that it kept his act fresh, and, anyway, he decided, he still had weekends on his farm in Wisconsin to recharge and keep things in perspective. "As a radio vet I've come to accept that everything done in this business doesn't have to make sense," he says. "And, of course, the older I get, the more I realize that applies to lots of things. Like, Iraq, for example."

As you know, WJMK is now a thing of the past.

•

"Working in format radio is like talking in calligraphy, where one little piece can be a whole paragraph." Winston pauses, apparently not thrilled with the analogy. He tries again. "As a performer, sometimes you can fly like Michael Jordan. But you're lucky if that's twenty to twenty-five percent of the time. Otherwise, you've gotta do prep, you gotta hammer it out — come up with some tease lines, create a beginning, a middle, a payoff and a bailout line just in case the whole thing doesn't work."

Winston says he's always done show prep and that it's as much a part of him as understanding that, in format radio, job one is to make sure your personality complements the station's total aura and doesn't dominate and take over. It's a mindset and discipline he learned from the jocks he watched when he was a baby newsman; from tapes of Robert W. Morgan on KHJ and from what he absorbed from Chuck Browning back in Indiana. He says he understood it when he went to Dayton in 1968, and also on Memorial Day — May 25, 2007 — when he did nine to noon on WLS during the Big 89 Rewind.

Does he have any advice for radio performers?

"Study your market," he advises. "Listen to everybody. Pay attention to technique and content. Get the flavor of where you live. A smart performer will absorb all of it and evolve. And," says Fred Winston, "No matter where you are in your career always strive for greatness."

Chapter 58

Wolfman Jack: Clap For The Wolfman

Rhythm and blues was one of the first things to ever grab Bob Smith's soul.

He grew up in New York City listening to Alan Freed on 10/10 WINS. But, it was Jocko Henderson on WDIA, and John R. on WLAC — both sliding in on a late-night skip from Memphis — that gave him the fever and made him want to be a disc jockey. Now, you gotta know his father was no easy sell. Eventually, though, the old man caved to the kid's dream and came up with the cash to send him to the National Academy of Broadcasting.

From the start he was an aberration; while the other students wrapped their mouths around the names of classical composers, Smith created a jive-talking persona he called Daddy Jules.

There was a man named Richard Eaton who owned United Broadcasting, and it was at one of his stations, WYOU/Newport News, that Smith, as Daddy Jules, found his first job. The format, to the extent there was one, was soul, blues and jazz; yes, it was eclectic, but it was also profitable, so Eaton decided to cash out.

With the new owner came new call letters, WTID, and an easy-listening format, and in the spirit of continuing employment, Daddy Jules re-named himself "Roger Gorman" and lent his melodious tones to Mantovani, et al.

But, the name never rang true, and the music, at least to Smith, wasn't music at all.

•

Mo Burton did sales and Smith was the talent.

In December of 1961, the two men left Newport News and bought a small two hundred fifty-watt daytime only radio station in Shreveport, Louisiana — KCIJ AM. The format they inherited was both country and gospel, but it didn't generate enough money to pay the bills, so the new owners made up the difference by selling air time to a bunch of preachers, whose main attraction was that they paid cash up front.

KCIJ wasn't the only station to cash the preachers' checks. In the early '60s, religious programming (if you choose to call it that) was a staple of late-night radio and one of the most notorious stations the preachers took over was XERF, a 250,000-watt AM radio station that blasted out of a Mexican town across the border from Del Rio, Texas. On any given night, these charlatan evangelists sold prayer cloths, bibles, baby chickens and anything else they could get away with.

It was all very strange and explosive, and it gave Smith an idea. He had a radio character he'd been thinking about, even practicing in the production room. The character, he said, was going to be "a happy-go-lucky cat, real hip — someone who just wanted to make people feel good, nice, sexy and alive."

In describing the character's persona to his wife, Smith was even more detailed. "This cat will have a deep, 'growly' voice.

And his name will be Wolfman Jack."

•

XERF would be the perfect station for this Wolfman, thought Smith.

He faked an aircheck and, with two thousand dollars in hand, he and Larry Brandon, his new partner, drove from Shreveport to Del Rio, crossed the border into Ciudad Acuna, Mexico, and began looking for the station. It wasn't easy to find, but thirty dollars and a dusty taxi ride later, they arrived at the transmitter site.

The building had stucco walls and a red-tile roof, but its most striking features were its towers: shining metal grabbing for the sky and shooting out enough energy to fuel a man's ambition.

Originally, the plan had been for Smith to buy air time for the Wolfman — like the preachers did — and launch a mail order business. But, things didn't happen that way. Instead, when Smith and Brandon walked into the station that day they looked around and, for some strange reason, decided they could take over the entire operation.

The preachers, as you'd imagine, didn't think much of this idea and that's when the machine gun and shotguns showed up. Arguments ensued — call them fevered discussions, if you'd like. For the next twenty-four hours the two gringos were left defending their position. But, when the sun came up the following morning, the deal was done, and Wolfman Jack had found a home.

"Those border stories are really true," says Bob Wilson. Wilson, the founder of "Radio & Records" and the man who handled the Wolfman's syndication in the '70s, should know. "Yeah, he used to tell them all the time."

•

Imagine this: You're cruising in El Paso, or Oklahoma City, fiddling with your radio. All of a sudden, out of the ether, comes this voice. "Aaaaoooooooo! Have mercy! Good Golly Miss Molly! This is the Wolfman Jack Show, baby. We gonna party tonight! We down here in Del Rio, Texas, the land of the dun-keys!"

For Bob Smith, there was no turning back.

Overnight, the Wolfman was a goldmine. Checks, cash and money orders flew in the door and baby chickens, photos and other "items of value" flew out. ("Order today and I'll send you — ABSOLUTELY FREE — an autographed picture of me that glows in the dark.") One of the best-selling items was "The Wolfman Jack Official Roach Clip" ("You get ready with the clip and catch those speedy little buggers as they run across the floor.") It was all very bizarre, and then the story took another twist.

After eight months of doing the show live from Del Rio, Smith and his partner bought a radio station in Minneapolis. Smith decided to pack up and head north to Minnesota.

This meant, of course, that the Wolfman had to move, too. So, by day, he was Bob Smith, radio executive. But by night, on tape, he was Wolfman Jack. And nobody in the Twin Cities, the bastion of white-bread America, ever knew.

•

L.A. was where the action was.

In January of 1966, Smith packed up the family again and moved to Southern California. He established offices on Sunset Boulevard and worked out a deal with another border station, XERB/Tijuana, that involved selling time to preachers — cash up front, please — and launching an L.A. version of "The Wolfman Jack Show."

For five years everything was peachy and the Wolfman's fame and notoriety grew at a ferocious rate. But in 1971, the walls came tumbling down. That year the Mexican government decided that broadcasting "evangelical religious" programming was detrimental to the Catholic youth of Mexico. This decision effectively meant that eighty percent of XERB's revenue disappeared. It also meant the Wolfman was off the air. Bob Wilson, then the PD of KDAY/ Los Angeles, explains what happened next.

"I sat Wolf down and told him what I thought he needed to do to come into the new generation." Smith agreed. KDAY put the Wolfman on at night and even hired writers to spice up his content.

Quickly, things started to happen. Building on this initial success, Wilson and the Wolfman started a syndication company. "What we did was way ahead of its time," says Wilson. "Wolf used to cut fifty to a hundred customized tracks for each radio station." This was new stuff for radio and smart programmers, like Buzz Bennett at KDWB, used the wild tracks to make the show sound live and local.

At its height, "The Wolfman Jack Show" was on over one hundred stations in the United States and on Armed Forces Radio around the world. "Wolf became a phenomenon," Wilson explains. "From that he got "American Graffiti" and "Midnight Special," and eventually that led to WNBC."

Wolfman Jack spent less than a year in New York, but by then he'd established himself as an American icon. Over the next twenty years he appeared in seventeen movies and made numerous radio, television and live appearances.

On July 1, 1995, after an extended time away, Wolfman Jack returned to his home in North Carolina. He'd been on the road promoting his autobiography, "Have Mercy" and, according to friends, he'd been complaining of feeling terribly tired.

He walked in the door of his home and greeted his wife, Lou, with a hug. Then, at that precise moment, he had a heart attack and died in her arms.

•

Wolfman Jack will always be with us. Not because he was real — though Smith would probably argue he was — but because the Wolfman character rang so true. If you're a doubter, do yourself a favor and watch "American Graffiti" again.

"In the history of rock radio," says Larry Lujack, "that whole Wolfman thing was pure genius."

On April 20, 1999, Wolfman Jack was inducted in the Radio Hall of Fame.

AUTHOR'S NOTE

Much of the work included herein was previously published in "Radio and Records" magazine and/or on the media website, www.allaccess. com. It is based on over one hundred interviews and a lifetime of conversations and memories that reflect a time gone by that was, decidedly, unique. The focus has been on music radio. Consequently, some radio personalities — Rush Limbaugh, Don Imus, Howard Stern and Dr. Laura Schlessinger, in particular — are not included, because their careers transcend music formats, their stories have been told often and well in other venues and, in the end, they will be judged more by their long-term influence on the public than their current immense popularity. Others weren't featured because they didn't want to be, couldn't be contacted or information wasn't available that would allow for more than a thumbnail profile.

This work does not pretend to be a complete history of American radio during those years, nor does it include every incident and/or person who contributed or influenced the medium during that time period. It is, rather, a series of profiles, most of which are based on one-on-one conversations with the principals. While I can't testify to the veracity of all the words quoted herein, I can attest that those who spoke the words were quoted accurately and that the perspective I provided in the telling of the stories represents the truth, as I know it to be. As for the anecdotes cited; well, they're anecdotes.

Disclaimers aside, this book wouldn't have been possible without the encouragement and support of Jeanette Alexander, Jerry Atchley, Rebecca Christensen, Dan Coughlin, Joel Denver, Chuck Dunaway, Erica Farber, Bob Gourley, David Graupner, Colin Gromatsky, Ira Lipson, Jim Long, Sonny Melendrez, Ray Potter, Ron Rodrigues, Neil Sargent, Dave Scott, Pat Shaughnessy, Don Sundeen, Craig Turner, Grant West...and, above all, my wife, Patti Shannon.

All mistakes are mine.

BOB SHANNON
CHRISTMAS 2008
BAINBRIDGE ISLAND, WASHINGTON

P.S. Mom and Dad, this is what all the commotion was about.

INDEX

H

KUTL, 305
KUTY, 245
KUZZ, 86
KVAS, 257
KVIL, 70, 74, 139, 349
KVOB, 16
KWBB, 369
KWBE, 304
KWK, 196
KWFT, 222
KWMT, 305
KXOK, 357
KXOL, 124
KYA, 100, 112-113, 119, 120
KYCW, 53
KYNO, 65, 67, 113, 154, 155, 189-190, 244, 274
KYW, 47
KYXY, 260
KXDD, 53
KXOL, 124
KXST-FM, 170
KZEW-FM, 266
KZLA-FM, 317, 326
KZZP-FM, 284

L

Laboe, Art, 210-213
Lacy, Jack, 337
Ladd, Cheryl, 261
Lake, Charley, 387
Lancaster, Burt, 299
Landecker, John Records, 214
Landis, Gary, 313, 332

Landsman, Dean, 45
Lane, Chris, 258
Lang, Michael, 312
Laugh, Laugh, 100
Lasorda, Tommy, 316-317
"Last Contest, The", 362
Law, Al Brady, 378
Lawrence, Dick, 17
Leach, Owen, 83
"Lean Cuisine", 151
LeBlanc, Dudley J., 233
Led Zeppelin, 4, 50, 81
Lee, Bob, 203
Lee, Peggy, 56
Lee Abrams Consulting, 5
Leeds, Mel, 252-253
Lennon, John, 117, 180, 266, 270, 273, 299, 311
Letterman, David, 218
Levine, Ken, 46
Lewis, Jack, 359
Liberty Broadcasting System, The (aka Liberty Network), 28, 226-227
Limbaugh, Rush, 133, 218
Lin Broadcasting, 307, 371
Lincoln Financial, 63
Lington, Michael, 83
Lipson, Ira, 266
Little Latin Lupe Lu, 314
Little Richard, 298-299
"Live Aid", 153
"Live From The Lonestar", 317
Lockridge, Willard, 81
Logan, Dave, 251, 255

X

TURN IT UP!

LaVergne, TN USA
14 September 2009
157793LV00001B/1/P